When
the Sparks
Fly

When the Sparks Fly

Resolving Conflicts in Your Organization

John D. Arnold

McGraw-Hill, Inc.

New York St. Louis San Francisco Auckland Bogotá
Caracas Lisbon London Madrid Mexico Milan
Montreal New Delhi Paris San Juan São Paulo
Singapore Sydney Tokyo Toronto

Library of Congress Cataloging-in-Publication Data

Arnold, John D.
    When the sparks fly : resolving conflicts in your organization /
John D. Arnold.
          p.   cm.
    Includes index.
    ISBN 0-07-002567-3 :
    1. Conflict management.   I. Title.
HD42.A76   1993
658.4—dc20   92-23939
                                                       CIP

1 2 3 4 5 6 7 8 9 0   DOC/DOC   9 8 7 6 5 4 3 2

ISBN   0-07-002567-3

*The sponsoring editor for the book was Karen A. Hansen, the editing supervisor
was Jane Palmieri, and the production supervisor was Suzanne W. Babeuf. It was
set in Palatino by McGraw-Hill's Professional Book Group composition unit.*

Printed and bound by R. R. Donnelley & Sons Company.

This book is printed on recycled, acid-free paper containing a minimum of 50% recycled de-
inked fiber.

To the many executives in the United States and abroad who, over the past 24 years, have strengthened their organizations by applying my conflict resolution/conflict prevention process so successfully.

Contents

Preface

This book is based on more than 20 years of experience resolving conflicts in major corporations, nonprofit groups, and government agencies through my company, ExecuTrak Systems, Inc. I've tried to present my approach as a blend of theory and practice, personal accounts, and prescriptive advice. Part 1 covers the core ideas and presents a methodology that has proven to be effective in many countries and in a wide variety of enterprises. To provide a context for applying the conflict resolution method, I've excerpted portions of the "ExecuTrak Files." (Of course, names and places have been changed to protect both the innocent and the guilty.) These "organizational whodunits," which you'll find in Part 2, are designed to educate; at the same time they convey the always fascinating human dimension of conflict resolution.

I've reserved the real "nuts-and-bolts" advice for Part 3, which offers detailed information about conducting conflict resolution and implementing conflict preventive maintenance programs. While you could turn directly to those chapters, you should read Parts 1 and 2. By reviewing the conceptual framework and the "whodunits" that I've helped clients solve by applying the methodology, you can avoid making basic mistakes and falling into common traps. Besides, why reinvent the wheel?

However you approach this book, bear in mind that conflict resolution is both an art and a science. I've provided the science. You'll develop a sense of the "art" as you get more experience with resolving conflict in your own organization.

Finally, bear in mind that there are no quick fixes in the field of conflict resolution. Whatever is causing the sparks to fly at your organization didn't materialize instantaneously. It developed over time and therefore will require time and a disciplined process for you to find a working solution. As I've often said to ExecuTrak client consultant–trainer candidates, "The meek might inherit the earth, but it is the patient conflict resolver who 'heals the family' and puts the organization aright." With that, I urge you to read carefully through the book, then combine theory and practice in your own organization.

Acknowledgments

I wish to thank three associates—Keith Parsons, Art Sullivan, and Diane Summers—who helped make my life a lot easier while writing this book during a particularly intense period. I also want to thank Bruce Anderson, Mike Snell, and my editor Karen Hansen.

John D. Arnold
Martha's Vineyard
September 1992

When the Sparks Fly

Introduction: Humans in the Midst

Case Study

Welcome to the Tower of Babel

After years of quietly acquiring chemical plants and related operations in Latin America, Deltron Corporation emerged as the leading supplier to many of the world's makers of paints and dyes. Yet, despite the strategic coups of Deltron, its senior executives failed to notice the animosity brewing between New York headquarters and the Latin American management teams. The fine-tuned MBAs populating Deltron's posh headquarters, for example, joked about their Latin American counterparts operating under the effects of "island fever," oblivious to time and the formalities of running a business.

The managers in the Latin American countries and Puerto Rico in turn cursed the "crazy gringos" who wanted 45 different financial control reports a month. Worse, when forced together during semiannual conferences, the Latin American managers would begin speaking in their native Spanish and Portuguese tongues (with a bit of French for emphasis) as a protest against the Americans' belligerent insistence on English as the official company language. (In one nearly comical meeting, two Austrian managers, stationed in Venezuela, began their own dialogue—in German—giving the entire meeting the aura of a Roman circus.)

The internal wrangling not only intensified already uncomfortable working relations between New York and the Latin American divisions, but it resulted in loss of business to competitors. As headquarters and the Latin American region further complained about each other, they began withholding information, causing delayed shipments and lost contracts, and playing "paper money games" aimed at improving their own image while diminishing that of their "enemy." Had senior management not stepped in and introduced a catalyst to build positive relationships between the warring factions, the company's future would have been seriously jeopardized.

¿Que pasa?

Organizational "civil war" is often even more blatant than it was at Deltron. Despite its obvious destructiveness, it is waged every day at companies, not-for-profit organizations, and government agencies throughout the world. And while Deltron's management was perhaps slow in realizing the depth of the problem, it cannot be blamed for allowing the friction to happen in the first place. In fact, it's fair to say that *whenever humans get together to do business, some degree of conflict is inevitable; it's just human nature.*

In all cases, organizational conflict involves a clash of expectations. These might concern the company's vision, business philosophy, competitive position, acquisitions, decision-making styles, operational procedures, interdepartmental processes, and so on. Often, an organizational conflict starts off small, affecting only a limited number of people. In some cases, the "virus" remains contained in an office or a division. But it can also spread throughout the entire organization, creating an unhealthy work environment and crippling the overall effectiveness of the organization. The following may happen when the sparks fly:

- People may cease to regard the firm across the street as the real enemy and instead focus on the department across the hall (as in Deltron's case).

- Irrational strategic, business, and marketing plans may get approved.

- Deadlines may be missed, projects delayed, and windows of opportunity lost.

- Good products may get killed while questionable products may be elevated.

- Accountability becomes impossible, and the company's coat of arms becomes a harried manager with arms crisscrossed and fingers pointed in the opposite direction.

- People may get promoted on a political, rather than a performance, basis, destroying the careers of deserving employees and pushing up "deadwood" into the management chain.

- Your best talent may no longer be motivated to perform at 100 percent, or they may defect outright and become your archrivals.

- Foolish acquisitions may be made. (It's no surprise that two out of three acquisitions are outright failures.)

- Upper management offices may become a revolving door as heads roll and replacement bodies report for duty.

- Your organization ultimately may be forced to severely downsize as the company is no longer able to satisfy customers and compete effectively.

Often, organizational conflicts are misdiagnosed as personality conflicts (which are also inevitable when human beings get together to do business). Unfortunately, when this misdiagnosis happens, limited efforts are made to identify the root cause, so that whatever actions are taken to correct the problem fail, and the situation festers. All top executives and administrators should be aware of the telltale signs that organizational conflict is afoot. While the causes and symptoms of organizational conflict will be discussed in depth throughout this book, consider the following basic signs:

Low-Level Conflict

- A hushed or deathly quiet atmosphere persists. Even in a formal culture, people will smile and interact. But when people are squirreled away in their cubicles or offices, avoiding eye contact with one another and talking only in whispers, and when the corridors look like an air raid has just been called, you can be sure that the organization is experiencing some level of strife.

- Meetings are conducted in "hub and spoke" fashion, the only one talking being the department head or highest ranking manager. Everyone else is silent unless asked a question, for fear of saying the "wrong" thing or rocking the boat.

- Rumors run rampant—even transmitted by people who should know better.

Medium Conflict

- Memos are riddled with excessive justification, "CYA" (Cover Your Ass), and "we-they" language. They also have a win-lose dimension. ("*We* did our part but *they* missed their bogey." "*We* tried but *they* never responded," and so on.)

- Backstabbing is the first line of defense when accountability or responsibility is called into question.

- The most common refrain is "can't do because..." or "but...." This defeatist attitude often results from the "NIH" (not-invented-here) syndrome or an expectation that the organization's projects are destined to fail.

- Meetings drag on because no one can agree or no one is willing to make a decision and commitment. People don't want to be held accountable because they don't trust other people in the organization.
- "There is paralysis by analysis" (studying issues "to death," often through an incessant chain of meetings).

High-Intensity Conflict

- Bids are won but shirts are lost. For example, a defense contractor might win a large contract but actually lose money on it because the different departments didn't make realistic projections. Each department may have only considered its own function rather than how it must fit into an integrated plan and budget combining all departments.
- The sales force consistently rejects marketing promotions because "marketing just doesn't understand or won't respond to our needs," or they half-heartedly push the products involved in favor of lucrative or "pet" lines. Such biases amount to sabotage and can severely diminish the market-share potential and profitability of otherwise excellent new products and services.
- Top management whipsaws the organization so that people take on the attitude, "This too shall pass—don't take it very seriously."
- The company has no unified, common vision or sense of the organization's mission, direction, or strategy. This leads to conflicting statements about where the company stands, and reinforces "we-they" boundaries. ("*We* hit our deadline—they missed *theirs*.")
- Major ship dates are missed because of internal fighting between the "realists" and the "dreamers" over the actual and the possible, and because of discrepancies about the product's design, function, marketing, and so on. (Just look at how Lotus Development Corporation and Ashton Tate lost significant market share when they failed to deliver their promised products anywhere near the expected due dates; disillusioned customers eventually flocked to competing software packages.)
- Compensation programs reinforce the individual win-lose mindset rather than the "united we stand" mentality.
- Internal competition eclipses the real battle for market share (as in the case of Deltron Corporation, mentioned earlier). Marketing and sales

accuse manufacturing of not being able to meet demand for product. Manufacturing complains that marketing and sales treat the production as a "black box" capable of spitting out any order at any time. Marketing and sales and manufacturing all blame engineering for not keeping up with product introductions and design changes necessary to stay competitive. The spears fly and the fingerpointing continues while the competition chews deeper into the company's customer base.

Have you ever experienced any of these in your company, or at an organization where you worked previously? Chances are, you have, in one form or another. Every company has some level of organizational conflict. But what action has been taken to counteract the situation? If your organization is like most, probably one of the following has been done:

1. Ignore it and live with it, or hope it will go away. ("Oh, that's just the way we do things around here....It's just the nature of our culture." Or "Things will get better at some point....They have to.")

2. Write it off as personality conflicts or "bad chemistry." (It's "just the folks locking horns—healthy jousting," or "The veeps of marketing and manufacturing are like oil and water—just can't get 'em to mix.")

3. Punish it out of existence, instead of probing for the root cause and taking corrective action. ("Beatings will stop when sales and morale improve—so hunker down in the meanwhile, folks.")

4. Send people to off-site sensitivity training—which is too often another way to skirt the real problems at hand. ("Maybe if George is shipped off to 'feely touchy' boot camp he'll come back a human being.")

5. Bring in a psychologist or consultant with interpersonal skills to build a team. ("Hey, for a $20,000 a month retainer, I bet we can bring in a top B-School professor. That'll solve our problems.")

All these approaches are doomed to failure *unless* they deal with the root cause of the conflict—and often they don't. An insidious side effect of not dealing directly with the root cause is that the more the conflict is allowed to escalate, the harder it is to resolve. The lack of action (or ineffective action) merely lets the virus replicate, allowing the infection to drive deeper and spread to other parts of the organization. The data becomes "contaminated" and distorted as you layer it with assumptions and suppositions. When this happens, the task of getting down to the core issues becomes ever more complex—and the probability of resolving the problem more remote. "Musical chairs" often follows—as in the instance of the New York–Latin American regional conflict in which eight presidents of the latter were hired and fired in seven years!

A Better Approach

The fact is, organizational conflict can be resolved—if you have a methodology that focuses on the underlying causes and yields solutions that work for all parties, not just the most powerful faction. In the pages that follow, you'll learn just such a methodology: the Arnold Conflict Resolution Process. It's based on my past 30 years of experience consulting with companies throughout North America and abroad, many of them in the Fortune 500.

The Arnold Process entails two phases. The first involves defining the issues and getting the facts, while the second is concerned with reaching agreement on, and implementing, the best solutions to the organizational conflict at hand. By applying the 10-step methodology, you'll learn what's really causing the sparks to fly at your organization, how to adopt a winning philosophy that enables your people to go beyond the conflict and seize opportunities, how to determine what everyone wants to "achieve, preserve, and avoid," and how to develop criteria for generating workable resolutions. By the tenth step, you'll have a set of specific actions for reducing organizational conflict so your people can focus on what they are paid to do.

While the Arnold Conflict Resolution Process works best with a mediator or catalyst, you can nevertheless make tremendous progress by using the 10 steps as a framework for reexamining your situation. Very often, things aren't what they appear:

- "Bad chemistry" may actually be an unworkable arrangement in which people are forced to compete for limited resources or are faced with conflicting objectives.

- Sales and production quotas may be consistently missed, not because people don't care, but because the boss demands at least 10 percent more product than that shipped in the previous month.

- Managers appear to make consistently poor judgments but in fact are acting on incomplete information. (This is known as the "mushroom effect"—managers are fed a lot of manure and kept in the dark.)

- People may be disillusioned because the management and decision style of their superiors places them in a "Catch-22" or "double-bind" situation—they can't do their jobs because the current system or approach is unworkable, yet they are not empowered to suggest or implement alternatives.

- Offices, departments, or regions may have banded into fiefdoms because the system unwittingly rewards the "feudal lords" most capable of deflecting arrows to others or the "robber barons" who "steal" the most from fellow departments.

Once you understand the real causes of organizational conflict, the method will also help you understand your options for dealing with the underlying causes. Even if you plan to bring in an outside consultant to help with the process and the implementation of the solutions, familiarizing yourself with the methodology will make you a better client and enable you to participate more directly in all phases of the analysis.

Once you have mastered the process, you'll notice a number of improvements in your working environment and the organization's performance, including

- A healthier and more productive workplace
- A team spirit that enables your company to take a true multidisciplinary approach to product development, marketing, customer service, and other key functional areas
- Faster new product-service development and market entry
- Integrated and actionable plans
- Improved customer satisfaction because the right products are shipped in the right quantity at the right time (i.e., the just-in-time approach).

The Global Imperative for Change

Now, if organizational conflict is endemic to all human enterprises, why bother trying to resolve it? Once you stomp it out in one area, won't it just rear its ugly head in another? Besides, haven't we gotten along just fine despite our so-called conflicted organizations?

At first blush, resolving organizational conflict may indeed seem like enacting the Greek myth of Sisyphus, condemned for eternity by the gods of Olympus to continually roll a gigantic stone up a hill, only to watch it career down the slope as soon as he reached the peak. True, every organization will always have some level of conflict; it's simply impossible to meet everyone's expectations all of the time. But "some degree" is the operant phrase. Every organization can live with a modest degree of unrest; none, however, can withstand prolonged internal strife that rocks the foundations and threatens to bring down the entire structure. Once you learn how to resolve large conflicts—those that if they were earthquakes would register 6.5 or greater on the Richter scale—you'll be able to spot others while they're still causing mild disturbances, then take effective action to contain them and minimize any damage. In other words, conflict resolution will become an everyday part of doing business at your company, nonprofit organization, or agency. You'll even learn how to take preventive actions that *anticipate* likely sources of conflicts and eliminate problems before they even surface.

As for the second question—"Why not live with conflicted organizations?"—the answer is twofold. First, we have an obligation to our stakeholders to make sure that our companies are as effective and competitive as possible. We have an obligation to our employees to make sure that their work environment is as harmonious as possible and that we can give them continued professional and satisfying employment. We give them the best tools to work with, why not the best environment?

Equally pressing is the new global imperative that is forcing every company on the planet to cut slack and waste. Energy consumed by fingerpointing and backbiting is waste. Scrap, rework, and unsold stock caused by warring departments is also waste that cuts into the bottom line and jeopardizes customer service. And in today's fast-paced Darwinian business world, there is little forgiveness; the fittest survive the race for global market share and products.

Yes, to cause organizational conflicts is human. But to learn how to prevent conflict that's harmful to an organization and its members, and to resolve conflict on an ongoing basis, is to accept our frailties and turn them into opportunities for growth and prosperity in the world marketplace. Think about that, especially if the sparks in your organization are so intense that you can read this page in the dark.

PART 1

Organizational Conflict and the Conflict Resolution Process

A genetic engineering firm merges with a major pharmaceutical company; in six months, what initially looked to the founder-CEO to be a strategic coup results in the dispirited shell of an acquisition.

Instead of trying to beat the competition, sales and the head office battle each other.

A Canadian subsidiary feels treated like a "fifty-first state." This "we-they" thinking reinforces U.S. headquarters' "paternalistic" and autocratic role and the "rebellious child" role of the Canadian "division."

Soaring customer complaints and plummeting customer

service levels combine to cause fingerpointing and cries of "sabotage" among sales and marketing, manufacturing, and engineering.

A chief financial officer, given his first senior line management assignment as president of a major international company, comes up against a knowledgeable executive who heads up both operations and sales. They each have very different management philosophies and styles, strategies and objectives. The organization divides into two camps.

Organizational conflicts—how they start and fester, how a small fire can turn into a conflagration. Once a chain reaction begins, conflict—unless resolved—moves through five increasingly damaging phases.

Companies throughout North America, and in South America and Europe also, have found that the 10-step Arnold Conflict Resolution Process helped them quench the fire, regardless of which of the five stages conflict had reached. Obviously, the earlier the detection, the less time, energy, and resources required to get it under control and turn it from a potential catastrophe to a real opportunity for improved motivation, performance, and reward.

Each of the above situations, described in detail in the following chapters, illustrates the five evolutionary stages of organizational conflict and how they can be resolved using the 10-step Arnold Conflict Resolution Process.

So fasten your seat belt, turn to the next page, and vicariously live these situations in order to identify why such organizational conflict problems occur and how they can be resolved; for, very possibly, one or more are occurring right this very moment somewhere in your own organization.

1

Anatomy of an Organizational Conflict: Understanding Strife

Case Study

The Ideal Marriage?

When Dr. John Kaslow agreed to merge his genetic engineering firm, BioTek USA, to Armco Pharmaceuticals, he considered his move to be a strategic coup; Armco would provide much-needed cash and access to international markets. According to the original agreement, the world-renowned Kaslow was to remain as president of his firm, and he would work hand in hand with Armco's top management.

BioTek was to function as an independent research and development operation, while Armco would handle marketing and administrative functions. BioTek had enjoyed a reputation for being a research haven for brilliant scientists, and it had been able to recruit the best minds in the business. But it had failed to make a significant presence in the marketplace. Armco, with its marketing muscle and savvy for turning great ideas for pharmaceuticals into blockbusters, seemed like an ideal partner.

On paper, the "marriage" seemed like it was made in heaven, and during the first-month "honeymoon" any skeptics appeared to have been proven wrong. But within six months, morale at BioTek began to drop; Armco clearly intended to play a far more intrusive role than anyone imagined. Rumors of Armco's "reporting and security mania" spread throughout BioTek's "shirtsleeve" and denim culture like wildfire. Key researchers suddenly felt censored by new limitations on what they could discuss at conferences. Upper management felt counterparts from Armco breathing down their backs. Despite lavish salary and perk offers, BioTek's best talent began seeking other "safe havens." Within a year after the merger, an embittered Kaslow left the company he had founded and worked so hard to build. Six months later, Armco divested itself of BioTek, leaving nothing but a dispirited shell.

BioTek (a composite company) would not be the first merger or acquisition to fail because of a clash of cultures and expectations. Just think of classic debacles, such as Mobil's disastrous foray into retail through its acquisition of Montgomery Ward, or Exxon's misadventure with Vydec, a maker of word processing gear. Mobil, seeking a quick return on investment, failed to understand that when you raise prices at Montgomery Ward, customers will simply go next door to Walmart or Hills. Exxon, unused to competing on the basis of quickly changing technology, mired Vydec in layers of decision making while competitors such as Wang took a (only temporary) commanding lead.

Or consider how W. R. Grace ruined Mr. Gasket, bought from former stock-car racer Joseph Hrudka (who started the company by hand cutting one dollar heat resistant engine gaskets and selling them to his friends for a dollar). After paying Hrudka $17 million for his company (Hrudka hoped to make $10,000 a year when he started the company in his mother's basement five years earlier), Grace replaced a number of Mr. Gasket's nonprofessional managers with an elite corp of MBAs and imposed its own highly sophisticated computerized system on a simple paper operation.

Morale sank, and so did Mr. Gasket's revenues. According to some analysts, decisions that Hrudka and his race-car cronies could have made in 15 minutes over donuts and coffee took four to six weeks of nonproductive meetings and committee revues; the new management looked at the product line as just a product—pieces of rubber. For the old crew, which lived and breathed racing, the gaskets and related products were an integral part of their lives. And the sophisticated computer system merely bogged down the company in mountains of meaningless numbers.

Grace eventually sold the company back to Hrudka (who was itching to come out of retirement—he was bored with restoring Victorian mansions). Hrudka gladly paid the $4 million, after which he restored the old simple systems, rehired dedicated racing enthusiasts, and expanded into related aftermarket product areas. Within four years, Mr. Gasket enjoyed $120 million in sales.

Even without an acquisition, internal culture clashes can tear an organization apart. Look at the situation at Biogen. Founded by Nobel laureate Walter Gilbert, the company (like our composite, BioTek) was an academic's paradise where researchers could explore the basic nature of disease. Eventually, Biogen's board began demanding tangible products on an accelerated timetable, and it accused Gilbert of running an open-ended program. Gilbert eventually left Biogen, by then a highly polarized organization, to work instead with companies not riddled with internal strife.

In all of these cases, the culture clash and ensuing organizational conflict grew over time. And just as an avalanche begins with a single snowflake, organizational conflicts can start with a simple, seemingly innocuous act. It may be an implied slight—someone not receiving what he or she considers should be adequate credit for an idea. Or someone might perceive a hidden agenda in a comment by a peer or superior. Like that proverbial snowball, the conflict may begin to grow and pick up speed as the offended individual gains supporters.

In other cases, the conflict may start more dramatically, with a broadside salvo from top management—a "housecleaning" or a dramatic new approach to doing business. Management might issue an "imperial edict," demanding a 10 percent improvement in sales. Or a manager might shoot first and ask questions later. (Perhaps he or she has learned about a complaint from an important customer, then, without researching the details, lambastes the people in order-entry, sales, or technical support.)

In professional groups, organizational conflicts often grow from pent-up resentment about compensation. Consider the common conflict between "rainmakers" and "worker bees" in law and accounting firms. The rainmakers often feel they're entitled to a larger piece of the pie because they've brought in the business; the "worker bees" in turn believe that they should reap a larger share, since they are actually servicing the clients.

Whatever the intensity of the catalyst, once the chain reaction is set in motion, the path in which the conflict develops is generally the same. It usually consists of the five stages shown in Figure 1-1 and the following sections.

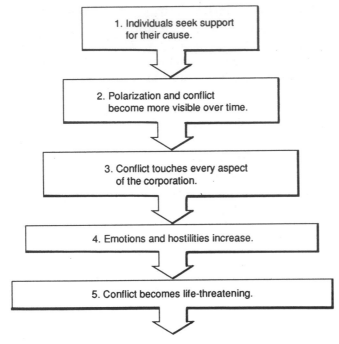

Figure 1-1. Five stages in growth of organizational conflict.

Five Stages of Conflict Development

■ *Stage 1: Individuals seek support for their "cause," forming "we-they" boundaries.* Those who aren't sympathetic are viewed as the "enemy." Consider the situation at Dently Corporation, a once highly profitable, family-owned discount store chain. Upon retiring, the chairman, who had built the business from a single store to a thriving business with more than 200 outlets nationwide, appointed his son to succeed him.

Unfortunately for the company, when the son took over, he cared less about operations in the field than the workings of the home office; in fact, he spent most of the time in his office and conference room. Communication with the field dissolved as the son focused his attention on affairs at headquarters. As one district manager put it, "When I call New York, I feel like I'm treated as a second-class citizen." Where his father had served as a kind of "glue," binding the headquarters and field organizations together, the son was a catalyst for mutual distrust. The field people soon banded together and began rallying support for their plight as the "underdogs." The seeds of destruction were thus sown.

- *Stage 2: The polarization and the conflict become more visible over time.* This reinforces the factions, which simply become more entrenched. At Dently, the conflict transformed the entire company. Almost overnight, the company became riddled with internal competition that shifted everyone's gaze from the marketplace to the internal struggles between the headquarters and field people. When field managers came to headquarters for meetings, they felt like they'd just "beamed down" to a hostile planet. (This was most noticeable in the cafeteria, where the field staff huddled together like a band of "untouchables." The beverage counter served as a demilitarized zone!)

- *Stage 3: The conflict touches every aspect of the corporation, from board room to boiler room.* As we described earlier, an organizational conflict is like a virus that invades the whole company and weakens its structure. Dently soon began to suffer from the conflict between the field staff and headquarters. The retail stores complained that merchandising (the buying operation) was losing touch with the market. Inventory was either late or incorrect, and sales were dropping off as a result. Headquarters, in turn, complained that the stores weren't setting up the merchandise properly, which was why sales were dropping. Of course, the company as a whole suffered from the deteriorating situation.

- *Stage 4: The more time passes, the greater the emotions and hostilities.* And the more the data becomes distorted, the more difficult, if not impossible, it becomes to focus on the original (and often smaller) issue! At Dently, the conflict between headquarters and the field soon mutated into conflicts regarding sales commissions, promotional budgets, and other related issues. As the "virus" spread, factions broke off within the headquarters and field operations; some fought the "outsiders," while others sparred with people across the hall. By this point, it is unlikely that anyone could have traced the original problem back to the favoritism that the founder's son showed toward operations at headquarters: refurbishing the head office while the field people languished in barrackslike quarters, instituting a policy that head office people could leave early every Friday, and offering higher compensation for positions at headquarters than for commensurate field positions. Of course, without focusing on the original problem, there was little hope of finding a lasting solution.

- *Stage 5: The conflict becomes life-threatening. It contaminates customers and vendors.* This final phase hit Dently hard. Not surprisingly, customer service began dropping as more attention was paid to internal bickering than to stocking the stores and maintaining top-notch displays. And in today's retail environment, dissatisfied customers merely have to walk next door to a competitor. Loyalty is ephemeral. So was the tenure of the young chairman at Dently; the board finally realized the root of the problem and summarily replaced him with an even-handed leader. He was able to bring in an outside resource who could help him identify the issues as perceived by key vendors and people in the field and by people at the home office; he then translated the issues into a common vision throughout the company's management. Within six months the situation began to turn, and within a year, the company was acting as a unified and profitable business entity.

Now let's consider two detailed cases from the files of my company, John Arnold ExecuTrak Systems. We'll examine how the "disease" progressed from one stage to another until the entire organization was compromised.

The Slouching Furniture Company

No one at Arland Corporation was surprised when the CEO announced he was leaving—immediately. Actually, he was fired. The once profitable $60 million furniture maker had been hemorrhaging badly during the past two years, and it might have slid into Chapter 11 if drastic action hadn't been taken. The board brought in C. W. Grant, a CEO-for-hire, for a six-month stint. During this time, Grant was to turn the company around and find a permanent replacement. Grant astutely recognized that organizational conflict was in large part responsible for Arland's problems, and he knew that the conflict needed to be resolved before the company could hope to get on its feet. He'd also read about the Arnold Conflict Resolution Process, and he asked if we would help out.

As Grant explained it, Arland had already reached Stage 5 (life-threatening conflict)—the most difficult stage to resolve. In fact, the company had progressed from Stage 1 to Stage 5 with alarming speed. The "we-they" boundaries had sprung up when Arland's major supplier couldn't keep up with nationwide demand for a new product line. As Arland's sales representatives were pushed for volume "to meet the numbers," they continued to promise delivery and put pressure on the home office staff. The home office accused the sales reps of being unrealistic, while the sales reps accused the home office of being unresponsive.

Already separated by distance from the home office, the sales reps banded together and tried to recruit "insiders" in the home office for their cause, while the home office sought sympathetic reps (Stage 2, polarization). The "problem" with sales or the "problem" with the head office became the dominant discussion theme (Stage 3, conflict expands). Sales and the home office managers soon found other "problems" with the way each other did business (Stage 4, hostilities increase). While the two sides bickered, customer service levels plummeted, endangering the whole enterprise (Stage 5).

When we arrived on site, our interviewing team began gathering information. During the course of the first week, we spoke with 40 internal constituencies—managers and supervisors at all levels, and a select group of hourly employees that included two union stewards. We also interviewed institutional customers and furniture designers to pinpoint external problems.

Within three weeks, we had analyzed the data and written a detailed feedback report. Then we conducted an all-day session with CEO Grant, presenting him with a "family portrait" that revealed how the people within and outside Arland viewed the situation. The discrepancies, as is often the case, were striking. The Arlanders blamed various internal factions. Service/installation and accounting, for example, pointed to sales as the source of the problem. "Oftentimes I wonder if the sales people ever get the message," complained one manager. Sales claimed that there wasn't enough support. And the fingerpointing went round and round.

Customers, of course, weren't privy to the internal problems, so they landed on the sales account reps, which was only natural, since the reps were the only tangible contacts. As one customer put it, "I constantly have to go to management to get action on an order. The sales reps can't produce on their orders or make things happen. It's a waste of my time to track down the answers to other people's mistakes." And a designer complained that "it takes so long to get any kind of answer from Arland. They have so much internal communication to go through that it frustrates the whole design process. The reps should be able to come back with answers by the next day."

After the feedback session, we held an all-day meeting with the 26 top managers from across the business. They were bloodied and bruised by the many issues revealed when they saw the whole picture. (This is one advantage of using an outside impartial interviewing team—the red ink, falling sales figures, and many anonymous quotes we presented were undeniable.) Most important, the managers wanted to arrive at answers to questions such as, "Where can we go from here?" "Is this even a viable business?" "Are we beyond hope?"

I outlined a proposal and process to help them identify the key planning assumptions and critical success factors for the business for the next one to three years. When these were agreed upon, we focused on the company's mission, direction, and basic strategies. The managers also agreed to reduce the number of product lines the company would carry, so they could concentrate their limited resources on particular market niches and on other areas in which they excelled and hence had a competitive edge.

Through our process, we were able to shift the focus from manager versus manager to the key strategic and tactical issues—on "what," "why," and "how" rather than "who."

We continued to work with Arland's management team for the next two months, helping to refine the company's objectives, rightsize the organization, and pinpoint role relationships as well as the lines of responsibility, authority, and accountability. At the end of that time, Arland had a team that was wired together and functioning as a unit with a shared vision and mission. Sales picked up significantly, and the company gained ground, even during the recession of the early 1990s. The secret was curing the disease before Stage 5 became terminal.

Trouble North of the Border

When Nelson Carter joined the New York-based financial giant ELT Group, he knew that of the company's three foreign subsidiaries, the Canadian group far and away outperformed the others. But he was somewhat shocked to learn that it was also the most troublesome entity within the group. In a nutshell, all communication between Canada and the U.S. headquarters had broken down.

The Stage 1 conflict began the moment the ink dried on the paper formalizing the purchase of the Canadian group. The very boundary between the two countries served as a symbolic "we-they" dividing line, as the Canadians perceived that their U.S. counterparts wished to make them a "fifty-first state." The we-they thinking soon led to squabbling over operational procedures and processes, and a mutual lack of responsiveness to routine inquiries. This merely reinforced the U.S. headquarters' "paternalistic" role, and the "rebellious child" role of the Canadian "division."

Stage 2 manifested itself in jokes about the other "side's" managers;

the U.S. managers referred to the "surround-the-wagon mentality" of the Canadians, implying that they were still in the pioneer stage. The Canadians talked about the southern "imperialists" and how great it would be to "secede from the union." (In one instance, the Canadian managers found a cartoon of someone sitting in the corner with a dunce cap. They typed in the caption, "I see you had another meeting with New York," then circulated it throughout the company.) ELT slid into Stages 3 and 4 as the jokes and resentment became institutionalized on both sides of the border. Had CEO Carter not intervened, chances are that ELT might have visited Stage 5, with its terrible consequences.

Carter, who had recently read a previous book of mine, thought that ExecuTrak Systems could help resolve the conflicts, and he invited us to help restore relations between the United States and Canada. We agreed, on the basis that the Canadian president, Ron Berenson, would decide whether or not I would be hired. "You can't just parachute me into the Canadian office and expect him to welcome me with open arms; you'll be sowing the seeds of destruction," I told Carter. He agreed that Berenson would have veto power, spoke with him on the phone about his plans, then briefed an associate and me on the situation before we headed up to the north country.

Not surprisingly, Ron Berenson was not pleased to see a team that U.S. headquarters was suggesting he hire. In fact, he was distressed. "There's nothing wrong up here," he had told Carter, and now impressed on me in rather strong language. "If New York would just stop treating us like second-class citizens and asking us stupid questions, we'd all get along fine." I explained to him that I wasn't being foisted upon him to conduct some sort of "espionage" or to help his people "see the light"; on the contrary, I was on a fact-finding mission that involved gaining an understanding of Canada's *and* New York's perspectives.

The goal was to work with both sides and arrive at a mutual understanding of the company's goals and strategy, not sort out who's right or who's wrong. Berenson couldn't turn me down at that point without seeming unreasonable, and he agreed to at least have me compile data. Depending on what we came up with, he'd decide whether he wanted to participate in a joint "summit meeting" led by ExecuTrak Systems.

The next week, we began interviewing the Canadian managers, and several days later we made a presentation to Berenson. The Canadian president was not surprised to learn that many of his people bitterly resented the U.S. headquarters' belief that the Canadians didn't understand the business. Said one manager, "There's a perception in the U.S. that all of the expertise lies in New York. While they seem to respect that we have some ability, it's not really a two-way street. I don't really think our input is sought on certain major items. This may be because we are so much smaller and our system is outdated—so they may believe that we're not in the same league. They also just make the problems worse by spending resources on U.S. problems and enhancements, not on solving our problems."

Another manager confirmed the feelings, saying, "The problems seem to be that New York doesn't have any confidence in us. Too many memos from my counterparts are crisp, cold, and sparse. The implication is that I'm not worth relating to. And there is far too much advice being given by them about our operational decisions."

Berenson nodded and smiled as we read off the list, shooting me occasional "I told you so" looks. But his demeanor suddenly changed when he learned that his people considered *him* to be a significant part of the communication problem. According to several of his managers, Berenson censored everything coming out of the Canadian operation. "We can't make a move or do anything to build relations with New York....[Ron] doesn't want us to look even the slightest bit conciliatory." This, of course, just further reinforced the feelings of being inadequate or second-rate that so many of the ELT Canada people harbored.

At first, a red-faced Berenson refused to believe that the interviews were correct, and he wanted to know who made those comments. But the interviews were done in strict confidence, and we couldn't betray the trust of those who spoke so candidly with us. After calming down, Berenson was ready to learn what he needed to do to change his style to "stop giving this impression."

Back in the "lower 48," Carter also had a surprise in store for him after we returned and had conducted on-site interviews with *his* staff. He and his colleagues had no idea that the Canadian managers had some very valid reasons for feeling the way they did. In fact, they mistook the Canadians' low profile as simply a "cultural difference" and their lack of responsiveness as just plain "orneriness."

Once both sides had digested our feedback, they agreed to a summit meeting on neutral turf (fortunately for us, in the wine country of California) at which we first compared and contrasted the key issues and opportunities as perceived by each side and later helped them understand their priorities. Eight top managers from the United States and six from the Canadian company attended the meeting. During the session, I reinforced the idea that our role was not to sort out who's right or who's wrong, but to get people to acknowledge that there was, indeed, "dirty laundry" and a lot of misconceptions on both sides. I impressed upon them that the key task ahead was to put together a mutually agreed-upon mission, agenda, and set of objectives for a common vision.

That three-and-a-half-day team-building conference, held in Montreal, went extremely well: the missions and objectives of the parent and subsidiary were wrestled through and agreed upon, and we were able to move on to developing a strategy that gave Canada its due input as both an independent organization in its own right and an important constituent of the corporation. Among the actions agreed upon and implemented were the following: (1) the top issues between the United States and Canada would be made visible, with plans and progress reporting, on a monthly basis; (2) certain policies and procedures would be modified; (3) a senior Canadian manager would be transferred to the parent headquarters; and (4) quarterly joint meetings would be held.

A year later we were pleased to learn that ELT now regularly sponsored joint meetings between the U.S. operations and *all* its foreign subsidiaries to ensure that the situation with Canada would not repeat itself. This was a wise move, given the high stakes of the game. And Ron Berenson's leadership had proved to be so capable that he was promoted to executive vice president of the parent company!

Summary

All organizational conflicts, though unique, contain the common elements described in this chapter. Sometimes the elements may be obscured by the time dimensions—a company might quickly progress from Stage 1 to Stage 5, or it might succumb slowly. Less frequently, it might stay at a particular stage for some period of time and never further decline, or it might remain at one stage for a protracted period, then rapidly progress to the final stage. But regardless of the time line, the consequences of not resolving the conflict are the same the defection of top talent, and key managerial and technical positions that become "revolving doors"; missed ship dates and windows of opportunity; impaired performance and lost productivity; diminished quality and customer service; and reduced profitability.

How can you staunch the progression from Stage 1 to Stage 5? The next chapter provides an overview of the Arnold Conflict Resolution Process. And in the following chapters you'll see it at work in many different operational contexts, countries, and cultures. Finally, in Chapter 11, you'll learn how to take preventive measures that reduce the probability of future organizational conflicts.

2

The Arnold Conflict Resolution Process

A Button-Down Sporting Event

The conference room at Jackson Limited looked like a bizarre sporting event in which the contestants wore suits and ties rather than athletic gear. Sales and marketing people sat on the left side of the table, while representatives from manufacturing and engineering sat on the right side. Both "teams" waited in silence for the "umpire" (actually, Len Craft, Jackson's general manager) to arrive. The topic: soaring customer complaints and plummeting customer service levels.

When Craft arrived, he cut straight to the chase and began asking for input. Within seconds, emotions erupted across the table. From sales and marketing's perspective, the blame clearly lay with the production side of the company. "Manufacturing isn't supporting us," complained the sales manager. "We gulp when we make a commitment to a customer because we know it probably won't be there when we say it will. And when it does arrive, 15 percent of it will come flying back because of defects. Then there's engineering....We know we can't count on engineering to make design changes that will keep our products competitive. They're sabotaging our efforts to get out there in front of customers!"

Manufacturing and engineering in turn accused sales and marketing of placing impossible demands on them. "You guys treat us like a black box," said one manager. "You make customer promises on the basis of what will earn a quick commission, not on what we can realistically produce. And when our backs are shoved to the wall, of course quality will fall. You can't just snap your fingers and have products instantly materialize on a customer's shipping dock!"

Craft let the bloodletting go on for half an hour—he figured it would be healthy. Then he opened the door and ushered me into the room. My mission: prevent a fight to the death and get everyone playing on the same team.

This was a milestone in my consulting career, because it was the first time that I had articulated a unified approach to conflict resolution. For 10 years prior to my engagement with Jackson Limited, I had used my total system for competitive problem-solving method. I had also helped warring factions at many companies to update their missions, clarify their goals, sort out their differences, and arrive at mutually agreeable solutions to problems ranging from annoying clashes about processes and procedures to catastrophic rifts that threatened to tear apart the organizational structures.

At Jackson, I would combine a streamlined version of my problem-solving method with my method of generating "win-win" resolutions to clashes in expectations and needs. By marrying the two approaches, I thought I had developed a generic approach that would enable companies to quickly home in on the root cause of the conflict, identify criteria for developing possible solutions, generate specific resolutions, then select the one that would lead to a win-win outcome.

The people at Jackson responded well; after two days of using the process (and helping me to "tweak" it), the opposing sides were willing to play together and march to Len Craft's drumbeat. Within a month, sales and marketing were working hand-in-hand with engineering and manufacturing to develop realistic schedules—ones that would allow enough time to produce quality product while remaining competitive in terms of lead times. It wasn't a perfectly smooth road to recovery, but within a year the company regained the confidence of its customers and grew significantly.

During the 10 years that have passed since I first walked into the Jackson "playoffs," I've kept in close touch with Len. He was able to apply the conflict resolution method to other issues before they snowballed out of control and threatened profitability. He then became CEO of a much larger organization and has successfully applied the 10-step conflict resolution process to other situations, once employing ExecuTrak Systems on a particularly sensitive strategic alliance.

Over the years I've changed some of the wording and descriptions of the Arnold Conflict Resolution Process (see Figure 2-1), but the core

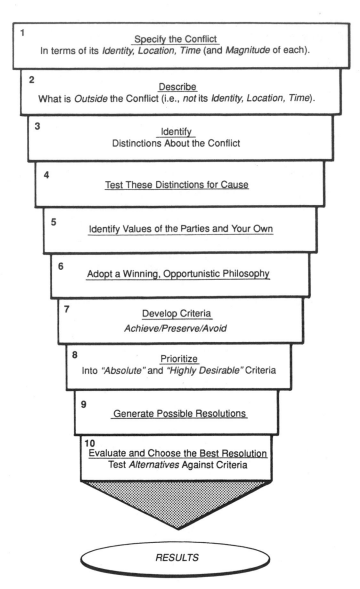

1 Specify the Conflict
In terms of its *Identity, Location, Time* (and *Magnitude* of each).

2 Describe
What is *Outside* the Conflict (i.e., *not* its *Identity, Location, Time*).

3 Identify
Distinctions About the Conflict

4 Test These Distinctions for Cause

5 Identify Values of the Parties and Your Own

6 Adopt a Winning, Opportunistic Philosophy

7 Develop Criteria
Achieve/Preserve/Avoid

8 Prioritize
Into *"Absolute"* and *"Highly Desirable"* Criteria

9 Generate Possible Resolutions

10 Evaluate and Choose the Best Resolution
Test *Alternatives* Against Criteria

RESULTS

Figure 2-1. *The Arnold Conflict Resolution Process.* Ten steps to resolving organizational conflicts. (*Copyright © 1991 by John D. Arnold, John Arnold ExecuTrak Systems, Inc., Waltham, MA. All rights reserved.*)

methodology remains the same. In this chapter, you'll learn the basics of each step in the process (subsequent chapters demonstrate how the method can be used to resolve various types of organizational conflicts). As you read the steps, don't worry about how they might be used at your company, government agency, or religious or nonprofit organization; once you've seen the whole process in action in the following chapters, you'll get a good sense of how they can be applied toward resolving unique conflicts at your own company.

The program is divided into two phases: (1) diagnosis and (2) issue resolution. The steps involved in each phase are described below. My conflict resolution process adapts these steps to the specific purpose of ferreting out the clashing expectations that lead to strife in the first place, and it supplies a method for preventing conflicts from developing or for correcting them once they do.

The Arnold Conflict Resolution Process: A Generic System

Phase 1: Diagnosis

Step 1: Reconstruct the "Crime" (i.e., the Problem). This phase involves describing three dimensions of the conflict in specific and objective terms.

- *Identity: What* is the nature of the conflict? For example, an acquired company might consider the new parent to be overbearing; middle management and employees might be up in arms because a popular leader was fired capriciously; or two groups might be vying for internal resources, making them competitive with each other rather than against companies outside the business. In every instance, general terms such as "overbearing," "up in arms," "capriciously," and "competitive" need to be specified further; that is, in what ways are they "competing" against each other? And just what is meant by "capricious"? The better the definition of words used to describe the identity of the conflict, the better everyone's understanding of the problem. So describe what the complaint or conflict is and what people specifically say about it.

- *Location: Where* is the conflict occurring, or where did it occur? Is the conflict only at the headquarters operations or only in certain regions? Or is it happening throughout the entire operation? Specify *exactly* where the conflict is happening: whether at a particular site, throughout the company, internationally, and so on. Specify also where the complaints are originating from. Who is involved in the conflict?

As with the identity dimension, the location dimension is extremely important since it can provide valuable clues about the root cause of conflict. Often, when we are in the midst of a conflict, we assume that the strife is occurring everywhere throughout the organization. In fact, it may well be limited to one location, and knowing that fact will help you identify the root cause. (The importance of root causes will become evident when we discuss the identification of distinctions in Steps 2 and 3 below.)

- *Time:* Pin down the date and, if at all possible, the time *when* the conflict began. If you don't know specific dates and times, think back to any specific event that preceded or commenced just after the conflict began in order to determine approximately when it began. Beware of one pitfall: you might be building in an *assumed* cause if you link up the conflict with a particular event or condition. The event or condition may, in fact, have absolutely nothing to do with the conflict.

Other temporal aspects to be considered include the *periodicity* of the conflict. Has it been ongoing since it started? Has it really been happening *all* the time with no "truce" periods? Is it sporadic or cyclical? Periodicity, too, will help you define what is unique about the conflict.

One fascinating client application from the ExecuTrak files involves a multinational conglomerate with significant holdings in the Far East. Relations seemed alright between U.S. operations and those in the Far East, although the business was falling off—until the annual East-West "get-together" when "all hell broke loose." From the telephone and mail correspondence, you never would suspect that the East-West conflict was as serious as it was.

By applying the methodology, we helped the company focus on cultural issues as a major cause of the problem. This in turn revealed a basic lack of sensitivity on the part of each constituency to learn about and respond to the other's respective business customs and values, which each side regarded as a personal affront.

Without considering the time dimension, this important root cause might never have been recognized, and it would not have been recognized that such underlying hostilities were, in part, eroding the business.

As you map out the three dimensions of identity, location, and time, be sure to include the scope or magnitude of each one. For example, how many people are involved (and who, specifically is part of the conflict)? How many instances of conflict can you document? Is there a unique periodicity or sequence to the events related to the conflict? Are they identical? If not, describe each, as there may be separate distinct causes, each of which must be corrected to resolve the conflict.

Finally, bear in mind that the key to reconstructing the "crime" is to cast your descriptions in *specific* terms. The process of "root cause analysis" is one of continually digging deeper and deeper, looking for additional specificity. Too often, people embroiled in an organizational conflict talk in general terms that actually describe the emotional tenor of the situation and how they view it rather than the specific, objective, factual elements that give the conflict a unique identity. This is especially true when people are in the midst of a bitter conflict that has reached Stage 4 (so much time has passed that the original cause of the conflict has long been forgotten) or Stage 5 (the conflict threatens the existence of the organization and the careers of those who run it). When people speak in generalities, they often try to prove their points or justify their positions rather than uncover the core nature of the problem.

If you're in the thick of the conflict, try to step back or bring in an impartial observer who can collect facts objectively. However you collect the data, the better the job of defining the identity, location, and time dimensions, the higher the probability you actually may unearth the real underlying cause of the conflict; hence, the more likely you will be to develop effective solutions.

Step 2: Describe What's *Outside* the Conflict.   Here, you will determine what is *not* the identity, location, and time. This step is important in that it will help you to draw identity, time, and space boundaries; this, in turn, will help you to definitively determine which are the core issues and to zero in to the most probable cause.

First, ask yourself, "What's *not* been part of this organizational conflict?" If, for example, you're dealing with counterproductive fingerpointing between design engineering and manufacturing, it's important to identify and distinguish between exactly who is involved and who isn't. That will help you to throw a spotlight on what caused the conflict—and it will help you to develop approaches to resolving it. Just what does "fingerpointing" mean? What is reported? What do you see that says to you, "fingerpointing"? Be specific!

Next, ask, "Are there locations that aren't involved in the conflict?" Perhaps the regional or field offices are free of strife, or vice versa. Is headquarters really the only "island of sanity"? In other words, you are pinpointing where the people or organizations are in conflict and where they are not, where conflict exists and where it doesn't.

Are there times when the parties involved are *not* in conflict? Perhaps the sparring that design engineering and manufacturing people are doing doesn't occur during the new-product design stage when you'd expect it to. But once several prototypes are put into production, the sparks begin to fly. This will tell you that the internal struggle may well involve and be triggered by something about the production process versus something in the design process.

As in the case of Step 1, specificity is crucial—describing what is outside the conflict in as specific terms as possible. If manufacturing seems to be at the core of the problem, is everybody in the department involved? Perhaps just assembly-line A is. And on assembly-line A, perhaps just those people involved with final finishing operations are. Does the problem occur on all shifts, or just on certain shifts? By carefully specifying the identity, location, and time of the conflict in terms of what it is and is not, you'll know the *precise* nature of the problem and can begin developing lines of attack. I cannot stress enough that precision is key. A brilliant solution to the wrong problem won't help you in the slightest; it will probably even make things worse!

Step 3: Identify the Distinctions.   This step involves comparing Steps 1 and 2, to determine what is *unique* about the conflict. Contrast the subject and object of the conflict with what is *not* the subject and object. Let's continue with a real example cited above—the design engineering and manufacturing departments. They got along fine until a new aircraft engine prototype went into production. By knowing that only when the prototype went into the production process did the sparks start to fly, you can begin asking what it is about this part of the process that set people at each other's throats.

What came out from this application of the conflict resolution process was that the manufacturing people didn't feel that they had enough input into the product development process; in fact, the company had put together a team of design engineers and manufacturing engineers to do the "thinking for manufacturing." As a result, they designed products that in prototype could be made in one's and two's but couldn't be made within budget or specs during full production runs—"producibility" hadn't been factored into the design equation. Yet, until this cause was determined, design engineering people felt that they were dealing with a third-rate production arm (a "wet blanket," as one engineer put it) and that whatever they did, their brilliant designs would be sabotaged.

The same line of thinking applies to any other organizational conflict situation. After describing each dimension (identity, location, and time) in terms of what the "crime" is and is not, you'll find yourself dealing with the core issues that motivate people to behave in a certain way at a certain time and not at another.

Conflicts stemming from restructurings, mergers, acquisitions, and so on, usually provide striking examples of the before-and-after phenomenon. In these situations some brilliant and creative people and achievers are often reduced to demoralized automatons with little desire to do more than punch a time clock; others, fearful for their jobs, become tyrants and project subtle currents of anger throughout their divisions; still others take up a call to arms and initiate a civil war.

In any case, by doing a good job of contrasting what is and is not involved in your conflict, you'll be able to identify what is unique or distinctive about it. That in turn will help you to zero in on the true causes and develop focused solutions to the problems that have led to the conflict at hand.

Step 4: Test the Distinctions for Cause.   Once you know what is unique about the conflict, you can begin testing one or more hypotheses about each of the differentiating factors or distinctions. In other words, how could each one have caused the conflict?

The importance of testing the hypotheses derived from distinctions for unique cause is well illustrated by the experience of the new director of organizational excellence at a large consumer-products company. This individual, whom we will call Bill, was hired to replace a weaker director of training and development. For the first six months, everyone thought Bill was doing a "bang-up" job. Beamed one division manager: "He's bright, dedicated, and a real achiever. He's really helped us get off to a terrific start!"

At the end of the year, the vice president of human resources, Walt, to whom Bill reported, asked the division managers whether Bill should get a raise. Eight managers said absolutely, but four said "No—he's doing a great job, but we really don't think he's ready yet." This puzzled Walt. If Bill was doing such a great job, why wasn't he entitled to a raise?

Walt had trained in our problem-solving and conflict resolution seminars earlier, and applied the method. He quickly discovered something distinctive to the four managers who had suggested that Bill wasn't quite ready for a raise; these four, and *only* these four, had received negative feedback about training and development activities in their division from Bill during the prior year. Now, none of these managers were petty or vindictive people in Walt's experience. And none criticized Bill's work. So what was the cause of the problem?

"Negative feedback from Bill" was the only distinction Walt could find in common to the four managers in contrast to the other eight. Further independent probing of the four managers yielded a surprising and consistent answer. Whereas the previous director of training and development would look them straight in the eye and point out areas of weakness that needed shoring up, Bill would look down and smile all the time he gave critical feedback. This made him appear disingenuous; each manager felt uncomfortable with Bill sitting there smiling at them, and they began to distrust him.

Walt confronted Bill with the situation and learned something else surprising: Bill was so enthusiastic and wanted so much to support the division managers that he was uncomfortable criticizing them!

Had Walt not analyzed the key dimensions in terms of what the "crime" is and is not, the feedback from the four managers might have remained a mystery dimension, no one would have learned anything, and Bill would not have gotten a well-deserved raise nor had any incentive to change his style. (He subsequently did—he became known as a kind but "straight-shooting" executive.)

In any situation, test *each* of the causal hypotheses derived from the distinctions against the dimensions of the conflict and see if it fits—that is, whether it explains not only what is but also what is *not* part of the problem in terms of its identity, location, and time (and the scope of each). Then validate whether a given cause is indeed the cause of the conflict by asking the participants whether or not your conclusions are on target. There may even be some ways to empirically test the validity of your conclusion as true cause.

The hypothesis-testing step is very important because it helps you crystallize a set of actions that have the best likelihood of eliminating the cause of the conflict and reaching a solution that's agreeable to all parties involved.

Step 5: Identify the Values Involved.   Whether you're a participant in the conflict or an observer, it's important to identify your own values, expectations, attitudes, and so on. If you're in the conflict, your values may be contributing to the events and conditions of the struggle. At best, failure to identify your values and attitudes may cause you to make erroneous assessments and judgments. As a participant, this will simply extend the conflict or twist it in new directions.

If you're an observer, understanding your values and attitudes is vital to your being able to understand the situation and take a neutral stance. That's because as an observer, you may make assumptions and draw conclusions that simply aren't true. (See Figure 2-2 for a graphic representation of the phenomenon.)

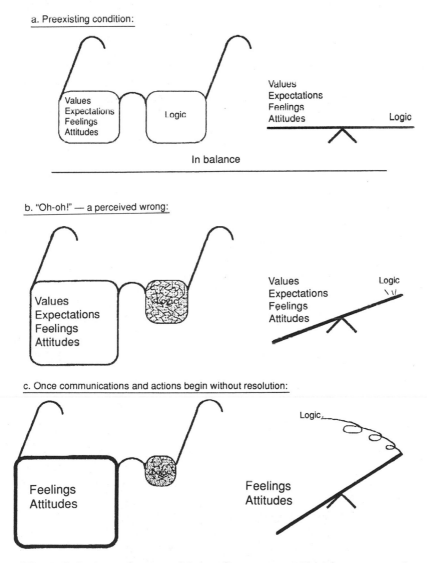

Figure 2-2. As an observer of the conflict, you must identify your own values.

Phase II: Issue Resolution

Step 6: Adopt a Winning, Opportunistic Philosophy. This step involves adopting a mindset that will enable you and your colleagues to see beyond what might appear to be mutually conflicting objectives. For example, sales and marketing might insist on having as many available product options as possible on the shelf, whereas those responsible for inventory control are trying to cut costs and reduce the number of stocked items.

In any case, no organization has unlimited resources, so there is bound to be internal competition for money, material, equipment, space, people, and so on. When you consider the potential for clashes of expectations, it's obvious that conflicts don't represent aberrations. Rather, they are part and parcel of the normal working environment. Can you think of an organization to which you have ever belonged that didn't have some degree of conflict? If so, it's rare!

The key is to develop an attitude in which people view conflicts as opportunities that can lead to "double-win" outcomes (that is, wins for all parties).

Fostering the attitude that conflicts are simply opportunities to negotiate a consensus might be difficult, especially when people are in the midst of an emotionally charged fray. But you can help them adopt a new attitude by pointing out that those who lose the "fight" will likely carry a grudge. And if you have to work with those people again, or depend on them for something at a future date, it probably makes more sense to seek a double-win than to force a win-lose situation. Note that this is very different from encouraging people to make compromises. When people compromise, no one feels satisfied, and the conflict may never be truly put to bed, as people will harbor ill-will and may take actions later in time to cripple you and your plans.

Step 7: Develop Criteria. With a clear identification of the issues and a proper mindset, you can now determine what each party in the conflict wants to *achieve*, *preserve*, and *avoid* (the three terms being known as the APA criteria). These three words truly apply to the resolution of any problem or issue. Think about it: when you're trying to find a solution to a problem, you will always want to achieve one or more objectives, preserve certain conditions, and avoid other problems.

Let's say that you're a manager in an insurance company and you want to see an increase in productivity. Your goal is more underwriting per month—that's what you want to *achieve*. But at the same time, you want to *preserve* the quality of work that goes into the underwriting process, and you want to *avoid* creating a stressful situation in which people feel pressured and resentful. A solution to the problem will be one that provides the tools to increase the amount of underwriting, rather than an edict such as "ten percent more per month or else...."

To find out what people want to achieve, preserve, or avoid, just ask! Part of our interviewing process simply asks people to describe their APA goals. People can anonymously let you know what they are through surveys or memos. However you collect the information, when you know everything that the warring factions want to achieve, preserve, and avoid, you can often begin to see possibilities for negotiating a double-win solution that will allow the organization to work together and go forward.

Step 8: Assign Priorities. Once you have determined what it is that everyone wants to achieve, preserve, and avoid, you can set about differentiating *absolutely essential* requirements from those that are important and *desirable* but not essential. For instance, an acquired company might be looking for more autonomy and less-demanding reporting procedures from the parent, among other things. The autonomy issues may be nonnegotiable, but some of the reporting requirements may not be as necessary as others or can wait until the acquired company feels more comfortable with its new parent.

Whatever the circumstances, translating the demands of the parties into APA criteria, and then assigning priorities to these, is a critical step in getting the conflicting parties to develop workable solutions. But too often in organizational conflicts (and often in conflicts between people), the parties tend to adopt an inflexible, "take no hostage" position. This leads to nonproductive head butting in which no progress is made and the conflict simply intensifies over time.

By getting agreement as to what everyone wants to achieve, preserve, and avoid, and then negotiating what is absolutely essential versus what is very important and desirable but negotiable, you'll generally find that creative and practical options can be generated. These in turn should enable all parties to find a reasonable resolution to the conflict.

Step 9: Generate Possible Resolutions. In the following chapters, you'll see many detailed cases of how companies have gone about creating solutions to their various conflicts. In fact, that's really what the remainder of this book is about. At this point, suffice it to say that the process of generating possible solutions to organizational conflicts involves drawing on your knowledge of the parties and their demands and wants as reflected by the prioritized criteria. In fact, use the criteria to generate possible ways of resolving the conflict. The criteria are *how* you might go about "achieving, preserving, and avoiding."

As with the other steps of this process, specificity is crucial; the more specifically you describe each option, the easier it will be to evaluate it against the absolute requirements and compare/evaluate it with other possibilities against the desirable criteria to determine how to resolve the organizational conflict (Step 10).

Often, by the time you have reached Step 9, the best conflict resolution steps will be evident, as was the situation at the aircraft engine company where it became painfully clear that new-product development simply couldn't rely on manufacturing engineering to "think" for the manufacturing department; instead, appropriate representatives from design engineering, manufacturing engineering, and manufacturing all had to be on new-product development teams. The same was true when Walt probed for and discovered the cause of four managers' uneasiness with Bill, his organizational excellence professional. He spoke with both the manager group and Bill, and Bill was able to modify his feedback-giving style accordingly.

Clearly, putting the focus of a conflicting organization on generating conceptual or specific resolutions to meet the agreed-upon criteria helps in one major way: you provide a much greater opportunity and incentive for people to shift from wallowing in the conflict to finding a double-win solution.

Later chapters present a number of applications of Step 9 to situations with clients, showing how possible solutions to conflict can be generated from the criteria list.

Step 10: Evaluate the Proposed Resolutions and Choose the Best Resolutions.   Once you have developed potential resolutions to the conflict, the final step is to evaluate each one and select the ones most likely to end the conflict. You do this by testing each resolution against the criteria identified in Step 7 and prioritized in Step 8. "Shoot down" any of the resolutions that fail to meet any of the criteria deemed *absolutely essential*. For those that pass the crucial test of meeting absolutely essential criteria, compare and evaluate them against one another in terms of those deemed *desirable*. In this way, you can determine which ones do the best overall job.

Do these steps seem somewhat mechanical? Actually they are not—as long as you have factored the values, expectations, attitudes, and feelings of the parties to the prioritized criteria (Step 8) and have evaluated the options objectively in Step 10.

In some cases, the bulk of the work will involve ferreting out the root cause; once you've found it, resolution is self-evident. In others, the focus will be on developing innovative optional solutions, on getting agreement on the prioritized criteria, on ensuring that you have a valid database on the options to test against the prioritized criteria, and on getting the appropriate representatives of the conflict to do the evaluation collaboratively.

The next chapter presents an actual client example that illustrates the process of smoking out the issues and locating the root cause of an organizational conflict; Chapter 4 presents a typology of organizational conflicts. In Chapters 5 through 10, you'll then see how the process works in the six types of conflict situations.

3

The Scene of the Crime: Identifying the Roots of Conflict

ExecuTrak File 175: "Shootout at the OK Corral"

At the young age of 46, Roger Weston had already served as chief financial officer of Kelco Corporation, a billion-dollar-a-year holding company, for six years. An aggressive executive eager for new challenges, he was thrilled when Kelco's CEO asked him if he'd like to take over JPK Industries, a struggling operating company consisting of a $300 million consumer-electronics business with 3300 employees. Despite a strong sales force of 600, the company was losing its market share to both a very aggressive American upstart and a major Japanese manufacturer.

Phil Howard, the incumbent president of JPK, had failed on several consecutive occasions to meet goals, despite the efforts of his much-lauded executive vice president, Mal Beatty, a man with a solid 15-year record of operations and sales accomplishments in one of the blue-chip computer companies. After considerable deliberation and discussion with several colleagues whose advice he trusted, Weston agreed to take the position. Howard was given a liberal severance package and allowed to "pursue personal business interests."

ExecuTrak Systems became involved with Kelco through an executive recruiter, Bill Evans, with whom we have at least a half dozen mutual clients. Bill had served Kelco Corporation's senior management staffing needs, and had worked with Roger Weston over a period of years. Since Weston had no line management experience, Bill contacted me about working with the new president to make his transition easier.

The Case of the Missing Market Share: Searching for Root Cause

Evans suggested that Weston meet me at a nearby resort hotel where several of us were conducting a turnaround conference for a heavy equipment manufacturer. The timing was tight, but the opportunity too important to miss.

Weston was a very trim-looking man with a no-nonsense demeanor. In contrast with many chief financial officers, he showed considerable sensitivity to the importance of corporate culture, the need to meld different business philosophies and management styles within an organization, and the brevity of a new CEO's "honeymoon period"—especially as a firm's prospects sag and profit pressures increase. This was all the more remarkable given the fact he had no prior line management experience.

Weston was also a very task-focused executive; when I suggested that we meet at 6:30 a.m. for breakfast, he said, "What's wrong with six o'clock? That will give us at least an extra half hour before you start your seven-thirty conference."

As good fortune would have it, we finished our discussion at 7 a.m., just as the president of our client's firm arrived. I introduced the two executives to each other, mentioning that Weston was exploring the possibility of using us. I then suggested that our client talk candidly about my work with him while I left.

The following day, Weston gave me some feedback by phone about both his favorable reactions to our meeting and to the discussion he'd had with our client's president. He agreed to return to the hotel to meet at 10:30 p.m. following the conference; this would also provide some time frame to prepare a proposal for what could be an initial project: to shrink Weston's take-charge time during which he would learn the key issues and develop a cohesive team and common vision. The goal was to increase JPK's market share and profitability.

Weston arrived at 11 p.m., and, given the late hour, we got right down to work and began looking at my proposal. As we discussed the situation at JPK, Weston spoke quite glowingly of Executive Vice President Mal Beatty's computer products experience and how aggressively he seemed to be taking charge of operations and sales. As the parent company's chief financial officer, Weston had observed several presentations by Beatty which he said were "impeccable." While Weston had not agreed completely with some of Beatty's basic ideas, he felt this was more a case of the prior president's views coming through the presentations than Beatty's own beliefs.

In any case, Weston clearly felt he could heavily depend on his executive vice president for effective results. To ensure that our project had Beatty's approval, I suggested that we should meet with Beatty to explain who we were and how our program works. Weston agreed wholeheartedly. (I had been alerted by executive recruiter Bill Evans that Beatty might not respond all that positively to our involvement; he had begun building tremendous loyalty, at least in operations and sales, and might therefore view us as a threat to his plans.) Indeed, when I spent several hours with Beatty, although he was formally friendly and shared a good deal of information with me, there was no question in my mind that he was "on guard."

Beatty candidly told me he wasn't sure that Weston's idea of using us as a catalyst to help accelerate Weston's learning time, foster team building, and strengthen Weston's leadership was in the best interest of the organization. The reason: now more than ever, it was Beatty's own marketing/sales and technical leadership that would be needed to provide direction for the company. While he greatly respected Weston's financial acumen, he felt that Weston's lack of any line operations experience would mean that he would be learning from Beatty more than from anyone else, rather than the other way around.

Beatty also indicated that Weston had the reputation of being not only a "green eyeshade type" but also a "nitpicker." Said Beatty, shaking his head: "He worries over every word in a sentence and requires all kinds of detail about everything in presentations to him."

I responded that a potential benefit of our project would be Weston's receiving feedback about his own leadership and management style, something that Weston had told me he would welcome. Beatty listened with the flicker of a smile, and I thought I understood! Weston had already questioned and then changed a number of words I had used in stating seven project objectives that would be "desirables" in terms of the resolutions we developed.

"Oh, I gather from your face that you've already experienced this," Beatty said, and then stated that he would "cooperate to the fullest since, apparently, this is something that Weston is going to do despite the reservations I have already expressed to him. I only hope your work, Arnold, won't derail the progress I've already been making with this organization."

Now it was my turn to smile. Specific objectives with JPK included updating the strategic plan of a year ago; strengthening functional interfaces; and determining how to select and integrate new products in a way that would increase volume, market share, and, it was hoped, profitability.

Reconstructing the "Crime"

In total, my company conducted 45 confidential interviews with key managers (including a number of executives from corporate headquarters), and we also met individually with 15 customers and suppliers. In analyzing the data from the interviews to reconstruct the "crime," it became evident to us that there were major distinctions in the value systems and business philosophies espoused by Weston and Beatty. Beatty, for example, was convinced that the company should invest heavily in new-product development—as his former employer had done—moving primarily with a newer electronic product line and, at the same time, developing ancillary products, systems, and services.

Weston, in contrast, being quite conservative, felt that the company's research and development function had still not proven itself and that the company's investment should not be in revolutionary new products. Instead, he thought that refinements to the existing product line were needed, with a strong emphasis on upgrading product and service quality, capitalizing on existing company strengths, and complementing current work methods in their market niche.

There was another reason that Weston wanted to focus on refinements to the existing product line. From what he had perceived at the parent company level, he felt that neither Beatty nor the vice president of research and development had sufficient experience, nor had they delivered on the objectives they had committed to in product planning and development under the leadership of the prior president.

Weston also felt the need to become more intimately familiar with the market, the products, the people, and the culture of the company into which he had just been parachuted. He had worked for many years under the very hands-on management style of Kelco's CEO, which was also his own orientation, and he wanted to become comfortable with what was going on and become accomplished before making a judgment to invest considerable money and time in developing a more cutting-edge product line.

Those on my staff who had been involved in the interviews, data analysis, and development of the feedback report carefully troubleshot Weston's (and Beatty's) likely reaction to our findings, conclusions, and recommendations. And there was some explosive material to report to the new leader of JPK. First, 41 percent of the managers we interviewed stressed that Weston must "set a firm company direction" and "focus on product planning, with *one* set of marching orders." Fifty percent of the managers stated that the key success factor in determining market leadership was "effective product and technology development," particularly emphasizing the need for product innovation as well as an expanded range of products.

What was likely to be most distressing was that 77 percent of the managers viewed product planning to date as an "utter failure." They said that "we're followers; we can't become leaders" and proceeded to compare the company unfavorably with its two main competitors.

Forty-one percent also claimed that lack of product development was responsible in large part for the low morale, attributing this to lack of direction in new-product development. Twenty-five percent stressed that "viable product planning is urgent." Customers and other outsiders interviewed concurred, the majority stating that JPK was *"always* a follower, never a leader in product and technology development." At the same time, however, *everyone* agreed that there were a number of promising product opportunities mentioned by participants.

Now, how did this fit with the two diametrically opposed views of Beatty and Weston? Beatty's idea was to remain with the core business, expanding the sophistication of the product line and adding high-tech multifunctionality to it. Accomplishing this goal would require further investments in research and development and significant building of skills. Weston's view, and that of a minority of managers, was to sell low-tech products and related services.

Overall, our analysis clearly showed that there was no single rallying cause or theme, no charismatic individual or strategy or tradition, no single clear "trumpet call" that would generate pledges of loyalty from employees or customers. In contrast, JPK's key competitors were viewed as having some or all of the above.

The second-highest priority issue for the managers we interviewed, after new-product planning, was leadership and management style. Of the managers we interviewed, 66 percent claimed that "lack of leadership" of the company was the primary basis of low morale. There were many statements in the interviews such as the following: "People are not clear as to how they should align their loyalties. Beatty and Weston's status could change very quickly. They are two very different kinds of people. You walk the halls and hear that an idea of yours, though it would be received favorably by Weston, will not fly because Beatty will not accept it." Another comment was, "They have diametrically opposed management styles. They could complement each other, but haven't yet found a way to do it."

A key problem was expressed by one manager: "Weston gives all line authority to Beatty but then wants to pull it back and exercise control. As a result, many people become confused. Weston is so damned detail-oriented, whereas Beatty says, 'Don't bother me with the details. We've got to make a decision today, even if we find we have to overturn it tomorrow.'"

It became very evident to us that, although employees wanted to view the company as a "technical products business," many of the senior people at the parent company, and several in the operating company, were predominantly financial people, like Weston. They were not technical people—there were no technical gurus, no technical centers of excellence within Kelco, let alone at JPK.

There was also a fair amount of criticism of Weston, most of it gathered from managers who had limited interaction with him when he was corporate chief financial officer at Kelco. Some of this criticism also stemmed from the two months of interaction people had had with him before we began our interviewing. Criticisms seemed to be, "he micromanages things" and "he doesn't make decisions on his own, but seems to rely much more on others, which is okay in some situations, except that he's kind of remote and he seems to back off whenever Beatty disagrees with him; this hurts his credibility."

Beatty also was seen as having some liabilities, including "building a clique" of favored managers. In fact, seven respondents specifically complained about his favoritism, especially in his selection of five regional managers. In this regard, Beatty was viewed as "playing politics" and "not looking beyond the 'yes-men' team he's constructed"; "all the favors, such as promotions, increases, and so on, seem to go to the 'new' people Beatty has brought in, and all the 'downers' go to the 'old' managers."

Five other respondents (with definite trepidation, despite the guarantees of anonymity) also spoke about their fear of being candid with Beatty, especially concerning the product-development and sales areas. Each feared retribution for criticism of Beatty's special passion.

A review of the composition of JPK's sales force showed that it indeed appeared to consist of representatives who had been with the company less than a year (other than 125 account and territory managers). People whom Beatty put on top were viewed by many as being promoted on the basis of "personality" and "kowtowing" to Beatty rather than on performance. There also was some concern that "people are in the field who don't know what the hell they are talking about."

Adding to this concern was the fact that "Beatty needs to get closer to senior field management and come to grips with the need for market segmentation." He was also criticized for his need to spend some time in the field to understand "what the problems are, both in sales as well as with field administration and service." This feeling was summed up by one respondent:

> Beatty is a "nonperson" to a lot of people in the field. He has this sense of urgency and understands the priorities, not in terms of the greatest mass of problems (like Weston seems to), but in terms of what needs to happen and in what sequence to move in the direction that *he* thinks is best. He definitely is success-oriented, whereas Weston is process-oriented. Beatty forces decisions and agreement on who's going to do what. In contrast, Weston keeps analyzing and discussing. He is too information-oriented, whereas Beatty relies too much on people's judgment and is too much a "shoot from the hip" type.

In all, 58 percent of the managers expressed concern about Weston's lack of decisive decision making, 27 percent stressed his detail orientation, with 5 percent commenting on his overdependency on Beatty for decision making and his willingness to cave in without challenging his executive vice president. Finally, to make things even worse, one key manager added another complaint: "I'm sure you found many managers—as well as customers and vendors—criticizing both Weston and Beatty for being inaccessible."

Recognizing that Weston was viewed as a "perfectionist," with a limited sense of humor, I knew this kind of feedback would be hard to swallow. But the fact that he was also exceptionally task-oriented meant that he would suppress his feelings and focus very "rationally" on the information. This had both negative and positive implications. On the downside, if he truly suppressed his feelings, I would not be able to reach the human being that was "buttoned up" inside, and Weston would not likely change his managing style. Since Weston's management style seemed to be to rely on others for their recommendations, and since he already had good input on how practical I am, I felt that my biggest task was *not* to get him to approve whatever I thought was in the best interests of the corporation. Rather, I should try somehow to get him in touch with his *own* feelings even though, at least initially, the more he got in touch with them, the more upset he might be with himself and the less "rational" about the company task at hand.

On the positive side, there was no doubt in my mind that Weston would leave no stone unturned to try and accomplish the task of correcting what were perceived as his management-style problems.

Presenting the Evidence

Weston's Reaction. I phoned Weston and confirmed my prior recommendation that he plan to spend the whole day on Friday in our offices reviewing our feedback report in detail, as there were several key decisions that had to be made.

"It's that bad, is it?" was his response. "You know how loath I am to invest that kind of time, John. I could have twelve to sixteen meetings on important matters in the time you're asking me to take with you."

I'd anticipated this kind of response and returned fire by saying, "Roger, I think you'll find it an excellent investment of your time. And any resultant decisions you make are going to save you and your people time, money, and frustration." He had already agreed to meet on Wednesday and now grudgingly agreed to fly in Tuesday night to meet us for breakfast the next morning and take the "bad news" standing up.

Following breakfast, we adjourned to my office where we proceeded together to go through our feedback report. Weston's reaction to the overall feedback was interesting: "A lot of new managers have been brought into the company in the last couple of years and there is a very obvious 'old versus new' mentality. Some of it has to do with the high tech side of our business—which we jettisoned or liquidated—versus what we've decided to go with for the next two to four or five years. But I had hoped that more progress had been made in melding the two groups of managers and employees than apparently has been the case."

Weston continued: "While I am not surprised that there is confusion in direction and management style—and there certainly are lots of product issues—it's possible that some of the managers will be surprised at just how much confusion appears to exist. In any case, they're probably going to be glad that everything is now being put on the table. I'm concerned, however, that they may feel, 'Since there aren't surprises here, will our attempt to resolve the issues be any different from our inability to solve them in the past?'"

One thing troubled Weston the most: "There are so many negatives on the operation of the current organization, both in the different directions Beatty and I are trying to lead people and just how we are organized to get there. I frankly feel this is going to block getting sound answers to the strategic issues, which is really where we have to cut into this 'can of worms.' Also, even though new Managing by Objectives and Profit Measurement System have been installed in the company, they are apparently not being implemented and certainly not viewed as leading to a clear direction."

At such a time, it's helpful for the counselor to be silent. Weston, too, sat silently for several minutes, staring out of my office windows at the duck pond. He finally replied in a quiet tone: "This is really bad. I don't know how I can share this information with my people. I had no idea the situation was so severe....It is no wonder my people are confused. I have to admit that a lot of what they say about me and the way I've handled decision making is unfortunately true. I really wanted to bend over backwards to show Beatty and our people that I respect his experience and that I want him to continue to provide leadership. But I recognize now that he and I are tugging in opposite directions and giving contrary signals to the organization."

Weston's analysis was still only at the surface. I had to dig deeper if I were going to accomplish the job that had to be done: somehow get him in touch with his own feelings so that he could deal with the findings as a human being rather than just "acting out" as a rather "prim and proper" manager. Only in this way could I structure a productive confrontation between Weston and Beatty that would have the likelihood of culminating in a double win in which *both* would feel good about the outcome—assuming, of course, that this was what Weston wanted.

"All this is true," I said encouragingly, "but a more basic question is, 'How do *you* honestly feel about yourself? Is this a deep disappointment? Do you feel you ought to beat your head against the wall, or what?'"

"No," he said thoughtfully, "I think I just underestimated the clash of our philosophies and styles. I haven't been in tune enough with the organization in terms of the impact I have had on them. And I haven't recognized and confronted the issue. But now, I am not sure what I should do. I certainly don't think this information ought to be shared with the team. It could rip them apart. Don't you agree?"

"Actually, Roger, I don't think there's much likelihood it would rip them apart. After all, each knows what he or she has told us so some will only be surprised at the severity of the situation. Of course, if this information is suppressed or watered-down, they'll feel 'used,' and they'll feel we've acted as your 'shill,' that we're only reporting what you wanted us to and therefore lacking integrity."

"I guess you're right about that, John. Well, what do you think we should do?"

"Roger, you're not the only president who has faced such a conflict in philosophy, direction, and style with key subordinates. It's actually quite common. Let me ask you: Do you really want a double win?"

"Absolutely," he immediately responded, as we had generally discussed the concept at our initial meeting.

"Well then, I do think it would make more sense for you and Mal to sit down with me and go over the data together before any information is released to the other managers."

"What do you really think that's going to accomplish, John? Isn't this information apt to make Beatty even more uptight and combative? It certainly gives him ammunition to use against me."

"He can use it that way if he wants to, Roger, that's true. But that's not what will happen if I've read him correctly. I think that if we set it up right, you and Beatty can have a wonderful 'heart-to-heart' talk, not personality-focused but rather in terms of, 'What's the best direction for this organization to move in?' and 'What should its mission and direction be?'

"Once you've agreed on that, then it's much easier to focus down and agree on the most appropriate strategy. That will help you determine the style of management that is going to be best for the company to get where it needs to go."

"Well, that all sounds logical, John, but aren't we apt to 'come a cropper' over that? I mean, Beatty and I have been working together now for a couple of months and you see we haven't gotten anywhere. We have had some 'heart-to-hearts,' as you put it, yet we've still gotten to the present, sad state of affairs. Having you in our meeting gives us a referee, but I don't see where that's going to help us much except bringing out into the open the serious conflict between us."

"I don't really feel there is conflict between you and Mal, Roger. Don't forget, I spent several hours with Beatty and although he may have been 'putting on a face' to imply that he feels more positively about this project than he truly does, my measure of him is that he truly wants what is best for this corporation."

"That may be, John, but he certainly has some very fixed ideas as to what that is, and they run counter to mine."

"Yes, he does. But let me suggest that if you, he, and I move off-site to work for one or two days, the two of you will mutually agree on the critical and divisive issues and be able to reconstruct the 'crime' and capitalize on the opportunity [Steps 1 to 4 of my conflict resolution process]. Then you can agree on what needs to be achieved, preserved, and avoided [Step 7] in order to achieve a double win. We'll then continue through my conflict resolution process together, evaluating alternatives against your absolutely essential and desirable criteria. I'll help keep the discussion focused on the task at hand—achieving the 'corporate good'—rather than on personalities."

"What is apt to happen as a result of doing that, John?"

"Well, together we'll be able to come up with a creative solution that not only will be best for the corporation but will allow both of you to work together far more supportively than has been the case so far."

"But what if that doesn't happen?"

"To be blunt, it may be necessary for one of you to think about resigning your post."

"You mean, there's a possibility that I'll be the one who should resign and may have to tell the boss that I need an assignment somewhere else in the corporation, or that I may have to find a job elsewhere?"

"That's it, Roger."

"Wow....And you think Mal would be willing to do the same?"

"I believe pretty strongly that he will. He is also very frustrated with the situation but hasn't dared confront you with his true feelings. He doesn't believe he's seen the same interpersonal sensitivity that I believe you possess but sometimes have difficulty revealing, especially to your direct subordinates."

"Well, John, I'm perfectly prepared to resign if that's the best thing for this corporation. But what I really would hope is that we somehow come out of the session having made whatever series of decisions are best for the organization. So how should we proceed?"

"I'd simply tell Mal that you spent a day with me going over the feedback and that there is a *lot* of tough information in there, especially for you but also for him. There's obviously a conflict in the direction each of you feels is best for the company, so before I'm asked to conduct a feedback session for the management group, you would like me to go over the identical feedback with him. Then, using me as a facilitator, the three of us will get together and review the issues and come up with a plan. I'll be happy then to phone him, respond to his questions and explain the process I plan to use, which includes your giving me permission to first sit down with him as he reviews an identical copy of the feedback report."

"Okay. I think that makes a lot of sense, John. I'll do it."

Beatty's Reactions. The next day, I spoke with Beatty over the phone, and he agreed to meet with me on Thursday. The one ground rule I established with him was that he *not* disclose the contents of the feedback report to anyone inside or outside of the company until both he and Weston agreed that such a disclosure was wise.

Thursday was as difficult a day for Mal as Tuesday had been for Roger. While he was pleased at some of the positives about his leadership and reinforcement for some of his views and philosophies, there was also a lot of distressing information for him. He agreed that it made eminent sense to meet with Roger and me to resolve key issues and map out a game plan.

The Rendezvous

On Saturday and Sunday that week, the four of us (the three of us plus my administrative assistant) met at a hotel near their offices, where we had booked a conference suite. Our goal was to determine, within the next 48 hours, the best mission, direction, strategy, and leadership style for JPK.

While my administrative assistant set up a word processor and copy machine, and got ready to process the output of our discussion, Weston, Beatty, and I started our discussion. I began by asking both how they felt. Each indicated, with some anxiety, that he wanted to do what was best for the company. Weston stated that he had no hesitation about resigning if that was where we came out. Beatty did the same.

I then reviewed our "reconstruction of the crime" chart, which helped Weston and Beatty agree on the key conflict issues. We then reconfirmed the purpose of our discussion. I had suggested that first Weston and then Beatty very openly discuss their reaction to and feelings about the feedback, and discuss their expectations and attitudes (Step 5 in the Arnold Conflict Resolution Process).

Weston essentially said that he found he had begun reacting to it in his typical fashion: suppressing his feelings and looking at the information in a very logical and "rational" way. He said that if I had not persisted in bringing to the surface what he actually was feeling, he probably would not have realized the impact of his own emotions when he allowed them to "seep down from my head into my gut."

He apologized for having worked with Beatty in a manner that probably made it difficult for Beatty to openly express his feelings and judgments about certain things, and he said that "this is probably the biggest single 'eye opener' I've ever had in my entire business career."

Roger went on to state that he really wanted to do what was best for the company at this difficult stage of its history. And in light of the parent company's objectives, if this meant that when he left the hotel room he needed to tender his resignation as president, he would do so.

Roger further stated that even though he had "some pretty fixed ideas" about the mission and direction of the company—how it should be organized and the style of management he preferred, "being detail-oriented and somewhat of a 'micro-manager'"— he would try to lay his biases aside and approach the situation with as much professional objectivity as possible. At the same time, he would rely on me to help him be as realistic as he could be in terms of his own personality and style.

I was impressed by Roger's remarks and believed that Beatty also felt very good about his openness and apparent willingness to approach the situation as flexibly as could reasonably be expected.

Beatty himself then spoke. "What we're about to do, I'm sure, is going to be difficult for both of us, Roger. I knew that you and I were headed in opposite directions and I have felt badly for our people because they sometimes feel as though they are 'on the rack,' being stretched unbearably between our two distinct philosophies and styles with no 'white knight' to save them from their daily torture....I'm not sure, frankly, even with John's help and the goodwill that both of us have, that the conflict is resolvable. But I will give it my best shot. If the best thing for the company is my resignation, I promise you, you'll have it.

"Let me be frank with you. I have been increasingly dissatisfied since you came into the organization over some of the things you read about in the feedback report. I could pretty easily tell—or think I can—which quotes were mine and, in some cases, which were yours. But whether I'm right or wrong, there sure were a lot of people who said the same kinds of things.

"I know this is not easy for you to accept, Roger, but I've gotten to a point in my life and career where there are certain things I *must* do. I have to admit that in the last several weeks, I've become increasingly uncomfortable both because I had no idea where this John Arnold project would end up and because I find myself chafing more and more at the lack of resolution of key strategic, organizational, and management-style issues. In fact, things have gotten to the point where I don't look forward to coming into work every day....I used to start here at six-thirty in the morning but now I am straggling in anywhere from seven-thirty to even eight forty-five. It's not because there's lack of challenge; it's because I've grown increasingly frustrated. So, John, I guess Roger's bringing you in will have a positive effect *if* we can resolve this dilemma of which direction to go in and if somehow we either meld our management styles or decide which is the appropriate one for the company's direction and get on with it."

The opening remarks from both men were heartwarming. These were two "good guys," and if we could avoid a "shootout," as I was confident we could, the best would happen not only for the company but for both executives.

"Okay," I said, "you've both expressed your feelings and I respect you both very much. Let's put my conflict resolution method to work."

The Denouement

Since the three of us had already worked through Steps 1 through 5 by agreeing on what constituted the "reconstruction of the crime and capitalization of the opportunity," and since the two had put their values on the table, I briefly outlined Steps 6 through 10. We then proceeded to apply the steps sequentially, after *first* agreeing on the key external and internal factors that determined the strengths and weaknesses of the organization. After some discussion, they hammered out the following draft mission:

> The mission of our [low-tech consumer product] business is to achieve a sustainable position of market and profitability leadership by satisfying customers' needs with high-quality [proprietary products] and related products and services.

After a late lunch, during which my assistant finalized materials transcribed from the morning session, Weston and Beatty agreed on the major strategic and financial objectives, and by 3:30 p.m. we went into the major organizational structure analysis. As you will read in virtually every client application in this book, setting criteria (Step 7: determining all the things you're trying to achieve, preserve, and avoid) greatly helps win agreement among conflicting parties and greatly facilitates the generation and then evaluation of alternative choices.

It took about an hour and a half to hammer out and refine their list of criteria, including:

1. Ensure we meet current year plan (revenue, profit, product planning, engineering, manufacturing, and all aspects of marketing).
2. Facilitate development and implementation of a clear direction for the company.
3. Maximize our ability to achieve long-range successful strategy.
4. Resolve the "we-they" schism in the organization.
5. Achieve resolution of product-development problems as quickly as possible.
6. Avoid loss of emphasis on our core business.
7. Preserve the (parent company) CEO's confidence in our company.

8. Strengthen Roger's leadership:
   a. Keep him "in touch" with what's happening.
   b. Recognize his need for detail.
   c. Improve his decisiveness.
9. Resolve perceived uncertainty of Mal's commitment to the company.
10. Achieve clear definition of responsibility/accountability and authority.

Weston and Beatty both left for the evening at 6 p.m., wearied, but ready for a wrap-up session the next day. The following morning, we started at 8 a.m. with Weston and Beatty's review of the criteria. We then started prioritizing the criteria (Step 8), which is "where the rubber meets the road" in this process, because you separate the absolute requirements from the desirable objectives; this really makes explicit the basic values, philosophies, and objectives of all parties involved.

Early on in the prioritization process, it became evident what was most important to both executives. In the dialogue that ensued, I had expected that Beatty might be the less flexible of the two, but actually, after listening to Weston's reasons for saying something was much more, or less, important than another criterion, Beatty increasingly tended to agree with Weston! On several occasions, I questioned Beatty as to whether he sincerely believed that the resultant priority that came out of the discussion was indeed the most appropriate for the company. In each instance, he said, "Yes, I do." Several times, he added words saying, in effect, "that's not what I prefer to see but, given the strategic planning we did yesterday, the mission we devised, and our agreement on these criteria, I have to admit that where we are coming out is right for the company in terms of market and product."

At one point, Beatty added, "I guess I haven't been willing to admit the reality of the situation we face in terms of the market and competition and our own state of product development and quality. I've wanted us to get on a much faster, more exciting developmental track, but I guess I have to recognize that we lack the necessary products and resources."

Mal Beatty really was a pro!

We never did complete the prioritization of the criteria because, around 10:30 a.m., Beatty summed up his feelings: "I can pretty clearly project now what the structure of the company should look like from the priorities we've agreed upon. I have to say that my own background and experience has probably biased me strongly in the direction of new-product development and enhancements which, given all the feedback from customers, vendors, and our own managers and employees, and the strategic thinking we have done yesterday and even this morning, is *not* the way this company is going to best grow and prosper. That means to me also that the kind of organizational structure that would be best is *not* the type I've envisioned.

"Also," he continued, "I really don't believe I'm the best person to be executive vice president under your leadership, Roger. In fact, I don't believe the company at this stage needs such a position over both operations and sales. It's too big a roadblock. It gets in the way of your learning the business and having sufficient hands-on ability to work with people so you become knowledgeable and comfortable with the way things work. So I'm going to give you my resignation. I don't want to spend the next several years at this stage of my life doing what I now feel *our* company needs to do. I trust you'll give me sufficient time to land on my feet in another situation that I'll find much more professionally challenging and satisfying. In the meanwhile, I'll do everything I can to pull the organization back together under your leadership and help you learn as much as possible through my own experience and relationships, both inside and outside the company."

Silence prevailed. I felt tears well up in my eyes, and saw them in Roger's also. What a super human being Beatty was turning out to be!

Weston, as task-focused an executive as I've ever met, seemed affected by Beatty's remarks and shook his hand warmly. "Mal, I deeply appreciate what you're saying," Roger offered, "and how much you're giving up just in terms of your personal investment of time and energy. I'm really sorry that we won't be working together. I truly admire you and wish that we could have found a solution that worked for both of us. But I do agree, given your rationale, that it probably is best for the company that we follow the route we've embarked upon. Believe me, I'll do everything possible to help you not only land on your feet but secure a superior situation to this one, one in which you're the president and have an opportunity to exercise your superb leadership capabilities."

We had already accomplished so much in resolving the conflict that we all agreed it would not be helpful to continue with Step 7. At this point, it made a lot more sense to postpone the prioritization of the organizational criteria until after the feedback session with the management group. Then, during what we call the "Common Vision/Issue Resolution/Modus Operandi Work Conference," the group could develop its own list of organizational criteria. Weston would assure the group that the final list made complete sense to him as he drew upon his own notes from his session with Beatty. The group would then move through Steps 8 through 10, generating and evaluating various organizational structures, and selecting the best one to fulfill the new corporate mission and objectives.

So what had looked initially on the surface as a possible win-lose confrontational situation between two high-powered executives had, indeed, resulted in a double-win resolution of the problem. Weston, Beatty, and I worked out what would be presented to the management group, to the company at large, and, of course initially, to the parent company. Beatty would have as much time as necessary to find, with Kelco's help, the right situation as president.

On Monday morning, Weston and Beatty met with all company employees in the building. They announced Beatty's resignation and the reasons for it in the context of the new mission and how Beatty really wanted to invest the remainder of his career in a direction that would draw more on his particular experience, talents, and orientation. Beatty lived up to his voluntary commitment to Weston that he would do everything he could to support the thrust of the business they had agreed upon, and Weston lived up to his commitment to help Beatty find a new job that would meet his need.

The management team feedback session we conducted the next day also went very well. Following that, 10 days later, Weston and 11 senior managers (without Beatty) met for four and a half days of intensive work and developed a strategic growth plan and an organizational realignment, generating much the same organizational criteria that Weston and Beatty had begun to develop. Most importantly, Weston did not force the criteria on the group; rather, he let the members develop them, only giving input to the discussion when he felt strongly about a given point. In other words, Weston understood process.

At that point, we closed the ExecuTrak file. We still check in with Roger (see the following postscript), who has continued applying the method himself as new challenges arise. Yes, he had come into the job with no line management experience whatsoever. But he hit the ground running and is now winning the race.

Postscript

It took Beatty five months to find a suitable position. He did indeed "land on his feet" as president of another consumer-products company. Under his leadership, the company has moved forward very aggressively in terms of new-product development, and its name today is far better known than it was before Beatty became president.

Weston led his company to capture increased market share and realize a significant increase in earnings during each of the next three years. At this point the parent company CEO had him "leapfrog" over the heads of several peers to take over the largest group of operating companies in the multibillion-dollar corporation. As of this writing, he is the number-two senior executive in that "Fortune 100" company.

PART 2

Six Types of Organizational Conflict

A major company with a formal culture acquires a
free-wheeling entrepreneurial one; the entrepreneurial
company chokes under the shackles of its new parent, cutting
off the flow of creative ideas.

The autocratic leader of a large financial services firm has
made a number of poor decisions that have diminished the
competitive position of the company; key managers who can
put the company back on track know that any criticism of the
chief may result in severe reprisals or the loss of their jobs.

The sales and marketing arms of a consumer-electronics
company believe that they should be developing new products
to stay ahead of competition; research and development
believes that enhancing existing lines is the best strategy to
pursue.

Certain key members of a major manufacturing company are
split over whether headquarters should close a plant in a small
town; the closing makes fiscal sense, but would devastate the
community.

Top management and design engineering at a furniture

manufacturing company squabble over launch schedules for new products; top management demands that the design-to-production time be cut by 20 percent, while engineering believes that such edicts will compromise product integrity and come back to haunt the company in the future.

At an appliance maker, people in inventory management and sales and marketing argue over stock levels; inventory management wants to reduce component and finished goods levels to as little as possible, while sales and marketing want every possible configuration available to meet customer demand instantly.

Every day, we hear or read of tales of organizational conflict like the above. And while the details of every conflict are distinctive, I have found, based on my years as a counselor-catalyst, that all conflicts fall within one of six categories (which, it so happens, are represented by the six brief scenarios just presented):

1. *External* (conflicts related to competition, the marketplace, regulation, or an adversarial takeover)

2. *Management Process and Style* (conflicts stemming from leadership style, the decision-making process, or organizational structure)

3. *Strategic Direction* (conflicts over the company's mission/direction, objectives, and strategies)

4. *Operational* (conflicts related to issues such as "quality versus schedule" or "design-to-production transition")

5. *Interdepartmental* (conflicts that occur when divisions compete with themselves rather than with other companies)

6. *Value System* (conflicts over business philosophy)

In the following chapters, you'll get an in-depth picture of each type of conflict: what it's all about, and guidelines for resolving the strife. Bear in mind that labeling a problem does not necessarily solve it; nonetheless, recognition of a problem type is helpful in ferreting out the root cause and devising an effective solution to the problem at hand. Some conflicts, depending on how global your descriptors of them are, may reflect more than one of the six types. It's helpful to determine the basic one (or two) types you're dealing with, so you can quickly get to the root causes.

Also, since some companies experience several organizational conflicts at the same time, it is useful to have a grid that sorts out the different problem types. The more order you can impose on chaos, the greater the chance that you'll find double-win solutions. Now turn to the next chapter and read about the first type of conflict, external, which can be among the most destructive. Fortunately, with the right tools, you can learn to reduce the impact of external conflicts and channel the hostile energy into productive ends.

4

Pressures from Without: Managing External Conflicts

Case Study

ExecuTrak File 372: "Firing the
President Was a Dumb Thing to Do"

When Garber & Sons, Ltd., a diversified furniture and related
products manufacturing company, acquired Bradford Corporation,
Inc., a once-profitable but now ailing office furniture producer,
industry analysts hailed the maneuver as "a natural," one that
would surely benefit both parties. While the press speculated that
Garber would no doubt make some management changes, no one
was prepared for wholesale housecleaning by Garber's CEO, J. L.
Tomlinson, who replaced every top executive except one division
president, Reginald Davis. Davis seemed to be doing a good job of
turning his division around. The "bloodbath," as one reporter put it,
sent "shock waves from one end of the company to another," and
some analysts wondered if the conflict would damage Bradford
beyond repair.

Davis, a veteran of several acquisitions, had dual difficulties:
establishing rapport and building confidence with his new fellow
senior executives from Garber, and assuring the people whom he'd
managed for five years that the "massacre" was done and that
he'd be around for the duration. In fact, Davis spent many an
evening wondering when Tomlinson's axe would visit his neck, too.

Postacquisition "massacres" like the one that took place when Garber & Sons bought Bradford Corporation are all too common these days, and they are frequently responsible for what I refer to as "external conflicts." In the first part of this chapter, we'll cover the basic causes of external conflicts and their effects on people and company performance. In the second part, we'll return to Bradford Corporation and find out what happened to the proverbial axe hanging over Reg Davis's head.

Overview of External Conflicts

External conflicts, the "boa constrictor" of conflict types, can squeeze the life out of a company. They create enormous pressure on a company's resources and ability to perform; they can also create high levels of tension and stress for all levels of employees. External conflicts have three primary causes: takeovers, market/competitive/ economic pressures, and regulatory actions.

Takeovers

Any kind of takeover, whether hostile or friendly, can cause significant turmoil within an acquired company. Just look at what happened when a friendly merger of two high-tech companies created Stardent Computer. Stardent failed, despite $200 million in venture capital and a $55 million additional cash injection: cultural clashes and management turmoil made technological problems all the more unsolvable.

Westinghouse's takeover of Unimation ended in a similar disaster. Unimation at one time was the unquestioned leader in the robotics industry, with rapid growth (from $4 million to $75 million in sales in just eight years). An entrepreneurial, informal high-tech company, it was crushed under Westinghouse's formal structure, business practices, and constant staff intrusions. Unimation's market share fell from 15 percent to 9½ percent, and according to one former executive, the company was becoming a "me-too" contender in the robotics market. In desperation, Westinghouse finally sold off the shrunken hulk of a once-profitable company.

I followed the Westinghouse debacle with great interest, because it illustrates why acquisitions fail. In the words of the head of a team planning for the integration of Unimation: "We have a jewel in the company we're purchasing and an opportunity that we will never again have if we don't do it well. Our record for acquisitions, I must say, is truly abysmal. We don't know the first thing about how to integrate them, and maybe that's one reason we are always reorganizing our groups and divisions. We are taking over a company four times the size of our own business unit, and we simply have to become educated, not only in what they know from their own experience but, in the process, how to integrate other companies."

At the top level of Westinghouse, however, there was a very different understanding of the problem. The vice president of technology (who actually wound up replacing the transition team following a top-down corporate restructuring) considered the integration to be a simple task of melding systems, not of integrating people.

No wonder that the acquisition was a disaster! Melding technologies is the least of the problems; melding cultures is critical. If the parent is "button-down" and the acquired company is "denim," the potential for conflict is significant. IBM and Rolm discovered this the hard way. To IBM's credit, it waited one full year before parachuting in a key "Big Blue" executive down the hall from the vice president of operations (who had been my client). From then on, IBM imposed more and more of its management process on Rolm, and it became increasingly disappointed in Rolm's performance. Eventually, IBM sold Rolm for a fraction of what it had paid.

Marketplace Pressure

While takeovers represent a major cause of external conflicts, the second cause—marketplace pressure—can be equally devastating. An upstart competitor might introduce a groundbreaking technology that leaves your products in the dust; another might force you into a price war that you can't afford; the "fickle hand" of the customer may tire of your wares or services; or the economy may take a downturn that sends customers scurrying for less expensive alternatives. The list of reasons for market and competitive pressures could fill a book. The point is, no matter how well-entrenched your company may be, there is always the possibility of unexpected whirlpools in the marketplace causing internal strife.

Consider the case of ARAM Foods, a premier maker of fancy preserves. For years, family-owned ARAM Foods had been regarded as the undisputed king of jams and jellies, with 65 percent of the upscale market. In the late eighties, the company found itself challenged by Jane's Farm, an upstart whose main credentials were "made in Vermont." At first, ARAM ignored the new competitor, figuring that Jane would simply go back to the cow pastures once the "Ben and Jerry's–type Vermont craze" died down. But Jane's popularity continued to grow, and the company succeeded in achieving a national presence through a major distribution channel.

By that time, ARAM's marketing people awoke to the fact that the company had its first real competition in 30 years, and they started developing new marketing programs and point-of-purchase displays. Meanwhile, regional sales managers began making price deals with the distributors and wholesalers. This infuriated marketing, since it violated their new value-price strategy. A contingent of disgruntled sales representatives began a vocal campaign to undo marketing's efforts, saying they were wide of the mark. Their own recommendation was to develop a new line of products that had the same "homey" feel as Jane's. "Change the packaging, come up with a new image—a 'jam for the '90s,'" complained one ARAM regional sales manager we interviewed. "Meanwhile, we've got to compete on the basis of price—until the new product is rolled out."

While ARAM's marketing and sales groups became bitter enemies and spent an inordinate amount of time in head-to-head combat meetings, Jane's Farm was quietly starting to pick up more market share. To keep his company from ripping apart, and in the belief that this action would cause fewer convulsions, ARAM's president asked for the resignation of the marketing manager, figuring that it was the only way to restore the chasm that had formed between the marketing and sales organizations. And because it was obvious that the national sales manager had lost control of his price-cutting regional managers, he was also fired.

ARAM did eventually introduce a new product line. But it never regained the market share that it had lost to Jane's. All companies should ponder ARAM's situation and take to heart the lesson to be learned from the incident: never become oblivious to the pulse of the marketplace. Even companies the size of IBM can be caught off guard. With "clone" personal computers digging ever deeper into their turf, IBM, DEC, and other key computer companies found themselves in the early 1990s faced with slumping sales. This drop necessitated restructuring and massive internal turmoil that in turn led to early retirement programs; these in turn led to diminished morale, an exodus of talented people, and eventually layoffs.

Regulatory Actions

Finally, consider the effect of the third type of external conflict: regulatory actions. Government regulation (or deregulation) is also a significant cause of organizational turmoil. Consider what happened to Bell Laboratories following the landmark divestiture ruling that opened the door for new long-distance service companies. Judge Green's ruling opened up to competitors markets that at one time were monopolistically held by AT&T, and it also allowed AT&T's Bell Laboratories to engage in profit-making activities. While that was a blessing for AT&T, it created enormous conflict among the scientists. Whereas Bell Laboratories had been a research haven, scientists and engineers suddenly had to live with restrictions on what they could write about in scholarly journals and what they could discuss at seminars and conferences. Pure knowledge suddenly became transformed to the realm of trade secrets. A number of top thinkers could not tolerate what they perceived to be censorship, and they simply returned to academia or consulting.

With deregulation, companies that once had to restrict their acquisitions to targets outside their industries—unless the target was a far smaller, weak competitor—could legitimately swallow their biggest rivals. Megamergers have consequently taken place in the food, airline, banking, brokerage, cable and broadcasting, tires, appliances, insurance, retailing, commercial real estate, and pharmaceuticals industries, to name a few. The list goes on and on.

The impact on hundreds of millions of families in this country has been enormous, to say nothing of the immediate shock to those employed in the affected companies, acquirer and acquiree alike. New structures, changed jobs (if one was lucky enough to keep his or hers), and new reporting relationships and work have created situations in which conflict is all the more likely; insecurities and anxieties will rise, and people will act in self-protective crisis modes. The rumor mills will churn, escalating the feelings that lead to despondency, decreased productivity, increased absenteeism, increased staff turnover, failure to meet product-delivery service requirements, and so on. All this adds up to a potential drain on a company's performance.

Effects of External Conflicts

Regardless of the cause of an external conflict, the effects are the same because the conflict tends to affect the company as a whole. When an acquisition goes sour, for example, it is unlikely that just a single department will be affected. The repercussions will be felt throughout the entire to-be-acquired or just-acquired company. In fact, when an acquired company feels that it has a new tyrannical parent, its people tend to band together, forgetting their own differences and establishing an us-against-them mentality.

Similarly, competitive and market pressures tend to have company-wide repercussions. If a company is reeling from a new competitor or loss of market share, everyone is drawn into the resulting organizational conflict because of the universal stake involved—paychecks. Everyone is therefore likely to take sides about how to best respond to the outside threat. This can even lead to the formation of a life-or-death crisis mentality in which no one feels he or she can afford to sit on the sidelines.

Finally, regulatory pressures affect the organization as a whole. If a product line must be dropped because of safety or environmental concerns, that action will have an impact on the bottom line—which is every stakeholder's concern. Likewise, an opportunity opened by regulation (e.g., the opportunity to provide consulting services related to air quality as a result of the Clean Air Act amendments) can cause strife as people try to determine the best way to seize the opportunity or cope with changes in their job descriptions. (Deregulation, of course, can have the same effect.) In any case, regulation is likely to have significant impact that will be felt from the boardroom to the boiler room.

Guidelines for Resolving External Conflicts

Before the 10-step Arnold Conflict Resolution Process is applied to external conflicts, you should understand the nature of the "beast": You can't simply uncoil a boa constrictor from its prey and expect the victim to get up and walk away; there may be massive trauma. Regardless of the exact cause of the conflict, if you (or whoever is acting as a facilitator) use the following guidelines, you'll be increasing your chances of quickly finding a resolution with minimal pain:

1. *Handle the situation with extreme care.*   External conflicts represent massive blows that can shake an organization from top to bottom. Some people will be in shock. Others will be extremely angry and looking for a scapegoat. Still others will be dispirited, asking such things as "Why did this bad thing happen to such a good company?" The last point is especially important because those affected by an external conflict often feel that they're being treated capriciously and unfairly and are victims of larger forces. And when dealing with the victims' emotionality, you must tread carefully.

Based on my experience, in the midst of external conflicts, some people will hunker down and fight. Some will jump ship when the fighting gets too intense. And some who don't jump ship will lean back on the oars. In rare cases, disgruntled employees will actually engage in acts of "sabotage" as they try to derail new management whenever possible.

2. Since external conflicts can cause extreme strain, it's critically important to differentiate the *perceived* damage (i.e., pain) from real damage. Therefore, it's critical to get the facts. This is why Step 1 of the Arnold Conflict Resolution Process is so important. If you can't reconstruct the crime, you can't hope to find out what really happened and what needs to be fixed.

3. Be patient, let people vent, and don't take anything personally. This is perhaps the most important point of all. When people are reeling from an external conflict, they're going to be feeling a lot of pent-up emotion. And you really can't make progress until they've had a chance to vent themselves. As the facilitator in an external conflict, you're likely to become a "punching bag." Don't take it personally; that's what you're there for.

An important aspect of this guideline is that you ask specific questions that show real empathy and sincere interest. The more specific your questions, the more you'll show genuine interest. Specific questions will also allow people to find "hooks" that they can hold onto when venting themselves. Finally, specific questions are critical if you're going to get through Steps 1 through 4 and unravel the real seeds of the crime.

4. In the case of takeovers, be aware that people will be especially sensitive and may feel as though top management is trying to "sugarcoat" the situation with a consultant or "team builder" who's supposed to wave some magic wand and "make everything better." (In the second part of the chapter you'll see how my presence as a catalyst was met with open hostility on the part of the acquired company; the people affected by the conflict simply assumed that I was brought in as a cheap way to "smooth over ruffled feathers.")

From a practical standpoint, this sensitive situation means that you, as facilitator, should avoid pep talks and phrases such as "we're all in this together" or, after a takeover, "hey—we're all one family now!" The more you offer platitudes and patronizing slogans, the more people will distrust you. In contrast, the more authentic your questioning, the more people will believe that you are "for real" and perhaps have their interests at heart as well as your own. Don't speak in platitudes; the more obtuse you are, the more people will distrust you. The more specific you are, the more people will feel that you're authentic and really accountable for making happen what you said would happen.

5. Your choice of language brings up an important point: How do you feel about the situation? If you feel biased one way or another, it will be hard to adjust your language to a neutral position. What are your values and those of the involved players? It's essential to identify these (Step 5 of the Arnold Conflict Resolution Process) so that you can determine the best way to try to create a double-win philosophy, attitude, communications, and behavioral system (Step 6). This will facilitate implementation of the remaining steps (7 through 10) and raise the probability that the organizational conflict will be effectively resolved.

6. Pay particular attention to what people want to achieve, preserve, and avoid. Remember that with an external conflict, regardless of the cause, people often just want to preserve the immediately tangible: their jobs, their careers, next month's bonus, or whatever. Be aware that there are probably much deeper levels of "preserves" as well as "avoids" and "achieves." So pay special attention to Step 7 of the process, and probe gently but deeply into people's objectives, anxieties, concerns, and goals for the resolution of the conflict.

7. Don't look for quick solutions. When an organization has been hurt by an external conflict, the foundation may be shaky and you may have to do a lot of work to shore it up. The first step is to get everyone feeling that they're on more secure ground. Then you can think about building the edifice into its desired configuration. An excellent way to accomplish this is via Steps 7 and 8 (getting mutual agreement on the criteria to be met for a solution to be viable, and then setting priorities and getting people to buy into them).

8. Anticipate where people will balk with a resolution. While this guideline is important when resolving *any* kind of conflict type, it is especially so with external conflicts, because the stakes often seem like they're in the "life or death" category. Take your time in working through the generation and selection of resolutions (Steps 9 and 10). The first resolution that seems to make sense may not be the best. While there's the temptation to do *anything* that will assuage the troops, only the *right* choice will pay off in the long run. By running with a convenient solution that seems "alright," you might find yourself in more difficulty later on. So involve the participants in the generation and evaluation of alternative solutions insofar as feasible. What should their objective be? The participants, rather than the catalyst-mediator, must own the solution.

9. Part of the evaluation process, Step 10, should be troubleshooting what could go wrong with the selected resolution. Again, involving the

protagonists in collaboratively performing this task can help assure that tangible agreements and implementation plans are achieved. That will ensure resolution of the conflict.

10. One of the worst things many acquirers do to newly acquired firms is to quickly shift the interaction between the two presidents and downgrade the just-acquired firm to reporting to a lower level. This action is seen as a bellwether of how the firm will be treated henceforth; it is virtually guaranteed to create hostility and anxiety unless the maneuver was agreed upon during the negotiations. So often it creates the modus operandi that accounts for seven out of ten acquisitions failing to meet the objectives and expectations of the acquisition, which destroys shareholder value, and better than one out of three being failures.

With these guidelines in mind, we'll return to the case that opened the chapter (Garber swallowing Bradford) and find out what happened to Reg Davis. The case exemplifies how tempers can run high during an external conflict, especially one caused by a hostile takeover.

As the Guillotine Turns

Reginald Davis wasn't the only one who suspected that his tenure at Bradford Corporation was to be short-lived. The day I read about the takeover of Bradford by Garber, I jotted down in my notebook a prediction: in four to six months Davis would be out on the street. I had read about other Tomlinson-orchestrated takeovers and knew that he had a reputation as a hard-nosed "takeover artist," for brutal firings and frequently housecleaning following a raid. I sucked in my gut and called Tomlinson's office to offer my services during the transition period at Bradford. Remarkably, Tomlinson politely took my call after I explained to his assistant exactly what I do and how I can help when one company acquires another. Tomlinson listened to me, but he didn't jump at my offer. He did, however, encourage me to stay in touch. I felt this was sincere and made two more phone calls over the next four months, neither of which resulted in a contract. Then, five months after the mass firings, Tomlinson did "unexpectedly" contact me for an "emergency" consulting session.

The following is part of the story of a tumultuous, but productive, one-day firefighting experience. It is highly instructive because it demonstrates the importance of getting conflicting factions to understand one another's perspectives, preferably as soon as possible, not nine months later when negative attitudes become fixed and motivation and productivity have nose-dived. It also illustrates how an effective catalyst-mediator serves as a neutral sounding board for all parties involved. Tomlinson informed me that, effective next Monday morning (six days from the date of the phone call), he was replacing Reginald Davis (what a surprise!) with Harold Campbell, an executive with whom he had previously worked before taking over Garber. Could I possibly help with the rather abrupt transition? What a challenge! Given Tomlinson's schedule, I was only able to garner a 10-minute phone conversation with the CEO on the weekend (the president of Bradford was on a three-week trip in the Far East) and a 15-minute conversation with Campbell on Saturday night. We actually would not get down to business until en route from the airport to the Bradford division, which would give us only 45 minutes to discuss how best to facilitate the changeover.

Monday morning, Tomlinson, Campbell, and a driver (who turned out to be the vice president of human resources, known by Bradford Corporation survivors as "The Angel of Death" for engineering a number of high-level executive firings) flew in on their private jet, meeting me at a rental car agency.

On the way to the division headquarters building, I asked Tomlinson why he felt Davis had failed. In doing so I was looking especially for identity, location, and time dimensions. (Step 1: It's critical to avoid making value judgments at this point—"just the facts, ma'am.") As explained in Chapter 2, understanding these dimensions is essential for ferreting out the root cause. You can't begin piecing together people's perceptions unless you understand how they view the "what," "where," and "when" dimensions of the conflict; after that is accomplished, you can then focus down on the origins of the problem.

According to Tomlinson, Davis had taken far longer than expected to really turn his division around. More importantly, although Davis was proving himself to be a good manager, he didn't appear to Tomlinson to be a leader. (The difference between a manager and a leader was crucial for Tomlinson, as it increasingly has become for many CEOs.) And for Bradford Corporation to win the upcoming battles with global competitors who were buying out other furniture companies and cutting prices, the firm would need a powerful and dynamic leader to ensure future growth.

Tomlinson knew that the sudden firing would lead to resentment from the managers who had worked with and directly reported to Davis for the past five years; a few key people might even walk. But he also thought that the anger would "pretty much" subside once people realized that Davis wasn't the right person for the company over the long haul.

In fact, Tomlinson's assumptions couldn't have been further off-base.

As I soon discovered, his firing of Davis had ignited what could have become Bradford Corporation's equivalent of the Philippine volcano Mt. Pinatubo.

Tomlinson had met with Davis on Thursday and asked for his resignation immediately. Unfortunately, he had also already faxed a memo to the division management group on Friday morning regarding Davis's abrupt departure. The memo, which was short and blunt, announced Reg's resignation (with no explanation), and it stated that a "facilitator" named John Arnold would be accompanying Tomlinson, the new division president Campbell, and the "Angel of Death" sometime on Monday to meet with division management and "accelerate team building." (It was as if I or anyone could simply wave a magic wand and make all the shock, hurt, disbelief, anger, and so on, disappear!) Worst of all, Tomlinson concluded his memo with a request for each manager to be prepared to give Campbell a 10- to 15-minute presentation of his function or business, including key issues and business projections, the following day (Tuesday)!

I probed Tomlinson to learn what he wanted to achieve, preserve, and avoid (Step 7) at the "team-building" meeting. The discussion was pretty straightforward. In terms of achievement, Tomlinson had three objectives: (1) getting the management group to understand the soundness of his decision to replace Davis, (2) shifting the atmosphere from negative to positive, and (3) exciting the managers about his vision for the division and the corporation during the next three to five years. At the same time, Tomlinson wanted to preserve each manager's commitment to the business. And he certainly wanted to avoid lingering resentment in the management ranks.

Without challenging Tomlinson's assumptions, I suggested a three-stage game plan. (This phase of the conflict resolution requires the utmost objectivity on the part of the catalyst-mediator; the goal is simply to collect data in an impartial manner.)

The first stage of my game plan entailed meeting with the senior managers for lunch. (This is what Tomlinson had previously arranged anyway, since he felt the atmosphere would "be more informal this way.") During the meeting Tomlinson would introduce Campbell and explain my role. Tomlinson and Campbell would then excuse themselves, and I would conduct a confidential "team-building" session that would enable the managers to vent their feelings and frustrations. The goal of the session, in addition to relieving some of the resentment that had undoubtedly built in the management ranks, was to determine what each of the key players was trying to achieve, preserve, and avoid (in contrast to Tomlinson's sense of the same three dimensions). This information would be critical in determining how Tomlinson should present his point of view; the right approach would reduce the anxiety and any ill will of Bradford Corporation's managers, raising the chances that they would accept their new president. The wrong approach would simply confirm everyone's worst suspicions and cause organizational fissures that would only undermine Bradford Corporation's ability to compete and grow.

The next stage of my plan entailed my meeting with Campbell and briefing him on the essence of the managers' feelings and concerns. The two of us would then convey the situation to Tomlinson and recommend the best way to explain his decision. It would also be an opportunity to "bulletproof" Tomlinson's presentation by anticipating potential hot spots that might trigger an emotional eruption.

The third and final stage involved a group dinner at which Tomlinson would stand before the managers, acknowledge everyone's feelings, describe why he replaced Davis, and then move on to his larger goals for the company and division.

Cold Chicken and Cold Shoulders

When we arrived at the acquired division's headquarters, we headed straight for the conference room. (Tomlinson had called in from the car to have lunch brought in.) The charge in the air told me that the CEO was not really aware of how much hostility division managers harbored over his decision to remove Davis and his subsequent memo (which, it appeared, had the effect of pouring salt in the wound).

After introducing us, Tomlinson said virtually nothing about the reasons for dismissing Davis other than that it had become obvious to him that, although in the last several months the division had finally turned the corner, the progress "wasn't sufficiently rapid enough" and the initial confidence he had had in "Reg" was beginning to erode. Having worked previously with Harold, he knew of Harold Campbell's capabilities and felt that they were well suited to the difficult task that had to be accomplished to "assure a complete and successful turnaround of the business." Next, he turned to me and asked me to explain my role; then he announced that he and Campbell would leave us alone while they "toured the environment"! (Numerous eyebrows went up when Tomlinson and Campbell made this vague announcement. People seemed to be saying, "What? What did he say? What's that all about?")

Within seconds after the door closed, a sea of red-hot emotion flooded the room, which was in stark contrast to the muddled silence that had prevailed during the half hour of lunch. Then people stared at their chicken and tuna salads, avoiding eye contact with the three of us; now they were shouting. While I had expected a fair amount of anger, I was truly unprepared for the vehemence of the outbursts. (No matter how many conflicts I resolve, it's still hard to fathom the amount of negative emotion that people keep pent up on the job.)

Tomlinson had led me to believe that, although Davis was well liked, he was not generally regarded as a particularly good leader and was criticized for sometimes getting in the way of his subordinates. Tomlinson assumed that the abruptness of the firing would be the issue, not the firing itself. After all, now that the company had turned the corner, wouldn't it make perfectly good sense that a new leader should be brought on board to help the company gallop ahead?

Once I began asking questions and writing on chart paper as much as possible the crime is/is not matrix, the temperature in the room dropped a few degrees. The goal, in addition to allowing people to purge their venom, was to determine what each person had to say in terms of identity, location, and time: what in those dimensions appeared to be of concern and what did *not* seem to be of concern (Steps 1 and 2 of the Arnold Conflict Resolution Process); and also what seemed *distinctive* to the concerns in contrast with what were *not* concerns (Step 3). I also had begun to think in terms of hypotheses and testing for probable root cause (Step 4) as I listened to their outbursts. This would complement the inquiry that I had begun with Tomlinson earlier that day. And it would also show us how wide the gap was that would have to be bridged in order for the division to heal its management wounds.

Again, whatever the nature of the conflict, nothing will get resolved until the catalyst-mediator arrives at a clear understanding of everyone's fundamental perceptions.

Here's a very brief sampling of what some of the managers had to say:

> All of us in this division have spent 12 months under Reg's leadership turning the business issues upside down, and now, just when we've been implementing "the plan" and have turned into the black, the boss gets fired! It's unfair! Tomlinson is *crazy!*" [Note the *identity/location* (this division); the *time* (12 months); a key *distinction* ("Reg was a good guy and a good manager, doing what needed to be done; then all of a sudden he got fired, which is pretty unfair, especially since we're finally profitable! What's going on?"); and an imagined root cause ("Tomlinson is crazy!").]

> Under Reg's leadership, everyone is charged up, especially field sales personnel; bookings are up; and customers are beginning to take note of the new "Bradford Corporation." So, you bet we're mad!

I hope, Arnold, you're not here to try to teach us some vision or "team-building" crap. To try to discuss what our vision is for this company—and we do have a vision, mind you—is academic. Try it, buddy, and someone may just punch you in the nose! [This is the time to hold on to your seat and let the wave of emotions subside!]

As people expressed their views and feelings in just such terms, including a fair share of expletives, I wrote down their remarks on large sheets of paper taped to the wall. This is a very useful technique, because in an emotional firestorm, people often don't focus on what actually is being said; they just want to vent. In addition to identifying the root cause ("Tomlinson is crazy"), the writing on the wall revealed a number of insights about the group:

Achieve

"We want Campbell (note: that's the new president, not Tomlinson) to understand why we're upset."

"Even though Campbell is 'buddy buddy' with Tomlinson, we want him to know that he's going to have to do battle for us in the future and support our professional opinions and positions. We don't want to have to worry about getting short-circuited by crazy and rash Tomlinson acts, like firing Davis."

"We want to make it clear that we speak with a collective and united voice."

Preserve

"We want to preserve the confidentiality and anonymity of everyone in the room—especially since the 'Angel of Death' will be sitting in the postdinner session with Campbell and Tomlinson, and we've seen what happens after every one of his visits: somebody gets the axe!"

Avoid

"We're not happy he's here, but we aren't blaming him either. He's an innocent third party."

"We don't want Campbell to think he's taking over a bunch of vindictive clowns. We want to convey that we're a capable unit. Yeah, we're upset, but we're committed managers and we're going to make the turnaround happen, regardless of the monkey wrenches Tomlinson throws at us."

Once people had agreed that the statements on the sheets of paper had captured the complete sphere of thoughts and emotions, we could

Table 4-1. Chart Showing Assumptions/Understandings of Conflicting Factions

Management group's perceptions	Tomlinson's perceptions
▪ The company is on the right track and finally profitable.	▪ Reg is viewed by the division as a weak manager.
▪ Everyone is charged up under Reg's credible leadership.	▪ He lacks superior credibility with the sales force, the division, and the division's customers.
▪ Reg personally produced over $10 million in sales and stabilized the sales force.	▪ Reg spends some time selling.
▪ Reg gets fired, yet he was *the* technical expert.	▪ Reg knows the market quite well.
▪ Reg's firing was capricious and unfair; Tomlinson is irrational and not to be trusted.	▪ The timing of Reg's firing was perhaps a bit abrupt. But everyone will "get over it—they'll see the logic of my decision."

flesh out the process of "reconstructing the crime." Before describing that process, let's compare some of the assumptions and understandings of the conflicting factions.

The catalyst-mediator should always make up such a chart at some point in the conflict resolution process; you can't create a bridge without understanding what it is that must be spanned! The assumptions are shown in Table 4-1.

Reconstructing the "Crime"

At this point, I had a good understanding of how division management viewed the situation, and what they wanted to get out of the conflict resolution process. Once they gave me feedback that they were comfortable that I had really "heard" and understood, and once agreement had been reached on what they wanted to achieve, preserve, and avoid, it was time to begin to brief Campbell on the meeting and then work with both him and Tomlinson to develop a strategy.

Initially, the group had wanted me to collar Tomlinson, and drag him by the scruff of the neck into the conference room where they would confront him. But in reviewing what they really wanted as a value system (Step 5)—fairness in treatment and preservation of their jobs until they found better ones (although two had planned to give Tomlinson their resignations immediately)—it was clear to me that they wanted a double-win resolution to the conflict.

In fact, as I pointed out to them, it should be a triple-win resolution: for them, for their new boss (Campbell), and for Tomlinson. They reluctantly agreed with this, but I then demonstrated to them why it should be Campbell who should first learn of their pain, disgust, and anxiety. Let him meet with them *after* I briefed him and then let *him* bear the onus of representing the division management to Tomlinson. After all, from now on, he was their boss and he should do battle with Garber's CEO; if he lost, it would tell them a lot about leadership. In any event, what they had to say would test the mettle of both executives. And since so much heat had been generated by Tomlinson's abrupt dismissal of Reg, his curt memo, his vague announcement at lunch that he would "tour the environment" (when, in actuality, he and Campbell "buttonholed" people on the floor and interviewed them on a variety of matters, causing all the more apprehension and resentment by division management when they learned of it!), and his demand that at their dinner meeting he would "say a few words," they agreed it would be best if I privately briefed Campbell before inviting him to meet with division management in the conference room.

I left the group in the conference room, found Campbell, and quickly went through the process of reconstructing the crime with him (see Chapter 2), pointing out what the concerns were and what they weren't, as well as the nature of the root cause. I then escorted him back to the conference room, where he viewed and I summarized what was on the charts, without attributing them to individuals in the room. The group then added to what I had said and responded to some questions by Campbell. We then troubleshot his presentation to Tomlinson, recognizing that Tomlinson was a very strong and confident leader who could be somewhat insensitive to the interpersonal and emotional impact of his decisions!

When we were confident that Campbell could package the management group's issues in terms and language that would be acceptable to Tomlinson, we thanked the group and they left the room, not only concerned about what would occur at dinner, but anxious to learn further what Tomlinson was doing with his "interrogations" of their subordinates.

Campbell and I then found Tomlinson and began by asking him to *imagine* what the managers had said when I was alone with them. He reiterated what he had told me on the way over: that he thought they would be upset at the abruptness of the firing but would quickly realize the wisdom of his decision. So he was indeed astonished by what actually had transpired during the group meeting. At this point, he had to acknowledge the division managers' frame of reality; more important, he realized that to move forward, he would have to close the gap. We discussed how he could accomplish this difficult task, and for the next hour or so, Campbell and I critiqued his presentation. By 6 p.m., the three of us felt confident that Tomlinson was ready for his dinner engagement, and we headed to a nearby restaurant for cocktails and dinner with the group members who were already waiting for us.

Dinner at Seven

The atmosphere at dinner was somewhat calmer than that at lunch. The "venting" and a couple of drinks had already helped a lot, and most managers appeared hopeful that the discussion would at least eliminate future shocks. Better yet, they thought it might lead to a satisfactory resolution of the conflict. (Imagine what would have happened if a catalyst-mediator had not been involved or if he or she lacked a practical conflict resolution process: With a head of steam fired by a few drinks, furnaces would have been boiling! If you find yourself in a similar situation, settle for sparkling water; you'll need your faculties at 110 percent!)

When the waiters served the last round of coffee, Campbell tapped Tomlinson on the shoulder, and the CEO began his presentation.

Tomlinson started by sketching out his own past, how he had emigrated to America from Wales 10 years ago, and how proud he was to now be an American citizen. He also described his dismay at America's loss of competitive position and how his beloved adopted country's manufacturing base and global reputation for superior management expertise was being decimated by Japan, Europe, and "even" Korea.

The CEO then spoke eloquently about how essential it was to him to make both Garber and Bradford Corporation global, world-class business entities. He also described what that would require in the way of extraordinary professional and managerial excellence, especially at senior levels of the parent and subsidiary companies and divisions. As he described how Bradford Corporation would most certainly become *the* premier company in its market niche—through innovative products, by anticipating and responding to customer trends, with unparalleled customer service—even the most vocal critic began to nod her or his head as Tomlinson's infectious enthusiasm spread throughout the room.

Then it came time to discuss the matter at hand. With a sensitivity that I hadn't yet seen in my brief hours with the man, Tomlinson carefully praised Davis for his outstanding management skills and his ability to reverse the slump. But at the same time, he gently explained how Reg's talents wouldn't help the company achieve its full potential. He was more of a "keeper of tradition" than a visionary thinker; a firefighter more than a strategic thinker; and a good soldier rather than a four-star general. By contrast, Campbell had proven himself to Tomlinson in a previous assignment as an able thinker under fire (as division management had, to some extent, observed several hours earlier) with the skills necessary to help the company reach newfound heights.

Tomlinson then opened the session to questions, many of them direct and hard-hitting. But he handled them with aplomb, and when the queries stopped just after 11 p.m., it seemed like the division was ready for a new day of business. After a round of applause, one of Tomlinson's most vehement detractors—the vice president of marketing, who had carried his resignation in hand—stood up and said, "Well, I still don't agree with your decision to fire Reg and certainly not the way it was handled. But at least I now understand your thinking. I respect you for your position. I trust you believe that every one of us here wants the same and that from now on you will believe in us as we continue the turnaround. I, for one, will support you in any way I can. The division can and *will* go further than any of us ever imagined." As this manager demonstrated, at least everyone seemed to understand Tomlinson's reasoning. Equally important, they had broadened their vision of where the parent company was going and how it planned to get there.

Without my organizational conflict resolution approach, Tomlinson would have tried to handle the problem with a speech, as he had indeed planned, after dinner. This would have most likely engendered argumentation and ended in mass resignations or, at best, a dispirited managerial force. The Garber-Bradford session succeeded, however, because it employed an orderly organizational conflict resolution process that identified both sides' understanding of the "crime"—what it is, and what it is not. Most important, it clearly identified three items: (1) the values of division management and of Tomlinson and Campbell; (2) the fact that everyone really wanted a double-win solution; and (3) the things that people wanted to achieve, avoid, and preserve by bridging the chasm between Tomlinson and division management, by whatever means.

Only by understanding the gulf between conflicting factions is it possible to build bridges that lead to mutually satisfactory solutions. Also important, the division's managers had been given an opportunity to purge themselves. It is impossible to resolve organizational conflicts if people are acting purely from the gut. In this case, Tomlinson's trying to "sell" Campbell without allowing people to vent their frustrations would have led to tremendous resentment against both executioners. And the harder the sell, the more the resentment. Anger and hostility can only lead to a lose-lose situation; but once strong negative feelings are purged, it is possible to begin laying the foundation for a double-win understanding.

Finally, the game plan involved *anticipating what could go wrong* with the new president's [Campbell's] and CEO's presentations. As the session demonstrates, when you take *preventive* actions, you can keep the sparks from flying.

Case Notes

1. In external conflict situations, people are very quick to label what's wrong with the other side. For example, Tomlinson felt that "they're going to criticize me because I was too abrupt in dismissing Reg, but since they're reasonable people, they'll also come to see that he was an impediment to progress." In contrast, division management believed that Tomlinson was "crazy": "How could he fire anyone as dedicated as Reg, who was leading our turnaround? What a dumb thing to do!" So, it's critical to understand the crime, and get specific about what a conflict is/is not (in terms of its identity, location, and time) and look for distinctions. This will help you get to the root cause of the conflict (Steps 1–4).

2. Once the cause of the conflict (the distinctions between Tomlinson's and division management's points of view) became clear, it was possible to understand everyone's beliefs and values. Everyone wanted to achieve the same goals: to make the company work; to preserve the integrity of the division management team; and to avoid further strife that could ruin the company.

Understanding that both parties wanted to make the business work was critical; it formed the foundation for a double-win situation (Step 6). Knowing that both sides ultimately had the same goal made accomplishing it easier. If I could just get everyone to cool down, they'd see that their value systems were on the same track, and the solution would lie in everyone agreeing as to how the common goal would be best achieved.

3. Once I knew that everyone was trying to achieve, preserve, and avoid the same things, I was able to counsel Campbell and Tomlinson privately, to make them aware that despite the hostile environment, both factions wanted to get to the same place. With his years of experience as a CEO, Tomlinson was able to take in all the feedback and realize where his own perceptions were off base. It was unnecessary for me to suggest specific solutions (i.e., presentations that he could give to di-

vision management). Tomlinson's mind was already working through Steps 8 through 10: testing his options and selecting a strategy that proved successful at dinner and in the months that followed.

4. Again, this case demonstrates the importance of giving people the opportunity to purge themselves; it is impossible to resolve organizational conflicts if people are acting purely from the gut. In this case, Tomlinson's trying to "sell" Campbell without allowing people to vent their frustrations would have led to resentment. And the harder the sell, the more the resentment. Anger and hostility can only lead to a lose-lose situation; once they have been purged, it is possible to begin laying the foundation for a double-win understanding.

Postscript

Reginald Davis eventually found a job at another furniture company, where he led them to a creditable record as a competitor in certain product lines. Unbeknownst to him, a secret admirer, J. R. Tomlinson, had been watching his development from afar. Three years after his summary termination, Tomlinson offered Davis a job as the new president of a recent acquisition. Davis, with some trepidation, accepted, musing how strangely the wheel turns.

Meanwhile, Harold Campbell won the hearts of everyone at the division, continued the turnaround, and was promoted to president of Bradford Corporation. Campbell gave Bradford the kind of leadership Tomlinson knew the company would need to grow in a marketplace increasingly populated by aggressive American and offshore firms. And Bradford's managers grew to realize that they were lucky to have as talented a leader as Campbell. With the organizational conflict behind it, Bradford has lived up to its potential, and today it is one of the premier producers in its selected markets.

5

Business as Usual: Management Process Conflicts

Case Study

ExecuTrak File: 412: "Between a
Rock and a Hard Place"

In the late 1980s, Clayton Ltd. had become one of the most successful
footwear manufacturers in the United States, and one of the few
American companies to actually retake market share from Pacific
Rim competitors. Clayton accomplished this by adopting the same
manufacturing techniques as the Japanese used, such as the just-in-
time technique, and by instituting a total-quality program that
allowed the company to make superior products at a lower cost.

Clayton was about to embark on an exciting new project that
involved creating a sister company for specialty markets. Everything
looked good on paper, except when news of the deal leaked from a
high-level executive source. Clayton then found itself caught in a
fascinating management process conflict involving two top
executives with very different styles, each of whom had interest in
the new company. Whoever won the top position would bring his
own supporters, which guaranteed that a warring team of managers
would be running the new company and the parent company.

One of the executives, Peter Rand, then executive vice president,
had built his reputation on the impression that he would do
whatever he had to do to get the job done—no matter whom he

steamrolled. While it was true that during meetings, people would sometimes hold their breath as he skewered someone who had failed to meet an important objective, even his most ardent critics acknowledged that he was tremendously productive and deserved a lot of credit for getting Clayton to where it was today.

George Kirsky, Clayton's senior vice president of sales and marketing, was also of a single-track mind. But to him, honor and integrity, fair dealing, and succeeding *through* people were all important. George's supporters tended to see Pete as a tyrant, whereas Pete's supporters considered George to be too smooth and glib. The new arrangement would put the two executives straight on a collision course, and it would put Clayton's current president, Ted Adams, in between a rock and a hard place.

Types of Management Process Conflicts

The type of conflict probably responsible for more strife than all of the others combined is a management process conflict, perhaps because people are dealing with issues that crop up on a day-to-day basis, regardless of the type of organization, level of management, or business.

Problems with Leadership Style

The most common type of management process conflict concerns leadership style. Consider, for example, what so often happens as a result of managers whose style is reflected in a hub-and-spoke power structure. During meetings, questions emanate from the hub and shoot out down the spoke. Though people's intent may not be hostile, invariably they tend to gather all the data they can in the event that they're called on by the hub to perform. For most people, this means having to overload with information in order to cover the bases and be ready to answer the hub's question. Preparation for information overload is not a good use of these persons' time, nor does it sharpen their skills. If called upon, and if they feel insecure, they too often simply give a "core dump" of what they know, hoping that something relevant will "stick to the wall" and that they'll have covered their posteriors in the process. This style of leadership also fosters a great deal of fingerpointing (usually under the table).

Another type of conflict-generating style is the leader who advocates participative management but in fact doesn't want input from anybody else. This fact becomes evident when the leader calls for suggestions and feedback ("I really want your ideas, Jackie") but, when the responder turns in her thoughts, the leader either does what he or she intended to do anyway or fires the idea back for rework, again and again, until satisfied with the answer.

A third conflict-generating leadership style is the executive who cultivates "yes" people. Subordinates quickly learn to read this type and constantly scan to see which way the grass is bending. Yes people quickly learn the ropes after getting stung once or twice. For example, they might early on question the executive's judgment and find themselves rebuked with answers such as, "Hmm, you seem to have a negative attitude. I want to see a 'can do' attitude!" The message is clear: don't make waves.

Some other popular destructive management styles that I've observed include the following:

Ostrich: An executive who "sticks his head in the sand" to avoid making decisions or who procrastinates, hoping the need for a decision will go away. This inaction can cause extreme anxiety and even grief as people try to do their jobs without direction or support for important choices that have to be made.

Gunslinger: This person operates in the old "ready, fire, aim" mode, shooting from the hip first, asking questions later. The gunslinger's trigger-finger usually bypasses his brain, leaving "dead bodies" throughout the organization. One sad consequence of this approach is that people tend to head for cover, everyone for him- or herself, whenever it's time to make a decision. As a result, there's little teamwork and a great deal of effort to preserve individual hides.

Chicken Little: Executives who practice this style of management believe that they have to act on the basis of what is known now (the sky is falling!) without getting further research and thought. This makes it very difficult for others in the organization to develop or implement well-thought-out plans, and it can cause a tremendous amount of strife at all levels.

Univac: This type of leader wants everything reduced to numbers, with no human element, feelings, or subjectivity. Subordinates often feel that there's little hope of being treated like people, which again can cause significant internal unrest.

Bleeding Heart: The opposite of Univac, the bleeding-heart leader is unpredictable because his or her decisions are made almost exclusively on an emotional basis. When people are led by an unpredictable executive, they tend to distrust him or her and their peers too, because they don't know how they'll react. Working as a team thus becomes difficult.

Janus: The Janus leader flip-flops like a modern-day politician, saying whatever will make a particular constituency happy or agreeing with the last person who leaves his or her office. Subordinates catch on to the game, and they learn not to trust such a leader. And without trust in an organization, no meaningful work can take place.

Mr. (or Ms.) Smooth: He or she is affiliation-oriented (and, one hopes, achievement-oriented), constantly scanning for how he or she can establish rapport with a group or an individual. Through business life, this type of leader has built up patterned ways of greeting people, communicating with them, sometimes putting his or her arms around their shoulders and making them feel good when they're in the boss's company. Mr. or Ms. Smooth tends to be good at people tactics, rather than strategically thinking in terms of the big picture.

Problems with Organization

In addition to these and many other painfully difficult leadership styles, many organizations are often crippled by a structure that blocks progress. For example, there may be too many reporting levels so that decisions take forever, which frustrates energetic, achievement-oriented managers and employees. Another problem is a complex reporting structure that forces a group to pay multiple allegiances to departments with conflicting goals. Management information systems often falls into this trap. It typically reports to the finance and accounting people, yet it's supposed to serve all departments in the organization. Many finance departments are primarily concerned with controlling costs, monitoring results, and getting early warning of emerging problems reflected by "the numbers." Too often, this preoccupation dominates information systems in an organization; instead, the focus should be on responsiveness to the primary users.

Human resources is in a similar category. Too often it reports to finance and administration as opposed to, say, the president. Given the fact that "people" make or break an organization, you'd think that human resources would be given a higher-level reporting relationship than is found in so many organizations.

Problems with RAA

A third source of organizational conflict concerns vague or nonexistent tables of responsibility, authority, and accountability (RAA). RAA issues are often confused with personality issues or the need to "realign" the organization (a favorite catchall solution of management consultants). In my experience, the root cause of conflict is often a lack of clearly defined and mutually agreed upon RAA structures. If various groups have all kinds of shared responsibilities, no one knows who has the RAA, and sometimes major action items drop through the cracks. This often leads to intensive fingerpointing and internal unrest, if not outright conflict. At the other end of the spectrum, there may be such a concern to make sure that nothing is missed that several functional groups duplicate one another's activities, actually fighting over who has RAA over particular spheres of activity.

At one consumer-products company that retained us, we discovered that conflicting ideas about RAA were the root cause of widespread strife throughout the entire organization. On the surface, the problem appeared to involve a turf battle between the research division and the consumer-products group. In fact, the company was to blame, because the RAA lines had become blurred.

This was most evident where new-product development was concerned. For example, no one knew exactly who should be responsible for developing line extensions and product proliferations. Should the consumer-products group leave it up to the research division, whose track record for this was abysmal? What was the real function of research and development (R&D)? Should R&D merely provide technical specialists and services on a temporary basis as needed and work on new technologies to enhance existing products? Or should it have direct responsibility for the outflow of specific, major new products? Should new-product development be a joint accountability, shared by the research division and the consumer-products groups' R&D, with each responsible for different phases of the process?

From interviewing the relevant managers and technologists in both groups, it was clear that poor coordination existed between the two divisions. We found ample evidence that the company was slow in getting new products to market and in making vital changes necessary to keep product lines competitive.

What was the solution? A new Business Development Unit was established that would draw on *both* groups. The unit was represented by product-line management as well as by the research division. Specific responsibility, authority, and accountability were designated for key issues. Everyone involved agreed that this approach resolved the current problem, in part because it clearly spelled out RAA lines.

Another fascinating RAA case from our files involves a cosmetics manufacturing company in which the board of directors handed the

CEO a goal of doubling the company's revenues in just three years. The CEO doubted that this goal would be obtainable because of what turned out to be an RAA conflict. Following the CEO's termination of the president, the general managers of the three divisions and the chief financial officer (CFO) all vied for the position. Managers and employees beneath them rallied to the cause, as if they were involved in a political campaign. All four had some qualifications, but the "election" of any one would cut deep across partisan lines. If the CEO promoted one general manager to president, the other two and the CFO might well quit, and the new president would lose the support of his "opponents'" divisions. If the CEO promoted the CFO, the human resources director and possibly the division managers would quit because they disliked the CFO so intensely. (He had earned the nickname "K-9.")

In short, in the words of the beleaguered CEO, "whatever happens, there's going to be a real 'disconnect' across all functional lines." Following numerous confidential interviews, we held a conference designed to resolve the issues agreed upon at our common-vision feedback session. Our feedback report had clearly delineated the major cause of organizational conflict in this company: poorly defined RAA for a whole host of management process issues, centered on the divisionalization of the company and the roles and relationships between the divisions and the corporation as a whole. For example, it was unclear as to what the appropriate degree of RAA should be for the divisions vis-à-vis the specific staff departments, the business planning/forecasting/budgeting/pricing processes, as well as the approval process for shutting down the line, changing formulas and vendors, and introducing new products.

Using the conflict resolution process, the managers were able to jointly agree upon the designated roles. By the end of the session, everyone, including the three general managers and the CFO, agreed as to the distribution of responsibilities and power. With everyone aligned to the same goals, the CEO recognized that he was better able to delegate RAA to give additional responsibilities to the divisions and functional staff. No longer would he be the bottleneck that he had clearly become. During the next several months, this delegation of RAA enabled the CEO to clearly determine which of the candidates was best suited for the position. The promotion of one of the general managers did not lead to civil war, because the RAA lines were clearly drawn and no one felt that their power was usurped. In fact with RAA working for the company, the CFO was far more comfortable in implementing his responsibilities and proved more valuable to the corporation.

Problems with Compensation and Reward Systems

RAA battles can indeed tear companies apart. But no less potent are the third causes of management process conflicts: "malfunctioning" compensation and reward systems. In some cases, reward systems are unwittingly designed to *promote* strife by encouraging people to take a competitive attitude toward their peers. Poorly designed compensation and bonus systems often do just that, as many a salesperson will testify.

In some cases, the reward system simply doesn't offer people an incentive to do things that benefit the company as a whole. We had several projects with an insurance company that had an excellent individual commission plan. Unfortunately, however, the company never gave the individual sales representatives an incentive to pass along other parts of the business when they had the opportunity to do so. For example, if the reps learned that they had customers who were expanding to other cities, they wouldn't try to make contacts for their colleagues in the appropriate offices. "What's in it for us?" asked one sales rep whom we interviewed. Clearly, this company's reward system lacked any incentive for team play, and the organization suffered as a whole.

The solution was developing a new compensation plan that met the APA (achieve, preserve, avoid) criteria. It rewarded teamwork by compensating both the referring and servicing branches.

Another example of a poorly designed reward system was at a blue-chip food processor. The new group vice president discovered that the quarterly sales and shipment figures were sometimes falsified. The "funny numbers" seemed to keep cropping up at the end of those quarters when shipments did not meet the "bogey." In an attempt to meet established sales and shipping quota commitments, if the products had been ordered for delivery at a later date, the shipping department either shipped them early or sent them to the food processor's own regional distribution warehouses. As long as product left the plant, no one would be judged negatively on performance reviews (during which raises were determined on the basis of whether or not the various divisions and plants met their quarterly targets). Again, the company's reward system (and the ethics of the managers involved) was to blame. It encouraged people to deceive their finance and control people, senior management, the SEC, and ultimately the stockholders and investors about the actual performance of the company.

Effects of Management Process Conflicts

Whereas external conflicts tend to hit a company "broadside," affecting the organization as a whole, management process conflicts are often felt by departments and individuals. While all executives may become irritated by one another's style, leadership style problems tend particularly to affect middle managers who individually feel discontent with the superior's decision-making and communication process. Eventually, individuals—and even entire functions, departments, and divisions—share their misgivings about the way a superior makes (or doesn't make) decisions, and they commiserate about their inability to do their jobs well or make a real contribution to the company.

Conflicts involving compensation and reward systems also tend to affect individuals. They can make people act like loose cannons or even adversaries of other functions and departments rather than as members of a unified team. Indeed, poorly designed reward systems can actually have the opposite effect than intended.

Organizational conflicts stemming from structural causes are distinctive in this category in that they tend to affect whole departments rather than just the individuals within them. For example, finance and accounting may feel pitted against individual departments or even the entire company. In the same vein, marketing and customer service may feel pitted against sales; engineering and production control may be against manufacturing; manufacturing may be against sales; and so on. If responsibility, authority, and accountability have not been clearly and appropriately nailed down and bought into by all parties, conflict between functions, departments, and individuals will just be further fueled.

But whether a management process conflict starts with a single individual and then spreads throughout the organization, or whether whole departments or divisions become involved at the same time, the results are the same: the organization will be weakened.

Guidelines for Resolving Management Process Conflicts

Management conflict processes are relatively easy to diagnose, but they are often difficult to solve because you're dealing with situations that may have long precedents. As a catalyst-mediator, you will always face a danger that you'll be "shot as the messenger." Therefore, take the utmost care and observe the following guidelines.

1. Be aware that when you set out to resolve a management process conflict caused by leadership styles, you're walking on thin ice. By definition, these conflicts reflect a way of leadership that has worked successfully for the individuals involved, even if it doesn't work for the organization. So the style is deeply ingrained in the personalities, and the perpetrators aren't about to change easily. It usually takes a traumatic or shocking experience for change to happen.

Knowing this, you *must* get at the beliefs and values of the executives (Step 5). By smoking out the APA criteria of each protagonist (Step 7), you'll know what he or she wants to get out of the resolution, and you can have a better basis for creating an environment for a double- or triple-win situation.

2. Any protagonist is operating within an ongoing environment. Regardless of that individual's strengths and skills, the person may still have adverse effects on the organization. Similarly, the organization's culture and climate may have negative effects on the individual. From the viewpoint of a catalyst-mediator, it's important to recognize the interplay. Bearing this in mind, you will probably come up with solutions (Steps 8–10) that will result in one of the following: (1) the solution will protect other people from the negative aspect of the leadership style while capitalizing on its strength, or (2) the person will feel compelled to make a change if he or she wants to stay in the organization and be rewarded.

The former solution typically entails insulating the company through a change in the organizational chart or assignment for the individual. For example, in one instance that we dealt with, a brilliant but extremely abrasive director of marketing was shifted to a "special" corporate staff assignment. There he could continue to help develop strategies, but he no longer had line responsibilities. This was not a true demotion, as he was able to contribute his conceptual and analytic acumen for the benefit of the company. Personally he was much more comfortable, as he knew he was antagonizing others in the marketing department in his line management capacity.

The second solution typically involves a long-term process of modifying a person's attitudes, communication, behavior, or performance. In other words, you can't take gunslinger-type executives and managers and turn them into sensitive, calculating leaders overnight. But through an ongoing process, you can help them develop a style that shows more awareness of the effect that they have on other people.

3. Conflicts caused by structural problems and blurred RAA lines tend to involve large groups of people. As in diagnosing and resolving the other types of management process conflicts, confidential interviewing can help to reconstruct the crime (Steps 1 and 2) and identify key distinctions and home in on the root cause (Steps 3 and 4), which lays a firm foundation for implementing Steps 5 through 10.

4. Regardless of the source of the management process conflict, the catalyst-mediator has a role beyond helping to resolve the immediate problems. She or he should also plan on providing ongoing counseling or coaching. (This is a key point. An important goal of the catalyst-mediator is to demonstrate to the protagonist that changing his or her management style is a process, a journey with a destination, rather than a "magic pill" or a one-stop action.) Chances are, the situations leading to the management process conflict have other ramifications. Therefore, part of the catalyst-mediator's responsibilities entails helping people to think things through by applying the 10-step process to other issues at hand.

For example, the catalyst-mediator might ask, "What new 'crimes' need to be reconstructed?" "What difficulties are you experiencing these days?" "What's going *especially well* in the area in which you had difficulty in the past?" and, "What, in contrast, is *not* going as well, or as well as you hoped?" Specifying the identity, time, and location dimensions in both respects, then searching for differences and probing them for the root causes (Steps 1–4) can provide vital information for establishing what everyone now wants to achieve, preserve, or avoid in *future* situations. Once these Step 7 criteria are agreed upon, experience often suggests the best *proactive* solutions. By keeping people thinking in these terms, you'll eventually help the protagonists and the organization get to the point where any remnants of the original "crime" have been resolved.

Bear these guidelines in mind as you read through the case of Pete versus George at Clayton Industries. This case from the ExecuTrak files is especially interesting because it demonstrates not only how a leadership style problem can be solved effectively but also how the conflict resolution method can be applied in a "pinch" with little or no preparation.

Clash of the Titans

Pete came from the other side of the tracks, from a very poor family in the Deep South. Quick and bright, he was determined to make good in life. He played rough on his football scholarship, and this trait became his hallmark in business as he moved up the manufacturing and operations route. Strong-minded, a "bull in the china shop," he lacked political savvy. Instead, he was blunt, challenging other managers with the attitude, "If you don't challenge me back, I'll run you over!" His determination to be successful may have accounted in part for why he became a hard drinker at such an early age and smoked two packs of cigarettes a day. A true gunslinger-type executive, Pete let everybody know how good he was, especially union rank-and-file employees who were intensely loyal to him.

In sharp contrast, George, who also came from a tough neighborhood, this one in Philadelphia, was neither the brightest nor the quickest but a steady solid citizen, and he was quite sensitive to others. Honor and integrity were very important to him. Despite his tough upbringing, George exhibited a true Mr. Smooth style, and he was terrific at bringing out the best in people and making them feel comfortable.

While George respected Pete's ability, he intensely disliked his style. Pete felt the same towards George. Still, they were somehow able to keep the peace together as they rose in the hierarchy.

I reflected on these two personalities as Ted Adams, a client with whom I had worked closely several years previously, told me of his quandary.

"So you already heard from Pete, and he told you that he and George decided to go with the business school professor instead of your firm, John?"

"That's right, Ted. It was good of Pete to call me so promptly following the meeting at which this was decided, even though the news was not what I had hoped for."

"Pete's good at that," said Ted Adams. "I mean, he's pretty good at getting back to people who are waiting to hear news, good or bad. That's one of many reasons I made him vice president of operations some time ago, despite some of his personal characteristics. Frankly, John, I don't think he made the best choice of an outside resource. But it was only a year ago, as you may recall, that I appointed Pete as executive vice president and I really feel that he has to make certain decisions now for the company. In the final analysis, the deciding factor probably was the fact that both he and George had taken a course or two under that professor when they went to the Advanced Management Program, and they both liked him."

"There could have been another factor," I thought to myself. Ted had led a senior management conference of his staff, using me and several of my staff as catalysts, years before at a particularly difficult time. He had recently taken over as president of the company, and his honeymoon period was ending without the anticipated turnaround occurring. At one point toward the end of the third afternoon, Ted had gotten so enraged at the obstinacy of Pete, his manufacturing manager, that I called a break. I could see that the conflict between the two was no longer smoldering but about to explode.

I had pulled Ted into an adjacent room and absorbed the brunt of his attack: "That S.O.B. I should fire the bastard. I'll be damned if I'm going to sit and listen to Pete's drivel when we have so many problems in the market and even with the Union, with whom Pete's had a historically good relationship. Instead of putting his nose to the grindstone, he comes up with some of the damnedest impractical ideas."

"I know how you feel, Ted," I said, "But I also know that you respect him. Isn't it true that it's only when he is overtired or had a couple of drinks too many that you've said he tends to go a bit crazy?"

"Well, I can't afford to have my head of manufacturing behaving that way."

"I understand. Tell you what: I'll talk to Pete before dinner while the other guys are having refreshments."

I did just that, and it wasn't an easy discussion. For one thing, Pete had had his invariable beer with lunch even though he was the only one to do so. Ted had chosen not to make an issue of this, and I felt I should have troubleshot this with Ted. Perhaps he would have suggested no alcoholic beverages so nothing would get out of hand.

We had already been working three and a half very intensive days since Saturday (on top of the managers' full workweek), and Pete was upset. He had a union problem on his hands that had caused him to leave the session to take a couple of emergency phone calls. He was obviously tired and frustrated.

I started: "I'm going to level with you, Pete. I want you to sit there and just hear me out, and then you can say whatever you please."

Pete's eyes were smoldering. He looked as though he was going to pounce on me: "What's eating my boss, John?"

In short order, I had told him he was on the edge of being fired. That sent ice surging through his system. He literally sat bolt upright and said, "You've got to be kidding! That's just crazy. I don't believe it! Ted going off half-cocked?"

By the end of that difficult conversation, Pete seemed to understand that he was viewed as increasingly insensitive to concerns that not only Ted but also some of his peers had about his digressions, abruptness, coarse remarks, and sometimes running roughshod over people. This was difficult feedback for Pete. To help him, he and I agreed on some ground rules by which he would try to redeem himself in the eyes of the president and win back some of the respect he had lost with his peers.

While I always felt Pete was grateful for my feedback and counsel—indeed, he had worked very hard from that moment to show somewhat more consideration to management and hold his temper in check—he was a very proud man and probably always had resented me because he felt embarrassed (the shoot-the-messenger syndrome).

At any rate, it was a good five years after that private discussion with Pete. Even though I had had a good exploratory meeting several weeks before with him and George (now senior vice president of sales and marketing) about my firm's helping Clayton to restructure, they had instead selected the business school professor-consultant. So I had just lost an excellent contract opportunity. I thanked Ted for having "thrown our name into the ring" as another resource that should be considered.

Dial 911

Two months later I received a frantic call from Ted. He announced that some high-level source in the company had leaked plans for a new spin-off company that would make waves in the fashion industry. Not only was the leak a competitive risk, but it could cause a commotion in the investment community. It also caused tremendous upheaval in the company; rumors ran rampant as to who would run the new company. Would it be George? If so, what would be done with Pete, who would lose a big chunk of his responsibility? Bets were being placed and sides had already formed as to whom people would pay their allegiance.

Ted informed me: "George is delighted that he's going to be made president of this spin-off. George also told me he will absolutely refuse to work for Pete if Pete is made president of the overall company. Pete and George both know that I've told my boss at the parent, who's chairman of our company, that I want to retire within the next year or so. But I didn't feel Pete was quite ready yet to become president."

Continued Ted, "Although George, as senior vice president of marketing and sales, has been reporting to Pete on an interim basis these past six months, he's chafed at the bit to get out from under him. He's been looking forward to the prospect of the spin-off as the chance to run with his own agenda. He's told me in no uncertain terms that he'll quit if his new company ends up reporting to Pete, even though it makes sense for that to happen.

"But if I don't make Pete president, and if we spin off this major operation as we plan to, then I've taken away a very big chunk of Pete's territory and he has just the mainstream business to manage. He's been in manufacturing and operations for the last 26 years, so there would be even less of a challenge from this point forward. So, going this route, Pete will lose face with his people and in the industry; in addition, he'll not be nearly as challenged.

"Complicate this by the fact that the CEO of the holding company wants to conduct an outside executive search before he is willing to see Pete as president of this outfit. So it kind of looks like I am caught between a rock and a hard place. Wouldn't you agree?"

I agreed and asked Ted if he wanted me to fly in for a consulting session. "There's no time, John. But start the clock."

Although I had a crucial appointment with a potential client that evening, opportunity knocked hard here. (Besides, the conflict resolution steps are just as applicable under a time crunch; doing it under time pressure sharpens your skills.) My client wasn't due to arrive at the airport until 7:30 p.m., so I had some time available. I was personally challenged by the situation: With my knowledge of the personalities and the company involved, could I use the 10-step method and provide some solid answers? I knew the answer. "OK," I decided, "let's make it happen!"

A First: Mouth-to-Ear Resuscitation

Often, when I feel that I already understand the basic reconstruction of the "crime" (Steps 1–4) and recognize that the clients indeed want a double-win solution (Step 6), I suggest to them that they quickly develop a list of things they want to achieve, preserve, and avoid as problems by whatever means (Step 7). (If they prefer to do it jointly, we both do it, sometimes by long-distance phone.) With the Clayton case, as Ted briefly explained, the big boss was arriving at Ted's office first thing in the morning to talk individually with Ted and each of the two men, so my gut told me that Ted and I had better come up with a recommendation fast.

While I was reflecting on this, I suddenly realized that Ted had started his musings again: "I really don't know what to do, John, because George has to start up and make this 'spin-off' company work. I've got to be sure his eye's on the ball at all times. But if I don't have him report to Pete, then Pete is liable to say, 'Well, if that's the way it is, screw it!' and give me his resignation—or just cruise. Pete is wealthy enough to do this because of the leveraged buyout of our company three years ago and the fact that he made a lot of money on his shares when we sold a good stake to the public. So he can just walk out the door, keeping his pride and reputation in the industry intact.

"At the same time, I can't afford to have the two of them go at one another like snarling cats. It will tear the company apart. As it is, Pete doesn't realize how George chafes about the possibility of working for him. He thinks he can manage the relationship as he has all along, which hasn't been nearly as smooth as he thinks it's been.

"It's been obvious to me and to several others that there is tension between Pete and George, but it really doesn't break out into open warfare. George is too smart for that. He knows that Pete is sometimes hot-tempered and might let things get out of hand, injuring the relationship beyond repair."

"That sure is a dilemma," I agreed. "Do they both want to see this new concept of managing the business work? And do they believe the 'spin-off' is the best way?" I asked, probing to get some values (Step 5) information.

"Sure they do. They both aim to get wealthier by it. Pete assumes George will continue to report to him as head of the spin-off, while George is ready to lay his hand on the tiller and head for open waters!

"So I've really got a dilemma; I'm damned if I do and damned if I don't!"

"What's your druthers, Ted?"

"I guess I'd like to make Pete president as well as continue as chief operating officer, but I don't think I can afford to do so. I'm really more dependent on George to get this new company up and running. If Pete were to submit his resignation, I could continue to run the mainstream company. But that's not what I want to see happen. So, what do you think I ought to do, John?"

"Is your boss willing to talk with both men and explain his position?"

"Yup, he sure is. And this puts real pressure on me. I have to come up with a decision *now*. I've plum run out of time, and I probably should have called you before getting myself in this fix."

"Do you know what he is going to say?"

"Yeah, he's going to tell Pete that he doesn't have enough confidence in him at this stage and they're starting to conduct an outside search for president."

"Does that mean Pete has no shot at it?"

"No, not really. But you know my boss. When his mind is pretty well made up, it is made up just about all the way."

"Do you think there is any chance that, with the proper determination and follow-through, Pete could convince him otherwise—convince him that he's capable of being named president?"

"I think it is possible, especially if Pete convinces me that he should be president. Then I would do everything I could to take responsibility for things with my boss. I think he might listen to me."

I thought for a moment, "What do you want for yourself, Ted?"

"Well, I want to retire within two years at the latest. I give myself perhaps another full year of hard work and then maybe a consulting assignment for a second year."

While Ted had been speaking, I had been listening intently and jotting down what Ted seemed to be trying to achieve, preserve, and avoid as problems by whatever decision he reached. An idea was forming in my mind as to the purpose of the decision Ted faced. Whatever the best solution, it should result in a triple win—for Pete, for George, and for Ted.

I now felt I knew enough about the values and some basic beliefs of Ted, Pete, and George (Step 5) and that Ted wanted a triple win (Step 6). Just to be certain, I tested this against Ted, and he agreed that that was the type of solution he really wanted. In such pressured situations, it's critical to make sure your thoughts are on track with the protagonists each step of the way; otherwise you might exhaust your time without achieving your goal. I then reviewed some of my notes from the phone conversation and, together with Ted, developed the following (Step 7) objectives:

1. Avoid having either Pete or George resign.

2. Continue to preserve momentum of the business.

3. Achieve Pete's recognition that he does indeed have a clear shot at the presidency.

4. Motivate Pete to consistently demonstrate more broad-gauged management while curbing his temper and stubbornness.

5. Motivate George to be receptive to guidance and to do a first-class job.

6. Minimize adverse surprises and disappointing results.

7. Demonstrate to the parent-company CEO that you have arrived at a thoughtful and practical solution to a serious management dilemma.

8. Demonstrate to all employees reinforcement of the promotion-from-within policy and the potential to move up in management.

9. Demonstrate to the industry that there is a solid management succession plan in place.

10. Achieve a transition period for Ted's retirement.

"OK," I said, "that looks like a good, comprehensive list. Now let's get creative and develop possible solutions [Step 9—I purposely skipped over Step 8 (priorities) because I felt we could get right to the possible solutions]. For example, how about this one, Ted? What if you were to move up to vice chairman and leave the presidency vacant for no more than six months? You and your boss can both sit down with Pete and explain that he is the only insider who will be considered for that position. He has got a clear shot at it unless someone from the outside looks better.

"It sure sounds as though he's got some real advantages. He knows the company through and through, and he has worked his way up from the ground floor as a production operator. He's also taken the Advanced Management Program and knows all the people in the company and the industry. Somebody from the outside would have to have pretty damn good credentials to beat him out.

"The strikes against him, I guess, are that he is not significantly broad-gauged and he has quite a temper and tends to be quite stubborn."

"You're right on all three counts, John. Plus, as you've experienced, he still can really get rather coarse with his language, especially when he has had a couple of drinks."

"Well, he is going to have to pull himself up from the bootstraps on that score if he really wants the presidency."

"I think you have a very intriguing idea there, John. Pete knowing he is the only company insider who would be considered should help reduce any disappointment. And he already knows that I am pretty much in his court."

"Right, and it also means that George is not going to have to report to Pete unless Pete demonstrates to your boss and to you that he really 'lightens his spots,' which should make George feel better. And let's face it, George is going to have his hands full starting up the spin-off, while he gets plenty of status in the business community and industry by running his own show."

"Are you fully comfortable appointing George as president of the spin-off? And, if not, what are your major concerns?"

"I'm pretty comfortable with him. He's certainly the best man qualified, inside or even in the industry, in my judgment. He's got plenty of sales, and some good marketing–management experience. But he's not the most conceptual or innovative person, and he can be stubborn like Pete."

"Well, what about George, at least for now, reporting to you for your 'elder statesman' guidance?"

There was a pause.

"Would Pete accept that the significance of this spin-off requires, on at least an interim basis, George reporting to you?"

There was a longer silence at the other end of the phone for a moment and then Ted spoke, with obvious relief: "That's a pretty damn good idea!"

"Would Pete accept this arrangement?

"I don't know. But I think maybe he will. It depends how I present it and what my boss says that's convincing to Pete."

"Well, how do you feel in terms of your own status if you were to move up to vice chairman?"

"I think it makes a lot of sense. As you say, I'm already somewhat of an 'elder statesman' in the industry. Lord knows, I've run this company long enough and 'turned it around.' Now, it is 1991, so I think I would look pretty good too. People will know that I've championed Pete as the insider to have a clear shot at the presidency. In fact, with my move to vice chairman, I could add the chief operating officer title to him as executive vice president. Now, you can be sure he'd like that. As you say it, John, I think it could be a 'triple win' all around!"

"Well, I am just delighted that we have been able to come up with what sounds like a reasonable solution, Ted. But honestly, we couldn't have done as well if you hadn't provided the kind of information that helped me to reconstruct the 'crime' and capitalize on the opportunity [Steps 1–4], worked toward a triple win [Step 6], and worked with me on what you were trying to achieve, preserve, and avoid as problems [Step 7]. All three were the keys."

"I guess you're right. You've always said that, and this is yet another example. Maybe if I had just thought it through that way, I would have not pestered you like this."

"Hey, it's no bother to me. I love it. I'm pleased that I could contribute this idea. It's really the basic Arnold Conflict Resolution Process through Step 7 that helped me reach my suggestions, as it has so many other times."

"Well, I feel so much better about my boss's arrival tomorrow! And I feel more confident about what I'll say to Pete and George if my boss approves the idea, which I think he will. Knowing your concern for results feedback, John, give me a ring over the weekend, if you wish."

I glanced at the clock, and realized that I'd have to race to the airport to meet my client. After bidding Ted good luck and flicking off the light, I thought to myself that the best of this line of work is that you never know what's going to come in "over the transom." I felt tired but satisfied, having helped a really good person solve a tricky management "whodunnit." There was a psychic as well as a financial payoff here, too. I guess that's what makes this all worthwhile.

Case Notes

1. In every management process conflict resolution, you'll get to the

point where it's essential to help the protagonist develop a list of what he or she is trying to achieve, preserve, and avoid. These become the blueprint for the "house to be built"—what the architecture will look like, what materials will be needed, what degree of craftsmanship is required, what the end results will look like, how satisfied the new home owners should be, and so on. So focus heavily on the APAs (Step 7); otherwise you may simply replace the current situation with a "house of cards" that will collapse when the protagonist's real needs emerge again.

2. As the catalyst-mediator, you must maintain objectivity. While I reflected on the fact that Pete probably resented the negative feedback I gave him years ago, and while I was disappointed that he and George gave the contract to a business school professor rather than to ExecuTrak (despite my prior work with Ted, which helped turn around the company), I was able to remain objective in the current situation. I subordinated my feelings, and my only concern was to help Ted think through his quandary. What enabled me to do that was following the 10 steps faithfully.

3. All readers should ask themselves, "What is my management style, and is there anything destructive about it? Am I basically a gun-slinger like Pete, a Mr. Smooth like George, or any of the other types listed earlier in the chapter? Labeling the style as such (i.e., admitting it to yourself) is the first step to truly resolving whatever waves you are creating throughout your organization.

4. As you can see from this case, my conflict resolution method is not a highly complex, time-consuming, and mechanistic process. On the contrary, it is simple and logical, and it works because it incorporates the protagonists' values, feelings, and perceptions. If you have the data in hand, as I did in this instance, you can perform the process right at your desk. Just be sure, as you reconstruct the crime, to look for distinctions. Try to shoot down possible causes, and then determine what additional information you'll need to obtain to arrive at the best possible solutions. Troubleshoot those solutions, and you're on your way to implementing an effective strategy for restoring peace and harmony within your organization.

Postscript

When I spoke with Ted on Sunday evening, things had gone like clockwork. Within the next 10 days, the business and industry press reported the new spin-off. George was its president, reporting for the moment to "elder statesman" Ted Adams, who was appointed vice chairman of the parent. Pete was continuing as executive vice president, but he had the additional title of chief operating officer of the parent; he also had an assignment working closely with the chairman of the holding company, which gave the chairman an opportunity to evaluate Pete. There was a clear possibility of Pete being appointed president of the parent company by the end of third quarter.

Sure enough, as of October 1, 1991, Pete was rewarded with the presidency of the mainstream company, while George, as president of the spin-off, turned in a plan to grow his new company from $30 million to $85 million in the next three years.

6

The Road Less Traveled: Developing Solutions to Strategic Direction Conflicts

Case Study*

ExecuTrak File 564: "Whew, That Was Too Close for Comfort"

The roots of the Bergstrasse Group reach well back into the 1800s. Its fortunes waxed and waned over time, but today it has a strong track record in three distinct market segments of the medical field through internal development and many small acquisitions.

The ninth chief executive in Bergstrasse's history, Gunther Hemmerl, was scheduled for retirement in the next two years. He wanted to leave as his hallmark a company that, at least in the medical equipment field, was recognized throughout the globe as a world-class manufacturer.

*The client application of the 10-step process in this chapter was the subject of "Overcoming Mutual Mistrust and Misunderstanding," by John Arnold and Keith Parsons, in *Acquisitions Monthly*, March 1992.

Hemmerl had already made three small acquisitions related to the medical field, two of which were not turning out as well as he had hoped. Now he had embarked on the largest acquisition in the company's history, a medical equipment maker in the southeastern United States, Clampitt Company, Inc. Hemmerl hoped that Bergstrasse, together with another company headquartered in St. Louis (Politz, Inc., in which it had bought a slight majority interest several years earlier), would have a competitive edge by offering a full range of products from the least expensive and simplistic to costly state-of-the-art devices.

On paper, the acquisitions had all made sense, and Bergstrasse seemed like an unbeatable force. But the two U.S.–based companies did not quite fit the traditional European model for acquisitions, and Hemmerl faced a tough challenge: convincing the U.S. companies' management to play by the same strategic rules as their European counterparts.

Overview of Strategic Direction Conflicts

Like external conflicts, strategic direction conflicts impact the organization as a whole. But rather than originating on the outside, the problem originates internally and usually at a high level within the organization. The conflict basically involves one or more factions wanting to see the organization move in conflicting or diametrically opposed directions.

One area ripe for strategic direction conflicts is product development. In Chapter 3, we saw how two top officials at the company we called JPK nearly paralyzed product development because of their opposite views on the direction of the company. One (Mal Beatty) had a strategic vision that called for cutting-edge, breakthrough products; the idea was to reposition the company as an innovator in the field. His new boss (Roger Weston) wanted a less dramatic course that focused on improving and refining existing product lines. Weston's goal was to make the company known as the best in the business in its current product lines.

A similar debate took place at Lotus Development Corporation during the late 1980s when CEO Jim Manzi determined that the company should focus on developing spin-off products that supported Lotus's current product offerings. Lotus's crack programming team, however, wanted to develop pathbreaking products (not a surprising desire for creative minds). As a result of the conflict, several top programmers left to start their own companies or work elsewhere. The annals of business are filled with examples like this.

Not-for-profit organizations are often plagued by strategic direction conflicts, especially since their resources are often limited and the choice of what they do and how they spend money can be crucial to the very life of the organization. Consider this brief example from the ExecuTrak files. In the early 1980s, we were brought in by the board of directors of a community hospital to help resolve a classic strategic conflict: whether or not to merge with a larger metropolitan hospital and consolidate assets. The chairman of the board made a persuasive argument that the hospital (which we'll call Mercy) had to find a partner with deeper pockets if the hospital was to survive.

Another faction at Mercy, led by its president, E. L. Garth, vigorously opposed the merger, saying that it would be synonymous with death; Mercy would "lose its autonomy and unique identity." "We can survive," he claimed during an ardent "sales pitch" to the board. "We need to project an image that we're the best in surgery, emergency medicine—you name it, and we're the *best*. Then we'll get some much needed support."

In fact, our interviewing revealed that the Garth position was really fueled by his ego. He wasn't going to simply hand his hospital over to another organization. Besides, in two more years, if he played his cards right, the chairman could retire and he would achieve the level of CEO. He wasn't about to let anything as simple as near bankruptcy derail his career opportunity.

After the board was given our feedback, they authorized the retaining of a public relations firm to help Garth line up speaking engagements and write articles, both of which were designed to reposition him as a top thinker in the health-care field, while a very discreet campaign was undertaken to search out a compatible merger partner. Within eight months, Garth announced his resignation because he had accepted a new job as the chief of a prestigious hospital in another region of the country.

With Garth 1000 miles away, the pro-merger board members easily convinced the anti-merger members that linking with another institution was not just their only option, but it could be a double-win solution. As it turned out, Mercy entered into a very favorable arrangement with a larger community hospital, and the two have forged a mutually beneficial relationship that has allowed Mercy to retain its individuality. Perhaps Mr. Garth headed east too soon!

Another area prone to strategic conflict is diversification and acquisitions. Unless a solo raider is at the helm, few acquisition, expansion, or diversification plans are made without internal conflict. In fact, conflict in these areas can be extremely bitter since those for and against the plan tend to see themselves holding the fate of the organization in their hands. Those who push ahead on the throttle believe that the expansion or acquisition will catapult their company to new heights; those with their hand on the emergency brake fear that the plans will possibly drive the organization to ruin.

Finally, in many companies the strategic direction is simply ambiguous. And without a strong leader, people just follow the strategy of the day. That leads to anxiety and unrest. From this perspective, imagine how anxiety-provoking it must have been at times to work for Unisys or W.R. Grace, both of which went on major acquisition binges in the hope of finding a strategic direction that made sense.

Perhaps most frustrating of all is a company whose strategy seems self-defeating to key managers. In the mid-seventies, for example, IBM developed what is called reduced instruction set computing (RISC), designed to greatly speed up computing operations. But IBM's strategy was to hold off commercializing RISC, for fear of cannibalizing its other product lines. In the mid-eighties, entrepreneurial ventures such as Sun Microsystems picked up on the technology and took command of the RISC workstation market. How would you like to be one of the IBM engineers who developed the RISC technology only to see it flourish elsewhere? It sounds like good grounds for a rip-roaring conflict to me.

Effects of Strategic Direction Conflicts

Because strategic direction conflicts tend to involve high-level people within an organization, they can cause heads to roll or people to resign acrimoniously if they are not resolved. Strategic direction conflicts also tend to polarize companies more than the other problem types, since the stakes are so high; everyone in the company is affected positively or negatively by their perceptions of whether the company is heading toward the right place. Salespeople are often among the worst casualties of unresolved strategic direction conflicts. It's very difficult to make a heartfelt presentation if you don't believe that your company is making the right products or offering the right services. Finally, strategic direction conflicts can lead to counterproductive fingerpointing: "We're in trouble because we followed *their* faulty strategic thinking and flimsy arguments. If only people had listened to us."

Guidelines for Resolving Strategic Direction Conflicts

Strategic direction conflicts are usually easy to diagnose; the factions usually lay their cards straight on the table. But these conflicts can be extremely difficult to resolve because of the intense commitment that people attach to their favored strategy. Still, if you follow these guidelines, you'll have a good chance at developing double- or triple-win solutions that benefit everyone involved in the conflict:

1. As mentioned above, people tend to have a lot invested in a strategy that they believe is best for the company. And this makes sense: their careers and futures are on the line. On the other hand, pursuing a strategy that they believe is incorrect makes people feel anxious and concerned. As long as their favored strategies make sense to them, then their attitudes, communications, and patterned ways of behaving become quite fixed, and they then can believe their position is substantiated. So, it is often difficult to "wean" people from their strategic commitment.

For the catalyst-mediator, it is particularly important to reconstruct the crime in terms of specifically identifying *what* is bothering people and what is not; *where* they are being bothered and where they are not; and *when* they are bothered and when they are not. Particular attention should be paid to the scope of each dimension identified. (For example: Is it always the same? Or is it worse at some times rather than others? Is it getting better?) You can then get to distinctions, which in turn will help you find the basic causes. At that point, of course, you'll have performed Steps 1 through 4 of the Arnold Conflict Resolution Process.

2. Once you've gotten to the root cause, you'll want to find out whether an opposing strategy, or a change in strategy, violates people's basic beliefs about where the company should be going or whether it contradicts their value system (Step 5). Do they feel that the strategy will result in a win-lose situation and they'll be on the losing side (Step 6)? Do they feel they can no longer achieve, preserve, or avoid things that they believe are very important (Step 7)? Once you get agreement on these three criteria, and once the absolute requirements are separated from the desirable objectives (Step 8), the battle is usually two-thirds won, because everyone has agreed on the specifications for the house to be built. What remains is to generate possible solutions and evaluate them to select the best ones (Steps 9 and 10).

3. While any type of successful conflict resolution demands that fact be separated from feelings, in the case of strategic conflict values the

separation is critical because people are so easily influenced by their desire to see their pet strategy carried out. By helping people to separate the facts from their feelings, you can help them become aware of their own preconceptions, misperceptions, and selfish interests.

Back in the early seventies, I was speaking with an executive from one of the "Big Three" automakers. I asked, "Aren't you concerned about the popularity of the Volkswagen and some of the new smaller Japanese cars that have rolled onto American soil?" He laughed and explained that these silly "toys" only appealed to Americans who couldn't afford "real" cars: "John, most people measure each other by the car they drive and the house they live in. Who wants to be seen in a VW Beetle or an impish-looking Japanese subcompact if that person's trying to get ahead in a career or climb the social ladder?"

As I later found out, the executive had been seriously wounded at Guadalcanal, and, like so many veterans, carried a personal vendetta against the Japanese. This, coupled with the American automakers' erroneous belief about American values and quality-deficient Japanese production standards, led to a strategic position that American consumers would prove dead wrong.

4. When working through a strategic conflict, ask the question, "Why bother?" In other words, "Why bother to go through with this strategy? What is it supposed to do for you?" When people start thinking in these terms, they can often be wrenched from their tussle over the "pros" and "cons" of one strategy versus another. Their focus can be shifted to the objectives they're trying to achieve by whatever is the best strategy. If agreement can't be reached on the objectives, go all the way back to the raison d'etre, the mission and goals, of the organization to reach agreement on the objectives and then look at the "how's"—the strategy to achieve them. This will invariably reduce or even eliminate the conflict. Formerly competing parties can then reach agreement on a set of goals and a mission for the organization.

Now that you have a sense of what strategic direction conflicts are all about, let's return to the story of the Bergstrasse Group, which, through two major U.S. acquisitions, found itself on the brink of a strategic direction conflict that jeopardized a major investment of money and time.

Conflict Across the Atlantic

Normally, Bergstrasse would have moved slowly when acquiring Clampitt. But in this case, due to the need of the seller to consummate a deal for cash and of the buyer to do it before the end of its fiscal year, the due diligence had been compressed. The two companies looked like a good fit strategically, and the financial projections looked good if a healthy investment were made in Clampitt. But not that much was known about Clampitt's management and infrastructure since its president, Kurt Meckler, had been the negotiator for the company; he had managed the interaction without drawing heavily on his staff. Bergstrasse had no desire to ruffle Meckler's feathers since it would be very much dependent on him, at least for the near future, if not the longer term. In any case, Meckler's management group remained a relatively unknown quantity.

CEO Hemmerl knew that cultural contrasts, both national and business, could get in the way of achieving the acquisition objectives approved by the board, so he turned to the broker who had made the initial contract with Clampitt, Richard Fern, for advice. Fern suggested that Bergstrasse take out an "acquisition insurance" policy in the form of a catalyst-mediator. He or she could analyze potential difficulties and help bridge any strategic, competitive, cultural, personality, and other gaps between the two firms. Fern had read an article about my work, and he passed our telephone number along to Hemmerl. Three days later, I was en route to Munich, where I'd meet with Hemmerl and his staff to discuss how my firm could help.

On the way over, I practiced my German. Having helped a former employer set up an office in Wiesbaden some years earlier, I was familiar with the country and could speak passable German. But I was rusty and didn't want to make it look like I was patronizing my prospective client. (As you'll see elsewhere in this book, demonstrating a respect for the protagonists is crucial to gaining their trust. Speaking the same language, figuratively or literally, is an important way of showing that respect.)

I had built in a day to overcome jet lag, take in the country and people, and practice my German. After landing in Frankfurt, I took a long drive along the "Romantic Road" to Rothenberg and Dinkelsbuehl, which rejuvenated me before I went to Nurenberg and flew on to Munich. Two days after arriving in the country, I met with Hemmerl and his staff in their executive dining room at Bergstrasse's headquarters. Hemmerl's choice of such a formal dining room, with its starched tablecloths and napkins and a hushed atmosphere, reflected Bergstrasse's traditional and formal nature. I conversed in German as best I could with the various senior executives who, out of deference to their guest, spoke much of the time in English.

Hemmerl asked me to explain how I would help Bergstrasse overcome cultural and other hurdles with its new acquisition. I explained that the process would involve confidential interviewing with managers in the United States and in Europe. Once we'd analyzed our data, we'd present feedback reports and work with the key managers involved to arrive at a common strategic mission, direction, and objectives. Then, we'd take a look at the best strategies, product mix, and organizational structure to implement these. Our doing so, while accomplishing some "culture blending," would facilitate Bergstrasse's achieving smooth relations with its U.S. acquisition.

I also insisted that our interviewing process would include managers at Politz, the other company from St. Louis with which Bergstrasse would be working. It would be impossible for Bergstrasse to build smooth relations with Clampitt without understanding the dynamics of its relationship with Politz, too. (Politz, it turns out, had its own can of worms to deal with.)

Following my minipresentation, Hemmerl's associates began chattering away in German, mostly too fast for me to understand, although I did pick up a phrase that sounded like *"wenn nicht gebraucht, keine fixiere,"* which roughly means, "If it ain't broke, don't fix it." A few minutes later, Hemmerl asked me to wait out in the lobby while they talked a bit. For the next 45 minutes, I cooled my heels, troubleshooting mentally what concerns they might have and how to respond to them.

When I was invited back into the dining room, I tried to read the situation, but everyone's formal demeanor made that impossible. Without expressing any emotion, Hemmerl turned to me and announced that I was hired! (As I learned later, I was competing against two other groups: the German subsidiary of a major American consulting group, which had the advantage of having staff in both Germany and major cities of the United States; and professors from a leading Swiss business university. So something I had said clearly had made a deep impression on them!)

The only stipulation was that I was to start next week. As Hemmerl admitted (and I suspected), Bergstrasse wasn't just concerned about smoothing relations with Clampitt to avoid future problems. He was also concerned about the majority-held acquisition not delivering the numbers agreed upon and the subsequent strain in the relationship—"all because of the attitudes of the Americans."

I thanked Hemmerl and his staff for the opportunity and assured them that I'd be back with a full interviewing team the following Saturday. After a few calls to my home office to announce the news and mobilize the "troops," I was winging my way across the Atlantic, exhausted from the whirlwind travel but also elated at the opportunity to solve an exciting international management "whodunnit."

Three-Pronged Attack

Back in Boston, two of my staff and I sat down to design the interview strategy and a business values survey to be administered to the three companies. Two professionals and I would head to St. Louis to interview Politz, and three of us would go to Clampitt's headquarters in North Carolina. These teams would also interview key customers, vendors, members of the board of directors, and other influential external constituencies.

First, however, three of us left for Munich where we conducted interviews with Hemmerl's senior staff and other Bergstrasse managers who either would interact with the American companies or had been previously acquired by Bergstrasse. Our European interviewing process eventually took us to Bergstrasse sites throughout Germany, Austria, Holland, France, and England.

Prior to our arrival, Hemmerl had sent a memo to all managers announcing that we would be conducting *confidential* interviews and business value surveys with managers, key customers and vendors, and members of the boards of directors of the two U.S. companies. We also would be doing the same with those executives from Bergstrasse who either would interface with one or both of the U.S. companies or had already experienced what it was like to be bought by Bergstrasse. The quantitative and qualitative data would be analyzed, and feedback reports would be prepared that detailed our findings, conclusions, and recommendations. We would then conduct a series of feedback sessions, first individually with the CEO of each company, and then with the CEO's senior management group, beginning with Bergstrasse and ending with Politz.

Within three weeks, we had completed all the interviews in Europe and in the United States. I had personally interviewed the three CEOs, other key executives from the three companies, and several key customers and vendors.

A month later, we had completed our interview and business value survey data analysis and had developed a comprehensive feedback report. En route to completing the report, I spoke several times with Hemmerl to keep him apprised of our progress and to answer some specific questions relevant to decisions he had to make that couldn't await our complete findings. Note: Every conflict resolution must run its own course. In some cases you can proceed in a lock-step fashion, from interview to private feedback session, to group feedback session, to work conferences and related consulting. In other cases, you must reveal your findings and make recommendations earlier to keep the protagonists from making serious mistakes. After all, the conflict resolver's job is to do real-time analysis and provide real-time solutions, not simply administer a formulaic therapy.

I first held a private feedback session with Hemmerl in Munich. For several reasons he was appalled at what I shared with him, even though he had some inkling from our conversations of what lay in store for him.

First, he had no idea that Clampitt was in as bad a shape as it was. He had believed the Austrian president, Kurt Meckler, who said that all Clampitt needed was cash: with Meckler's team's strategy in place, and with the right resources, Clampitt would emerge as a market leader. In fact, this statement expressed wishful thinking, as so often is the case in an acquisition. There had been the belief that an infusion of capital, close monitoring of Clampitt's European president by Bergstrasse, and some good strategic direction were primarily what would be required. While Bergstrasse thought that with the purchase of Clampitt it was buying technology and a new product line, instead it found that much of the former proved to be outdated, and the latter was a questionable fit with Politz.

Not only did Meckler's own managers have serious misgivings about the viability of key elements of the product line, but they strongly resented Meckler's autocratic style. They felt that virtually all important decisions became bottlenecked at his desk. They also expressed concern that key decisions to stop the hemorrhaging were being frustrated by Meckler's almost total involvement in the "back and forth" between concerned groups: first, between the owner and prior interested parties, and then between the owner and his "last hope" (Bergstrasse) in the negotiations for selling the company.

Now let's move on to Politz: Bergstrasse had purchased its majority ownership of this company almost three years ago. Its members on the Politz board of directors had largely relied on quarterly meetings to get an overview of what was going on. Apparently, Politz's CEO and, to a lesser extent, its managers were hiding many things from its majority parent. (Sins of omission, not commission.)

There was also the distressing perception that managers from Politz had of Bergstrasse. Politz viewed the Germans as "pompous," "rigid," "autocratic," and "dictatorial" in contrast with the Americans, whom they saw as being typically "relaxed" and having more informal attitudes and mores. In addition, Politz management displayed an overwhelming negative attitude and lack of respect toward Clampitt; they thought the company had poor-quality, less-than-full product lines, a poor image, "woeful" marketing and sales groups, and no effective distribution. Overall, Politz's managers felt that "Clampitt will need a complete overhaul and tons of money to resurrect it." While some of this attitude could have been explained by the fact that certain product lines of each company competed against the other, the Politz managers we interviewed were quite specific in detailing their perceived vulnerabilities of Clampitt.

Perhaps most distressing to Hemmerl was the fact that Politz's view of Clampitt was not too different from Clampitt's view of itself! Although Clampitt's managers, in contrast with those at Politz, perceived their product and name as a strength, they agreed that the name and image had deteriorated in the marketplace. This decline was due primarily to lack of profitability and the fact that Clampitt's electromechanical products were no match for Politz's microprocessor-controlled line, especially since Clampitt's products were riddled with problems with quality and late deliveries.

Interestingly, the company's parts and service component was viewed as a grave weakness by many of its managers and distributors. Yet it was perceived by Bergstrasse as a major *strength* upon which the company could build a strong base in both North and South America!

To further complicate the matter, while in some respects the product lines of Politz and Clampitt complemented one another, they often *competed*. (Clampitt's high-end devices and Politz's low-end models were similarly priced and had close functionality and performance.) And the key new product line Clampitt brought with it was not nearly as solid technologically as Kurt Meckler had purported it to be. Clampitt and Politz also each had Mexican subsidiaries with a long history of feuding and the use of subversive tactics to steal each other's people and market share.

The next day, we held a feedback session with Bergstrasse's top managers. Because of the hurried nature of the negotiations for reasons previously described, their due diligence of Clampitt had been less than it should have been. It was obvious that they had failed to detect a lot of what our strategic and organizational intelligence disclosed. This embarrassed them, causing them to direct most of their hostilities at me. (I've been the victim of the shoot-the-messenger syndrome several times before.) The group was also upset that I had put their criticism of Hemmerl's management style into the feedback report. While they had certainly vocalized their feelings privately about Hemmerl before, their concerns had never been made this "public." Even though they knew that our report would be quite specific in terms of what we had learned, with no attribution, they felt in some jeopardy of retribution or reprisals in the form of thwarted careers; and at a minimum, they thought that they would be seen as being disloyal to Hemmerl and having embarrassed the CEO.

I had expected this. The impact, however, was somewhat more than I had anticipated in my discussion with Hemmerl the previous day.

I smiled assuredly and said, "Look, you canst strengthen how you manage geographically remote operations until you strengthen your own working relationships here and develop stronger channels of communication. You now have an unparalleled opportunity to make real changes. If you harbor misgivings about the way Bergstrasse is run and have suggestions for improvement, now is the time to get them on the table."

Herr Hemmerl reinforced my comments by stating that "no one is going to suffer from participating in this process," as he and I had agreed.

The Bergstrasse executive team seemed relieved to hear these words. By the end of the feedback session, they had agreed that the only way to go forward was to uncover the problems at home and abroad, then collaboratively determine the best ways to resolve them. I left Munich feeling that we were on good grounds with Bergstrasse. Now for the tough job—going back to the States and facing a feedback session with Kurt Meckler and his management group.

Not Welcome in the Carolinas

The day after touching ground, I flew to North Carolina with one of my staff who had conducted many of the interviews with Clampitt and customers. I expected hostility from Meckler, but not quite the level of anger he displayed when he finished reading the executive summary of the report. "You've probably cost me my job, you $#$," he shouted at me. "And at the very least you've cost me the respect of my management group!" (Situations like this are the ultimate test of your willpower. No matter how "wronged" you may feel, you must be the rock of Gibraltar. If the protagonists suspect that you've been drawn into the fray, your credibility will be permanently damaged.)

I let him fume; then I explained to him that it was "your management group that gave us so much of this information." By revealing both the problems that Clampitt was experiencing and the concerns that Meckler's managers had about his style, I had gotten all the "dirty linen" on the table—and that was the only way to move forward. "Look," I said, "my staff and I didn't make up this feedback; you're reading your managers' words, verbatim. Let's face it, there are problems with your management style. This has probably, to quite some extent, kept this company from turning around faster. There's so much potential for improvement. But not much is going to happen until everyone acknowledges and begins addressing the actual problems and issues.

"Besides, this is history. What's important is what happens from here on. How are you going to manage the business once you get the cash infusion from Bergstrasse that you're looking for? And as for costing you your job, in reality, I'm *saving* you your job. Eventually, when the extent of the problems became apparent to Bergstrasse, you might have gotten fired."

At that point, Meckler melted and confessed that he had *been* authoritarian. But he claimed that it was necessary. "I've had three fingers in the dike, and under Winthrop (the former owner), I was cash-strapped. Winthrop's group simply drained cash out of the company and refused to think about making investments to retool and modernize, which are both essential for the company to become competitive. I needed to take charge when negotiations with various parties began. And when Bergstrasse took over as the final interested party, I had to show strong leadership since there was little chance that another company would agree to give us the money we needed to turn Clampitt around."

In effect, he was admitting that he didn't want Hemmerl's people to see how bad off the company was, and by taking a firm authoritarian position, he was able to control the flow of information. While he didn't withhold information in a fraudulent sense, he cleverly manipulated Bergstrasse people into believing what they wanted to believe. In essence, I had removed the curtains that had shielded Clampitt from Bergstrasse's lens, so it's no wonder that he was upset. But as we talked he began to agree that this was really an excellent opportunity to get all the issues on the table and deal with reality. It was unreasonable to expect Bergstrasse to make the necessary cash infusion until they knew the real story. And it was also unreasonable to expect that anything would change at Clampitt until certain stumbling blocks were removed.

The next day, the rest of us from ExecuTrak Systems who interviewed Clampitt held a joint feedback session with Clampitt's management. Like Hemmerl, Meckler didn't want me to share the feedback reports, but as soon as I reminded him that everyone already knew what they had told us in the interviews, he agreed that he might as well get the issues out and work toward a common set of resolutions.

Before beginning this management team feedback session, I recommended that we do something about the room. (Part of the job of conflict resolver is to be sensitive to the physical environment in which the sparks are generated.) Like the company, the conference room had a stale feel. The drapes, which smelled as if they'd never been cleaned of tobacco smoke, prevented any sunlight from entering the room. We threw them back and opened the windows, an act that was metaphorically inspirational for the process that we were about to begin. Like their

German counterparts, the Clampitt managers were very uneasy about leveling their criticisms directly at Meckler; those who had publicly challenged him or openly questioned his style were no longer with the company. As with Hemmerl, I discussed with Meckler his opening, tone-setting remarks. I must say he was eloquent in this regard, admitting how difficult the feedback, particularly regarding his managerial style, had been for him—especially given that we were about to share it with the group. He thanked the group members for caring enough about the company to be as candid as they were, and he assured them that this feedback provided an excellent basis for going forward. Slowly they responded to the opportunity to find a meaningful resolution to the company's problems.

By the end of the session, everyone felt rejuvenated. Clampitt's managers felt that their operating environment had been given a shot in the arm. They were excited about working together, gained new respect for Meckler, and became more enthusiastic about using the Bergstrasse cash injection to make the company competitive once again.

They were, however, fully aware of the problems lying in wait for them at Politz and in the team building they themselves needed to do. These perceptions were reflected in their end-of-feedback session evaluation:

- "It [Arnold's report] shows that there is a major conflict brewing between Politz and us. There is a lot of 'we/they' between us, Politz, and Bergstrasse. It shows that *we all* must become more team oriented."

- "This is a totally slanted bias against us and our management. There are a lot of distorted views on what we are all about."

- "It is clear that our management team is viewed by most of us as noncommunicative and somewhat disorganized."

- "Politz and its distributors have no real interest in working complementarily with us, but they would like to rob us of benefits they deem useful to themselves."

- "Many opportunities exist for both us and Politz in a complementary fashion; however, only we realize this. Politz sees no real value of maintaining us alive."

- "We hope that the oneness of this study should provide the starting point for identifying the right solutions."

Meckler was pleased—so much so that he invited me for dinner at his favorite gourmet restaurant, usually reserved for special occasions such as visits from the Bergstrasse people.

I was exhausted, but satisfied, by the two-day ordeal occurring on the heels of the Bergstrasse sessions. The results were worth it, though. This case was beginning to come together. Now for the final component— Politz. This couldn't be any worse than my initial dealing with Clampitt, I assured myself. Little did I know what waited for me under the city arches by the Mississippi River.

Singing the Blues in St. Louis

I knew that Politz's president, Edward Hurley, was not pleased about my working with Bergstrasse. We tussled over the phone (using his secretary as a go-between) about how much time he would give me for the feedback to him. I told him it necessitated a full day; he insisted on only two hours. By the third call (and the threat that he would be seriously embarrassed and at a disadvantage compared to Meckler and Hemmerl if he denied himself the opportunity to receive full feedback), he grudgingly set aside the necessary time. I figured that he'd been sufficiently alarmed to play ball (or at least several innings) with me.

In fact, it was difficult to tell who was the more agitated of the three leaders. Hurley greeted me with the same epithet as that used by Meckler (perhaps this behavior was an unwritten part of Bergstrasse's corporate culture); then he told me that following Bergstrasse's purchase of Politz, he'd developed a "perfectly fine arm's-length relationship with them." He admitted, "Oh, sure. They poke their nose around here once a quarter and make silly requests for information that cost us time and money, but hey—they've never really gotten into our underwear. Now you're here and all of a sudden they're breathing down our backs like a pack of wolves stalking a calf. Just because Bergstrasse made a dumb move and bought that dog of a company, Clampitt, you've decided that we need to be investigated, too. You're gonna botch a good working relationship and make everyone sorry Hemmerl ever hired you. Why can't you consultants take a good flying leap off this planet?"

"And what skeletons is Mr. Hurley hiding in Politz's closet?" I asked myself (always a fair question when you're dealing with someone who refuses to make time for you). I gave him the same explanation that I gave to Meckler: that this was a terrific opportunity to strengthen the working relationship with Bergstrasse, straighten up a lot of problems in his own company that were common knowledge and discussion among his own people, and begin working toward a set of mutually beneficial common goals. I asked him why he was so negative about Clampitt, and he answered that Bergstrasse was going to have to pump a lot of money into Clampitt to revive it. That would probably put extreme pressure on Politz for performance and profit contribution. Politz would undoubtedly have to shoulder much of Clampitt's weight.

Eventually, two real problems emerged. First, like Clampitt's Austrian president, Hurley ruled with an iron hand; he was autocratic and tight-fisted. But Hurley had the additional problem of Project X, a top-secret new product about which only he and two top engineers knew details. Politz managers kept seeing enormous sums of money allocated to Project X, even though the project was disguised. Bergstrasse was only dimly aware that it was part of Politz's long-term strategic plan, but it had never successfully probed for more information about it. Expenditures for this project not only caused tremendous resentment among Politz's staff, who were denied funding for more immediate needs, but revealed a great deal about Hurley's lack of trust in others, except for close confidantes. To make matters worse, this project was failing!

There was also a second embarrassment. Several years earlier, Politz had purchased Execor, Inc., a small medical equipment maker that Politz had never really integrated. While Bergstrasse was aware that Execor made a minor contribution to Politz's overall revenues, it had no idea that there was so much we-they friction between the two companies. Hurley had not recognized this; the friction had been hidden from him by his own organizational structure, which shielded him from knowing Execor managers. It would assuredly be an embarrassment to Hurley if Hemmerl really knew the problems at hand.

I finally convinced Hurley that the truth would have to eventually come out. Better that all the cards be placed face up on the table rather than Hemmerl discovering the truth on his own. Hurley reluctantly agreed that this was indeed a good opportunity, especially since Hemmerl already knew something about it from the feedback report. He asked what would happen next, and I explained that we should go through the entire feedback report together, then prepare for the group feedback session with his key managers, as scheduled for tomorrow. After completing our review and discussion of the report at 5:30 p.m., we troubleshot what could go wrong at the management session and discussed our respective roles and tasks.

The next morning, we met with Politz's management committee. As with the Clampitt and Bergstrasse managers, there was no small degree of apprehension at the outset. But they more rapidly got over their fears as they saw Hurley admit to a number of glitches. As people opened up, they were able to more readily identify the real, burning issues, the key ones of which are embodied in the following quotes from Politz managers:

- "A serious communication problem exists between us and Bergstrasse that has continued to fester and needs resolution. The view Bergstrasse has of our company is shocking. Both 'sides' are unhappy with each other, and the whole relationship is detracting from our ability to run the business."

- "The ownership issue is key to much of the poor attitude, since we serve two groups of owners."

- "I'm shocked at the apparent miscommunication and bad feelings over the last three years of efforts in all of the merger activities. Why didn't we get 'professional' help trying to execute the merger activity instead of now 'professionally' trying to sort it out?"

After airing their feelings, the group was eventually able to set priorities and develop an action plan to resolve certain issues that they themselves could resolve.

With Politz under control, the time had now come to distill the output from all three company sessions and prepare to bring all three management groups together to iron out a common vision and game plan. This is exactly what took place 10 days later, back across the Atlantic in Germany.

The Summit Meeting

Before flying back to Munich, my staff and I "crunched" the output of the company feedback sessions with Bergstrasse, Clampitt, and Politz, and we prepared an executive summary with supporting material that compared and contrasted the issues as viewed by the three organizations. In Munich, we presented the document to the top 38 executives from the three companies, including the two Mexican subsidiaries, during a two-day joint feedback session. We began the session with a simulation designed to thaw the ice, give everyone a chance to loosen up, break down we-they polarization, and "open the opportunity lens." Then we engaged them in a business acquisition simulation: they were divided into acquiring and newly acquired companies and given the opportunity, in a relatively "danger-free" environment, to manage the relationship and then critique the performance. From both simulations, they then developed ground rules by which to manage the productivity of the conference.

I began the proceedings this way because there were such strong contrasts in perception among the three companies and because of the hostility of Politz toward Clampitt and even Bergstrasse. In this highly structured "in-basket" merger simulation (drawn from three files of actual client merger experiences), each executive, acting as a member of an executive committee of the acquiring or acquired firm, was given a general statement and description of the position plus some situational reports, memos, telegrams, and so on. He or she had to quickly assimilate these before convening with the other executive committee members to begin the task of making the marriage work.

Through the simulation, the Bergstrasse, Politz, and Clampitt executives recognized the importance of communicating in a way, and taking actions, that would lay a foundation of mutual trust and commitment to a common goal. They quickly found, however, that this was more easily articulated than accomplished, as became evident by their performance. They then critiqued (in a very animated fashion) their performance in the several phases of the simulation. They used this common frame of reference to develop ground rules by which to manage their analysis of the issues and productivity of the real-world meeting.

As we then revealed in plenary session the congruencies and "disconnects" of the key issues perceived by the three parties, open discussions ensued, facilitated by the simulation experience. Gradually, misperceptions and misconceptions were put to bed and mutual trust began to form.

At the end of the two-day joint-feedback session, consensus had been reached on what the true issues were and what process and plan would be used to address them.

Actually, with all hidden agendas flushed out, Hemmerl had an easier time than expected developing a common vision among the five companies of the priority issues. They then could easily identify which issues were best addressed by which managers amongst which companies, and which required task teamwork.

The session was viewed as a major success for the company, as evidenced by some of the written evaluations from the participants:

- "A wide variety of people have been given the feeling they are contributing to an important decision-making process. A great deal of information has been well assembled in a readable forum under sensible headings. Issues important to each participant have been brought out through the interview process in a nonaggressive, confidential environment."

- "Our relationship with the major part of what we regard as our core business is awful. Both companies [Clampitt and Politz] are heavy-handed internally and are not functioning properly. Clampitt, with its products and the marketplace's perception of them, is worse than anticipated. All this exacerbates the typical acquisition problems and leaves less time for resolving them."

- "Accidentally, the interviews have cleared a head of steam within Politz and brought the divisiveness to the surface where, however painful, it can be addressed."

- "The feedback and discussion highlights the need to significantly improve communication channels between our home office and the operating companies, particularly the overseas companies with different cultures."

- "The need for clear objectives and clear communication throughout the organization has been made highly visible. Agreement on management objectives and 'the common vision' is a necessity."

- "Thought must be given as to how the main messages derived from the exercise can be communicated to the executives of [other subsidiaries of Bergstrasse] such that they are prompted into identifying and taking action to minimize similar weaknesses. We cannot afford a once-off communication 'blitz' but rather must create a sustainable communication procedure which reflects the people, locations, and types of businesses involved."

Hemmerl was so pleased with the results that he asked my firm to serve as diagnostician and catalyst to help a five-company task force (the two U.S. companies, the two Mexican firms, and Bergstrasse) determine the best way to rationalize Mexican business. This effort to modernize the business and make it more efficient was crucial because of the current cross-linking of product lines, manufacturing channels, and distribution channels, some of them congruent and some competitive. All in all, the project was acknowledged to be highly sensitive because of the "head-on" nature of the two Mexican companies in their market, with Mexico City serving as the battleground.

While the Mexican business rationalization project was being undertaken, a separate project would be launched in the United States to evaluate the true value of the businesses. Bergstrasse could then determine, from a financial perspective, whether buying out the minority interest in Politz would make sense financially, and if so, what amount Bergstrasse should offer.

Clearly, the remaining significant minority interest clouded Bergstrasse's role and impacted its ability to make operational decisions, including just how to do any melding of the two U.S. and two Mexican companies. Given the number of critical issues identified by our feedback report, only some of which Bergstrasse had previously been aware and even then not to the full extent, there were real questions about whether such a significant further investment was wise.

There were also questions as to whether the minority ownership acted as a considerable constraint on Bergstrasse's ability to really influence and direct Politz.

Aztec Two-Step

At least two general criteria would have to be met by any recommendation: (1) maintain the value of Bergstrasse's investment in both U.S. companies and in the Mexican subsidiaries; and (2) establish the quickest route to make 2 + 2 = 5 in the combined product-market segment for the U.S. and Mexican companies.

Among the issue areas that would have to be resolved were product image, share of the market, branding, location of sourcing, place of manufacturing (whether at both Mexican plants or just at one), distribution, transfer pricing, engineering management and organization, and sales and service for the two basic businesses.

The latter issue was complicated by two factors: (1) there was a considerable amount of integration remaining to be done within Politz regarding its prior acquisition of the Connecticut company, and (2) Politz management had criticized "the Germans" for "looking down on them" and treating them as "second-class citizens" when they went to the Continent.

While respondents from Clampitt suggested a number of possible synergies with Politz, the latter's attitude in most respects was viewed by people from Clampitt as tantamount to "rape and pillage." The low regard that Politz had for Clampitt was reflected in rumors that Politz managers had told distributors that Clampitt was reporting to them and that Clampitt was going out of business. This adversarial attitude went so far that stickers of Politz were affixed to several Clampitt district office doors and messages were left on several Clampitt district managers' voice-mail machines saying that Clampitt was being folded into Politz.

While these two companies' attitudes toward each other were poor, the attitudes of the two Mexican operations toward each other were abysmal. Neither had much respect for the other.

Team building with the five-company task force was therefore absolutely essential before any potential synergies could be objectively identified and any task teams could professionally analyze how to accomplish the goals. To this end, I developed a plan that Hemmerl approved.

We held an initial two-day conference of the nine-member task force in Mexico City. The goal was to establish the process and plan that would rationalize business in Mexico under the present ownership arrangement. Bergstrasse, through its U.S. companies, would still own 100 percent of Clampitt but only a slight majority of its competitor, Politz.

For the first time in my career, I was appointed as head of the task force rather than merely having to serve as catalyst-mediator!

Because of the antagonism of some of the participants and the volatile nature of the subject matter, we thought it best that everybody start with a role-playing game, which would help them to relax and open up. The game chosen was a zero-sum one in which participants found themselves fiercely competing—only to end up losing considerable money. Involving the members in the simulation gave them the opportunity to take a penetrating look at their own thinking and communication. The group then used this experience as a common frame of reference for developing ground rules for managing the process.

Much of the rest of the two days involved reconstructing the "crime" (Steps 1–4 of the Arnold Conflict Resolution Process), sharing information about the issues, discussing the values and basic beliefs of the participants (Step 5), reaching agreement about the type of win (a triple win) desired (Step 6), and agreeing not only on how to determine the best ways to rationalize the business but on what data had to be developed and shared at the next meeting. In addition, the discussion focused on the format in which the information would be presented for a detailed decision analysis.

When asked, "What do you believe have been the significant accomplishments, if any, of this work conference?" the members wrote the following:

- "An understanding of the difficulty of the task and the potential peril in group working. An acceptance of the need for a structured and disciplined approach. The achievement of a basic degree of trust and collaboration, including identification of data needed to make informed, intelligent decisions and data sharing across company boundaries. A common vision of the objectives and criteria to be applied in approaching alternative solutions."

- "The format of the conference helped us to determine what key elements must be discussed in order for the parent to conduct business in Mexico, all this being done in a peaceful, friendly, and open atmosphere. Steps 5 and 6, and Step 7, the technique of achieving, preserving, and avoiding, were very useful in determining the above. The sharing of each company's data was also significant."

- "Appreciation for key players at Clampitt. Established a sound game plan for completing our mission. Cleared the air (or established a better understanding) on several volatile issues."

- "The process reaffirms my feelings that all problems are surmountable given the right forum for the interested parties to express their concerns without being stifled by unrealistic goals and expectations or other encumbrances."

A week later we convened again and began the detailed analysis by agreeing that a triple win was indeed the objective—for Bergstrasse, Politz, and Clampitt. After setting criteria (Step 7), the group agreed that the best solution for this particular line of business "absolutely without fail" must do the following: (1) result in no material loss (defined in terms of percentages) of the other product line's agreed-upon potential; (2) avoid any loss of Politz's current business due to any disruption of its channels of distribution; and (3) achieve a single strategy.

In addition, the best solution should also accomplish, as much as possible, such goals as maximizing profit and volume growth, exploiting the installed customer base for future sales in the best way, and maintaining service support for customers.

Eight alternative strategies were evaluated, including selling a particular product line to a third party, which had been favored by a number of the group. In focusing down on the best information available in light of their respective experience and judgment as they evaluated each of the alternatives, first against the absolute requirements and then against the remaining criteria, however, they came to the consensus that this would *not* be a wise course of action. Instead, they agreed that some components of this particular product line should be downsized and others transferred to Politz's product line.

The analysis was completed by noon of the second day. We then spent the afternoon developing a detailed communication and implementation plan to accompany the presentation of the recommendation to the two U.S. presidents. If the plan was approved by both of them, we would then present it to their superiors, Hemmerl and Bergstrasse.

Considerable attention was paid to the impact of this solution on the dealer network, on manpower staffing and factory workloads, and on the control of documents as it was implemented.

At the end of the session, we asked, "What do you consider to be the most significant accomplishments, if any, of this work conference?" The following remarks captured the mood of the group:

- "A mutually satisfactory working relationship was established that addresses both the short- and long-term needs of all the parties."

- "Through the [10-step] process, we got down to the probable options and then arrived at good conclusions and a realistic approach to conducting business in Mexico."

- "A course of action was set that will ensure a win-win, 2+2=5 scenario for Bergstrasse's interests in Mexico *and* the United States."

- "The plan is doable and should not require excessive management time to implement it. The plan will posture the Mexican companies to continue to be profitable in the short term and will enable them to move closer together so as to permit consolidation in the long term."

- "We reached unanimous consensus against considerable odds, accomplishing a real, cooperative working arrangement with a framework to actually produce results."

Bergstrasse's chief executive was delighted with the task force's recommendation and by the fact that a third conference, which had been budgeted to assure sufficient time to complete the analysis (Steps 8–10 of the Arnold Conflict Resolution Process), was unnecessary since the task had been accomplished in just two meetings. (You'll often find that, as people discover the value and power of the process, they can accomplish more than you expected, accelerating your schedule. But it's still best to plan for the maximum amount of time you think it will take to sort out the issues and arrive at mutually agreed-upon resolutions.) We left Mexico feeling like we'd been around the world in 21 days. But that kind of global "hopping" is sometimes necessary to close the file on a struggling multinational concern.

Case Notes

1. The catalyst-mediator has to anticipate that in any merger or acquisition situation, conflicts over strategic direction are quite likely, even though they may be hidden by various "guises." (Interestingly, strategic direction conflicts are often accompanied by management process conflicts, and the two are often hard to tease apart.) In any case, special attention must be paid to reconstructing the crime and determining whether strategic direction is really one of the basic causes.

In this case, while it may have appeared that autocratic styles were the issue (and they certainly contributed to the situation), in fact it was the lack of direction from Bergstrasse that was at the hub of the matter. In the case of Politz, Bergstrasse couldn't give direction because of the rights of Politz's minority shareholder. Politz, on the other hand, wasn't totally straightforward with Bergstrasse about its own product direction and other problems. Hurley intentionally played it close to the vest and wanted to keep Bergstrasse at arm's length. At the same time, Clampitt had some obsolete products with an unclear direction, as well as much wishful thinking on the part of its CEO, neither of which Bergstrasse had ascertained until our involvement.

2. As a catalyst-mediator resolving a strategic direction conflict, you must recognize that "what's done is done." Everything that happens in a company until the point you enter it is history. Your job is to help the executives understand the past so that they can strengthen the future. The goal is to capitalize on what they can learn from the feedback in terms of their skills as leaders and managers.

3. Trust is crucial. As a catalyst-mediator or as someone who is dedicated to resolving the conflict, you have to build trust in people who may at the outset be cynical, if not downright hostile, toward you. You can and *must* relay accurate feedback in ways that build confidence rather than depression and that will lead to action. After all, people are putting their careers on the line, and they trust that you'll deal with the information forthrightly while protecting the anonymity of the respondents.

4. Sometimes when you're resolving a conflict, you have to be willing to be the "bad" person. As you can see from this project, I served as the "punching bag" for three different CEOs and companies. Had I taken it personally, I would not have been able to get them to the point where they could work through the issues, arrive at a common mission and agenda for resolving them, and then do the problem solving, decision making, planning, and communicating necessary to achieve their shared goals.

5. This point relates to the previous note (and takes us back to Steps 5 and 6 of the conflict methodology). You have to look carefully at your own values and be sure that you're not influencing the decision because of your feelings about a specific person in the group or the values one group holds in contrast with another. With people's careers in the balance, you're dealing with their ambitions and prejudices. Don't be "taken" because you happen to like one person's personality or not like another's value system. You're there to help your client and company ethically and legally achieve its objectives. If you become distressed or uncomfortable, or if you feel you're being manipulated, confront the situation with the protagonist. If you can't resolve it (and in my 35 years in the business, I've never seen a confrontation that couldn't be resolved amicably), do the best you can via the 10 steps to leave the protagonist in a situation in which he or she doesn't lose face.

6. A catalyst-mediator must never be intimidated by a high-power executive who says, "Don't show that data to anyone else; I don't want

my people seeing this information." The fact is, the managers you interviewed will know what they told you. If they don't see their feedback, they'll realize that the report has been "sanitized." The entire process will then be compromised, and you'll have undercut your integrity with them. In fact, you'll simply succeed in convincing them that you're the boss's "shill." The only feedback data we've ever edited from a report shown to a client have been statements that were viewed as either too inflammatory, too revealing of a plan not yet divulged, or too risky in terms of complicating legal matters.

7. In a sense, the mediator acts like a psychotherapist—the tougher the feedback data for the CEO, the more you'll have to deal with his or her sensitivities and "hot buttons." So you'll need to be confident that you have the wherewithal to get in situations like this; either that, or be prepared to call upon a professional as soon as possible. If, however, you've been implementing the 10 steps, if the ground rules on confidentiality, who will see the feedback, and so on, have been clearly established at the outset of the project, and if you've kept the client at least generally informed of matters as they have progressed, you should not arrive at a point where an alarm must be sounded.

8. In all conflicts, double wins are very important. With strategic direction conflicts, they're critical. If all members aren't driving toward the same strategic objective, the company will never achieve its goals, and indeed it may suffer drastically. When you can achieve a double win or, if necessary, a triple win, the company can better realize its full potential.

Postscript

One year after we closed the file, the two U.S. companies gradually integrated their Mexican subsidiaries once Bergstrasse purchased the remaining minority shares of Politz. Meckler could not adjust to life in North Carolina under Bergstrasse and returned to Austria. Hurley turned a new leaf, and with quite a bit of coaching and much closer monitoring, learned to delegate; unfortunately, "Project X" never developed into a viable product, but Politz—with some of Clampitt's products—became an extremely important profit center for the company. In two years, since the three companies began operating like a well-oiled machine, Bergstrasse's sales increased 25 percent, pretax profits increased 15 percent, return on capital moved up to 31 percent, and Bergstrasse became number one, two, or three in each of its major global markets.

7

Teaching the Elephant to Waltz: Solving Operational Conflicts

Case Study

ExecuTrak File 732:
"Trouble in Paradise"

Once the king of certain grades of paper and cartons, Deltron Corporation had been losing market share for several years to more aggressive competitors. One part of the company that was clearly weighing down the entire organization was the Latin American region (LAR). Earlier, when Deltron had first purchased a series of box plants and paper mills located on different islands as well as in Venezuela and Central America, it had gained a distinct competitive advantage by being able to produce and ship locally. But improvements in computerized papermaking equipment installed by its competitors, coupled with LAR's failure to increase productivity in most of its operations, had resulted in strife between the entire region and New York headquarters.

Perhaps most symptomatic of the conflict was the fact that LAR had seen seven presidents come and go within a six-year period. At Deltron headquarters, people talked about the "island fever" and the

LAR revolving door. The "LAR Seven" had either left in frustration or were fired after failing to turn around the potentially profitable but always ailing region.

The situation eventually reached a point that Deltron's board was actively deciding whether to sell off LAR's paper mills and box plants to cut its losses. Such a maneuver would have had drastic repercussions in the poverty-ridden islands and some of the remote areas where Deltron had its operations.

So why did Alex Clark, comfortably ensconced as president of Deltron's British division, accept the offer to take the helm of LAR? He did so in part because he couldn't resist a challenge and in part because, as he put it, he had "factory smokestacks" in his blood and couldn't imagine a paper mill or box plant that couldn't be turned around. With a successful track record and plenty of energy, Clark was about to face an operational conflict (combined with a management process conflict) that would test his ability as a leader.

Overview of Operational Conflicts

Operational conflicts are largely what I call "system-driven"; that is, they involve schedules, design-to-production transition, computer/ MIS incompatibilities, and differences in judgment as to how a company should be run.

Schedules represent a major potential area of conflict in terms of pressures to produce. Sometimes the pressure leads to quality problems. Just look at the problems Ashton-Tate had with the release of its popular dBASE program. Not only was dBASE IV long delayed, but when Ashton-Tate finally did ship it, the program was riddled with "bugs," enough so that one publisher issued an entire encyclopedia of the problems! Many other software companies, too, have been plagued by schedule versus quality problems. In their rush to release products into a highly competitive marketplace, they issue versions not quite ready for the consuming public. This causes no small amount of internal pressure and unrest, and of course it brings the companies into conflict with the marketplace, especially their own customers.

One of the most unusual examples of the negative effect of scheduling comes from our own files. In this case, the client company was involved in the highly competitive food-processing business. The new sales manager for this company (whom we'll refer to as "Nick Lothrup") decided that he would personally give the company a leg up on its competitors by letting a major supermarket chain designate how it would like a new cake mix modified. A buyer for this large chain instantly fell in love with the concept, suggested a few variations, and ordered 200 units for a special promotion that was already in process—if they could be delivered within 48 hours. A successful test would result in a guarantee of another order for 25,000 units. This, of course, was music to Nick's ears. But, Nick's symphony turned to thunder when he phoned the plant manager, who laughed at him and said, "not in this lifetime, buddy. We're just not set up to turn on a dime like that."

Nick was not one to be intimidated or give up. Before reaching the plant manager, he learned from his secretary that her boss would be out of town for a three-day meeting the following day. Nick quickly made his move, changing his plans and flying 1200 miles that night to the plant. Upon his late arrival, he picked up a rented truck, caught a few hours sleep, then headed for the plant superintendent's office. There he demanded that production start *immediately*: "I'm not leaving until I see the production line cranking these new mixes out. We can't afford to miss this opportunity; it's 'Big Time.' Do it, or else."

The plant superintendent caved in, and the facility went topsy-turvy trying to pump out the new mix according to novel specifications. At 6 p.m. that night, Nick grabbed the last part of the order from the shipping area and raced for the airport with his cartons of cake mix, which he had stuffed into five large hard-shell suitcases.

When the plant manager learned what had happened, he was furious, to say the least. After threatening Nick with bodily harm if he ever stepped foot within "a mile of my plant," he thoroughly admonished his superintendent and put in a formal complaint to the general manager. This in turn triggered civil war between manufacturing (which felt completely abused by an overbearing sales manager) and the sales force (which regarded Nick as a "can-do" hero who bucked an archaic system, "kicked some 'manufacturing butt,'" and made the right things happen).

Luckily for Nick, the product took off, and the plant was able to mix the defined ingredients and produce them in sufficient quantities to meet shelf life and other specifications. If it hadn't, Nick's might have been the only butt that got kicked. Nick did receive a reprimand from top management, but the president of the company realized that this event was symptomatic of a larger problem between manufacturing and sales, which is why we were called in. We succeeded in helping the president find the root causes of the conflict between both departments (Steps 1 to 4 of the Arnold Conflict Resolution Process), get them on the same wavelength with regard to values and a double win (Steps 5 and 6), and see that they were committed to a mutually agreed-upon modus operandi (Steps 7–10). We were able to accomplish these goals in part because we had nailed down the responsibility, authority, and account-ability concerning the key issues that had previously thrown the departments into conflict.

Closely related to scheduling is the issue of design-to-production transition (DTPT). Often, manufacturing people in so many industries, from aerospace and defense to consumer products, complain that engineers treat them as a "magic box," handing over products that can't be manufactured economically (or at all, in some cases). In one company that retained us, we saw a situation in which a product design became a volleyball pushed back and forth across the "net" no less than eight times. Engineering was often late with designs, causing time crunches for manufacturing. Also, engineering often overdesigned products, so that they were nonproducible. On several new products, engineering had 200 to 600 design changes per month! It was impossible and frustrating for manufacturing to keep up with the daily barrage of changes. To further complicate matters, customers changed their specs, and engineering would change the designs accordingly. But engineering would frequently *forget* to tell manufacturing, which of course intensified the conflict. And what was the issue that most irritated manufacturing? The department was simply not involved in enough design decisions.

While we did help sort out the process and prevent future crises, our treatment was unfortunately too late; the company had lost so much time that a major competitor, who did not experience DTPT problems, introduced a similar product that instantly locked up the market. The world didn't need a "me-too" version of this particular item.

Finally, systems incompatibility accounts for no small amount of internal strife. Consider the case at one consumer-products manufacturer that hired us to "break down the walls" between its own accounting and finance departments and those of a newly acquired company. The parent company tried in earnest to convince its acquisition that its own reporting system made a lot of sense, even though it required five times as much input as the acquired firm's existing system!

More importantly, the acquired company's executives believed that the reporting format of the parent did not facilitate the keeping of information needed to run and track the acquired company's business. So the finance and accounting people at the acquired company decided to solve the problem by keeping two sets of books—one for the parent company's inspectors and one for itself! Think of the time and energy wasted in maintaining this double-entry bookkeeping system! No wonder the parent felt the acquired firm was top-heavy in its financial control unit and leaned heavily on the president to "cut your damn F&A

headcount!" When the president repeatedly and vigorously complained that the problem was the acquirer's too-sophisticated system, he was fired. His replacement faced the same music until a new executive vice president of the parent hired us to help break down the we-they walls. He then paid heed to our feedback report, especially the "reconstruct the crime" section, and realized the burden his MIS system was creating. A common vision of managers of both companies was achieved, and the conflict was eventually resolved.

Another splendid case of system incompatibility comes from the halls of academia, in one of the nation's most prestigious research institutes. We were asked to help resolve the "personnel" conflict between the various departments and the central accounting office. As I suspected even before beginning the interview process, this wasn't a "personality" conflict at all—no one had any particular problems with anyone else. But because the central accounting office system forced the divisions into a style of recording that they found onerous and time-consuming, they preferred to use their own individual systems that they had either written themselves (not surprising for research scientists) or purchased "off the shelf."

The mishmash of programs made it impossible for the institute to get a clear breakdown of expenditures or to conduct a meaningful analysis of resources across all departments.

Within the institute, let alone the related teaching hospitals and other geographically remote units, central accounting proceeded to conduct an audit and discovered that six different management information systems were in use. Some 300 research scientists had purchased their own Macintosh systems.

The chief information officer met with his staff and proceeded to lay out criteria for determining what information architecture would best meet the needs of not only the research scientists but also clinical and administrative staff. Obviously, the design and implementation of the most appropriate, user-friendly system and technology would be influenced by the culture and values of the institute and its members—including their attitudes, preferences, and inhibitors. This is why we were hired, to guide the selection and implementation of the information systems and technology to ensure responsiveness to the users.

Because all parties involved had a sense of ownership in the new architecture, the transition from individual systems to a centralized system was relatively painless. Once the bugs were ironed out (after about only two months), the users willingly accepted the system while the institute was finally able to keep accurate tabs on the organization's vital signs.

Effects of Operational Conflicts

Operational conflicts tend to start at middle management and lower levels, which makes sense, since they are likely to experience the brunt of the problems. If there's unrealistic scheduling, those making the product are most likely to feel the pinch. This can lead to "grass-roots hostilities." (Let's not forget the famous incident at the Lordstown, Ohio, plant of General Motors where workers began intentionally sabotaging cars because they felt the production rate was unfair and humanly impossible to maintain.) Eventually, the dissatisfaction will work its way into the management ranks, at which point senior executives and upper management may well find themselves at odds, too.

DPTP-induced conflicts are also likely to be felt first at a line level and work their way up until an entire division or department mobilizes against the "enemy" down the hall.

Finally, systems incompatibility conflicts can affect any level of the organization. While they might originate with those who use the incompatible systems, they quickly become high-level issues, because they relate to how a division, subsidiary, operating company, or acquisition uses its own information to manage the business. This in turn has a significant bearing on how well or poorly the entity will manage itself. And, the greater the human effort, time, and cost devoted both to the outright and internal conflicts (in terms of reduced motivation, productivity, and so on) and to maintaining two systems, the less that organization contributes to profitability and other key corporate objectives.

Guidelines for Resolving Operational Conflicts

Of all the conflict types, operational conflicts are among the easiest to diagnose; that is, they're not likely to be confused with value conflicts or other types. Productivity and profitability drop. So does the quality of life in the workplace, when systems don't allow people to do their jobs efficiently or properly and when people are worn weary by daily frustration. Whether you're a professional or an in-house conflict resolver, the following guidelines for dealing with operational conflicts can help you to make your task easier.

1. While the "crime" is relatively easy to reconstruct (Steps 1–4), the APAs (achieves, preserves, and avoids—Step 7) are sometimes more difficult to pin down. That's because all involved have their own idea of how to best do their jobs. Engineers, for example, often believe that

their "artistic genius" takes precedence over "manufacturability." They also often think that manufacturing should "rise to the occasion" and translate their creations into tangible products. Or a purchasing agent or merchandiser might get a "great price deal" on a component that seems to meet important specifications yet isn't quite what was ordered and then get immersed in a shouting match with manufacturing or store operations. Or salespeople may accept orders that, for any number of reasons, can't be delivered; harsh words, and sometimes firings or resignations, often result when these salespeople then go head to head with designers and engineers, production people, and logistics personnel who can't find a way to deliver on the promised schedule.

The annals of management consulting are replete with examples of presidents and other executives who "promise" anything to get a contract and then are berated by the staff for having been "totally unrealistic" with their commitment to the customer. After all, "worker bees" can only put in so many 80- to 120-hour consecutive weeks.

Finally, because operational conflicts affect the way people do their jobs on a daily basis, they tend to be enormously frustrating and demoralizing. Although people at the top set policy, other people implement the policies; if these workers find that the policies hamper satisfaction and productivity, their work will be compromised, and you'll have widespread unrest throughout the organization. Again, focus on the individual workers as thinkers rather than as "pairs of hands" or "robots." Make them feel that they have something to contribute.

2. Both for-profit and not-for-profit organizations tend to get caught up in buzzwords like *centralization* and *decentralization*. People then get blindsided and forget about the details. Instead, they worry about whether the so-called centralization activity allows people to work better and more efficiently. Or they concern themselves with whether decentralization allows greater customer responsiveness and the product to flow more quickly.

As the catalyst-mediator, you sometimes have to (carefully and gently) make people aware that their buzzwords don't solve problems. Yes, centralizing or decentralizing the operation might, on paper, seem like a good idea. But it's not an end in itself. What will be the effect on the flow of services or goods? How will people do their jobs differently? Most significantly, how will people *feel* about the changes? When you can get people to see more specifically than centralizing or decentralizing, it becomes easier for them to understand the operational implications of the project. From there, you can move on to developing appropriate solutions.

3. All conflict resolution requires the parties involved to feel like they have a double- or triple-win situation (unless you don't care forever after how the "loser" feels: what happens to him or her, what he or she might do to you in the future, and so forth). With operational conflicts, it's critical for top management to acknowledge the expertise of the people involved at lower levels. Again, the top manager's decisions will affect all workers' day-to-day life in the company. As a conflict resolver, make sure that all parties feel represented in the development and testing of solutions, and that the solutions are not simply edicts passed down from "on high."

The total-quality management (TQM) movement is perhaps the best testimonial in America to the value of involving hourly workers in solving operational problems, many of them causing festering conflicts.

4. Arriving at a common vision is important with all types of conflicts, but it's especially crucial in operational conflicts. Sometimes, people do have to change the way they work; they have to implement new systems and procedures to meet the common goal. But if people feel that they're the only ones being asked to sacrifice their job familiarity and routines, they'll often resist, especially if they feel the mandated change is counterproductive. No progress will then be made.

At one insurance client, line-operations people had been asked to comply with a reporting procedure that they found onerous and time-consuming. In fact, the new system was only onerous and time-consuming when compared with the way that they currently worked. And the end results would truly help senior management understand the profitability of the company and where it could shore up weaknesses. The protagonists grudgingly complied with the system, but they often made "mistakes" that rendered it useless. After a feedback session conducted by an in-house catalyst-mediator, trained and licensed in my 10-step process, senior management was able to explain in specific, acceptable terms the value of the new system to the company. A transition process in which people could gradually ease into the new system was then worked out. This solved one of the problems: the "cold turkey" approach was causing part of the discontent. Within three months after the feedback session, line managers were in full compliance with the system, and senior management was able to make more informed decisions for the company.

With these guidelines in mind, let's return to the example at the beginning of the chapter and find out how Alex Clark set about doing three things: resolving the conflict between New York headquarters and his region; developing an operational approach that would unify the islands into a true, full-fledged regional team that shared the same goal; and revitalizing the eight individual box plants and paper mills.

R_x for "Island Fever"

When my plane touched down in Caracas, it was hard to imagine that anybody could be in conflict with anyone else, given the beauty of the day and the mountainous background to this somewhat down-at-the-heels city. But after chatting with Alex Clark for five minutes and learning about the difficulties at Deltron, "paradise" suddenly began to feel a bit less appealing.

Alex had agreed to meet with me after Deltron's director of organizational excellence, Eric Wanley, suggested that the two of us had "congruent values," and not only in business; we appeared to share many similar interests. (It turns out that Alex is the only other business executive I know with a passion for playing African musical instruments!) Eric had heard me speak on organizational conflict resolution at a conference in Geneva the month before, and he phoned me almost as soon as I returned to Boston. We struck up an instant friendship, one that turned out to be rewarding from many perspectives.

Following Eric's recommendation, Alex had called to say that he was too busy to come to New York. He was deeply committed to getting a first-hand glimpse of each plant and mill, and asked how I'd feel about journeying all the way to Venezuela. The gypsy blood in my veins responded with an enthusiastic "yes." I changed my plans for the weekend, and shortly afterward I was winging my way southward.

Alex and I instantly hit it off. He began by explaining that he "breathed smokestacks"—he was descended from a long line of manufacturing people. (His grandfather started as a factory worker in Scotland and rose to become a managing director.) He had taken the LAR post because he felt it was his duty to Deltron to save what many hoped could become one of its most promising manufacturing arms. "Besides," he said with smile, "what a challenge! It's easy to walk into a well-ordered company and take the reins. But this...it's like trying to build a skyscraper from toothpicks!"

I asked Alex what he thought the main problems were, while I mentally performed the 10-step process. Alex cited many problems. For one, the box plants and paper mills quarreled over quality. The plants blamed the mills for supplying poor-quality paper, and the mills in turn pointed a finger at the box plants for making unreasonable demands on them just because there was common ownership and, in some instances, geographic proximity.

Alex also described the intense friction between the home office and the operating companies. The LAR staff, box plant, and mill managers viewed the home office executives as "overlords" who ostensibly came to point out everything that was wrong about the operations, spouting ideas that had no merit and only made more unnecessary work. It was felt that they really came to enjoy the weather and be entertained by "the locals"—on expense accounts, of course. Most insulting, there wasn't a single person in the home office who spoke Spanish (the language of most of the operations) or who was taking a "total immersion" course to learn the language conversationally.

When forced to work together at semiannual meetings, the LAR people would intentionally speak amongst themselves in their native tongues (Spanish or French) rather than in English, just to irritate their North American "colleagues."

Executives at New York headquarters in turn regarded such behavior as further evidence that the LAR people were lazy and suffering from incurable "island fever." "They just don't think like *we* do" was a typical MBA complaint from New York headquarters staff to Alex during private conversations.

While Alex already knew that he was dealing with a culture clash, he also suspected that Deltron's centralized management organization was the real culprit. In fact, Deltron was indeed experiencing a classic operational conflict. New York was trying to run the Latin American regional operations as they did their North American ones. Having central operations manage people 2000 miles away in Caracas through the local LAR president simply undercut the authority of the local LAR managers; it made them feel that their decisions were really moot. After all, central control was not needed to produce and sell a fresh produce box in one country and an industrial package in another. What *was* needed was concentrated cost reduction and an engineering approach at the individual plants and mills.

I listened quietly, taking mental notes and conducting Steps 1 through 4 of the method in my head. (Again, with operational conflicts the cause is often apparent. The important thing is to focus both on the values (Step 5) to determine whether a double or triple win is genuinely desired (Step 6) and on the criteria developed in Step 7.

After pausing for a moment to collect my thoughts, I said, "Alex, my experience in Latin America coupled with the information you've provided cause me to feel that you're right about New York's centralized structure strangling the plants with edicts, financial controls, procedures, and so on. But while you may have eight separate companies here, they do face many of the same kinds of issues. They all have union problems (even though the two Communist unions present different problems from the others); they all have raw material and production control problems; they all have manufacturing, shipping, and distribution problems; and they all have problems repatriating money back to the United States. Most importantly, they all have *customer* problems. So why not treat the region as a team in which members deal with the unique differences of their individual situations while, at the same time, they're tackling their common problems together?"

Alex's face lit up, "I think I like that line of thinking, John. Please develop it further."

I explained what an opportunity he had to tap into the *collective* experience, know-how, and judgment of the box plant and paper mill managers, sales force, and other regional staff, focusing them on the toughest issues facing the region and each individual company. ExecuTrak would use our standard techniques, conducting interviews in Spanish and French when necessary, then show Alex the feedback in a private session. Next, we would conduct a joint-feedback session for all the senior managers throughout the region. No one from New York would participate other than Eric Wanley and the director of strategic planning, since both would, we hoped, be viewed as neutral parties.

Next, ExecuTrak would help Alex develop a common vision and set of goals, given the issues facing the entire organization. We would also develop a list of critical success factors and use these to help crystalize the best collaborative thinking of the team focused on each priority issue. The conference would end with decisions and workable, date-specific plans that Alex could present to New York. These would demonstrate specifically how both the region as a whole and the individual operations would shore up their weaknesses and improve production, quality, and customer service. By accomplishing these goals, LAR people should give Deltron cause to give the regional employees greater autonomy and the respect they deserved.

"How soon can you start?" Alex asked.

Island Hopping

I flew back to Boston to work with my staff. There we prepared an interview process and designed a business values survey tailored to the needs of both the region and New York headquarters. We also brushed up on our Spanish with the help of a tutor who spent some time in our office, and we reviewed some conversational French to show sensitivity to the managers from the two French islands. I thought it was critical for us to show that we respected their native tongue and culture. (Again, the successful catalyst-mediator will always show signs of respect for the various factions involved in the conflict; nothing builds trust like a sincere interest in a party's language, way of life, values, etc.)

A week later, I flew down to the region with two of my staff, and we began the survey and interview process. When possible, we spoke in the local language, although much of the time people understood and talked with us in English.

Alex had phoned, visited in some instances, and sent a memo to each of the top plant and mill managers announcing what we were doing. As he expected, the common response was a groan and a comment such as, "We've been through seven presidents and so many promises to 'make things better'; how is this gringo going to help?" Alex assured them that our approach was unique and that they would truly get a chance to speak their minds and work together to develop a common solution to their problems. (It is essential that the protagonists of a conflict buy in to the solution.) Moreover, he said, "Arnold recognizes that we have a tremendous amount of collective wisdom, insights, and experience. He's going to help us draw from that pool so that we can 'farm better.' He's not offering any quick fixes; rather he will help us tap into our built-in strengths and use our equipment better."

That statement helped, but according to Alex, what really piqued the top managers' curiosity was the fact that ExecuTrak would try as much as possible to work with them in Spanish and, to some extent, in French. This alone demonstrated the kind of simple respect that no one from the states had yet shown them.

Over a 10-day period, we "hopped" from island to island, then to several Latin American countries, interviewing key managers and customers. We then returned to Boston where we spent several weeks analyzing the data and preparing our feedback report. According to both Eric and Alex, New York was "dying" to get a copy of it. (Alex, of course, had to get permission from New York to retain our firm for the project, and therefore New York felt it was entitled to see the results.) In fact, the international chief financial officer phoned me and demanded a copy: "Arnold, unless you're some kind of miracle man, those operations can't be turned around fast enough or sufficiently to stop the hemorrhaging. We'll probably divest the whole shooting match first; in fact, we're in the process of seeking buyers now. That's strictly confidential, of course. Your report will save us time and help us know just how bad things are so we can determine whether we should modify our negotiating strategy."

I firmly held my ground: since LAR was the client, I would only divulge the feedback to Alex. Any breach of confidence would instantly erode trust and make it impossible for us to help his people achieve a consensus. If Alex wanted to share the data, it was his business. Between Alex and Eric, they had enough clout to strike a deal with New York: "Let Arnold complete his process, and let's see what happens. If the situation in the region improves, there's no need for New York to see the report. If nothing changes, we'll send a copy; perhaps it will give you some insights into what needs to be changed. But let us try, first. Besides, if LAR managers believe that they're speaking in strict confidence, they'll be much more forthcoming, and we'll have a better chance at developing a working solution. If they believe that New York is reading the report and will take unilateral action, they'll feel 'what's the use?' and will clam up." Eric's colleagues grudgingly agreed to give Alex the latitude he needed.

I flew back to Caracas and conducted a private feedback session with Alex. The topics brought up in the feedback reports included:

- There was low morale; cooperation was lacking; confidence was poor (LAR managers felt they were the "ugly ducklings" of the corporation). Also, many felt that the fate of their communities was in their hands. Alex was the last hope, and if LAR could not turn itself around, they believed Deltron would probably sell those plants and mills for which it could find buyers and close the rest. Plant closings could mean economic hardship for more than a thousand people who were earning a better living than most of their neighbors, some of whom were living at a marginal level. The livelihood and status of LAR employees in these communities was, they felt, clearly at risk.

- Deltron was smothering LAR in red tape and "absurd" reporting requirements. Of the 42 quarterly financial and control reports that Deltron demanded, few seemed relevant to actually running a box plant or paper mill. "We need a full-time staff just to compile all these reports," complained many managers. "Why do the Americans need these things? And the more New York tries to 'help,' the more they tie us up in paperwork."

- Continual fuel oil shortages often caused plant shutdowns. Sometimes the cost of fuel was so high that the plants could only operate in the red. In a sense, the LAR plants were at the mercy of Shell, Texaco, and the other major oil companies, which insisted on dealing with each individual plant or mill, pricing its commodity accordingly.

- Equipment was outdated. Because LAR had never met annual financial objectives, Deltron had refused to invest in significant modernization. Rather, it demanded that the LAR plants find ways to cut costs and "trim fat" as a means of boosting profits.

- Inventory was excessive and potentially obsolete. Because of the fuel oil shortages and problems with some of the unions, the LAR plants tended to overproduce to ensure that they would always have sufficient inventory. But this just tended to worsen a bad cashflow situation. (This situation in turn came about from a long backlist of accounts receivables and a customer list that changed every day as new accounts cropped up and old accounts went bankrupt.)

Alex sighed when he saw the report. But he also shrugged his shoulders, saying, "This is pretty much what I expected. John, it's painful to see it in black and white but necessary to know the actual scope of these problems in order to deal intelligently with them. And I think your idea for an extended joint-feedback session and retreat might give everyone the 'shot of adrenalin' we need to pull the region together."

View from the Heights

To call the proposed retreat "extended" was an understatement. Normally, a joint-feedback session runs one day—two, if the problems are particularly thorny or complex. Work conferences run anywhere from two to four-and-a-half days. In this instance, because of the cultural differences, language barriers, sheer number of issues to be resolved, and team-building and conflict resolution process development required, I convinced Alex to schedule a *seven-day* session at a resort high in the mountains. Perhaps the beautiful vista would stimulate everyone to rise above the problems of his mill's, plant's, or staff role's unique problems. (The thin air might cool tempers, too, I joked to Alex.)

We did everything possible to make this session different from anything that New York had "foisted" upon the LAR managers before. There would be no lording or lecturing, no sales pitches. The conference would be held in an intensive, though recreational, atmosphere, with day and evening sessions designed to resolve the most significant of the complex issues facing the region.

Managers were brought in from the operating plants, the regional sales organization, and the Caracas home office. There was considerable apprehension because some of the conference groups included direct antagonists. All of the groups also contained skeptics who felt that the exercise would be a waste of time. Eric and the New York–based director of strategic planning were MBAs, while the box plant and paper-mill managers had, at best, high school or equivalent diplomas. The mother tongue of 4 of the managers was French, and of 13, Spanish.

After the 22 LAR managers assembled in the conference room and exchanged greetings, we conducted an "unfreezing" simulation (similar to the ones described in other chapters of this book). We then handed out the feedback report, written in simple English, but with Spanish (and occasional French) phrases sprinkled throughout, and with an apology that I wasn't fluent enough to do the entire report in both languages. This was met with warm smiles and nods that showed everyone's appreciation.

All of that day was spent reviewing the report with the group who identified the issues. (Even if only 1 of the 22 managers felt something was an issue, it went up on the charts and eventually into the word processor.) Even though there were so many issues, the way we conducted the feedback session created a climate of hope and even levity, instead of feelings of inadequacy and depression at the myriad of problems.

By the end of that long first day, Friday, the group had identified the priority issues and opportunities. For the next six days, the managers addressed each one. In some cases, managers described problems which were distinctive to their plant or mill yet which had certain features in common with other plants, mills, or sales offices. The 10-step process served, together with a second team-building exercise, as an integrative mechanism providing both the "glue" and a focus, enabling peers to offer sensible solutions.

Among the most important issues addressed and resolved were the following:

1. *The oil crisis.*   Previously, each of the mills and plants from the islands and elsewhere had been subject to the pricing strategy of the major oil companies. In reconstructing the crime, we discovered that the identity and time dimensions were the same for almost all locations: prices dictated by the oil companies had for many years been exactly the same distance apart from one company to another. Each year oil bids were up by anywhere from 50 to 100 percent, yet no one had been able to prove collusion.

After agreeing on their values and that they wanted a "win" all around (Steps 5 and 6), the team of 22 managers developed a list of achieves, preserves, and avoids (Step 7). This then led to a clever solution: banding together and soliciting other companies on the islands and in the same general area on the South American continent where the other plants and mills were located to form a buying cartel. With their combined buying clout, they could probably drive a deal that would make New York drool with envy. Not only would the deal force prices to be very low, and competitive, but it could be structured in a way that would ensure a constant supply.

2. *The unions.* Unions in the LAR often called strikes (especially the two communist unions), which fouled production and caused people in New York to wince and local customers to push for a quick settlement (usually in the union's favor). The LAR managers decided that they would stage negotiations at different times and ship between countries when necessary. This wasn't particularly profitable, but it gave the LAR companies a stronger negotiating position (and it built stronger ties between the sister companies).

3. *Poor cashflow.* This topic was near and dear to everyone's heart. We asked frank questions,* such as,

> *What was the main cause of the poor cashflow? The largest box plant customer, it turned out, had very generous 120-day terms. Why? Would he take his business elsewhere if the terms were brought in line with more conventional arrangements?*
> Yes, everyone agreed.

> *What about pricing—could prices be raised without losing business?*
> Not with an aggressive competitor ready to move in.

> *Could a plan be devised to shorten the terms and raise the price at the same time?*
> A foolish question!

> *But then why does that one customer need such extended terms?*
> Because he's underfinanced and must carry a large inventory to satisfy his customers.

> *If he received faster delivery, could he reduce his inventory? What do your manufacturing and shipping people think? If this customer were not in such a short cash position, would he or she still need the extended terms?*
> Of course, but...

> *Do our finance people have any idea how he could obtain bank financing?*

The result of the questioning was a plan that included contributions from sales, advertising, finance, design, manufacturing, and shipping. The plan did call for a price increase and shortening of terms. It was later presented to the customer by the plant manager and sales representative shortly after the conference. In fact, the plan benefited the

---

*This dialogue, and the issues described in it, appeared in *Turnaround: An Anonymous Case History* by John D. Arnold, Paper Industry Management, 1975.

customer as well—he would be able to obtain bank financing, receive cash discounts, have a guaranteed supply, and reduce inventory. In addition, he would receive weekly delivery on key items.

When the customer saw that his monthly payments would be no more than they were now, he realized that the company had considered his best interests—and he accepted the terms!

The customer received about $690,000 from his bank immediately, without having to grant any discount. Labor and material costs were then passed along as they occurred. Because of its improved cash position, LAR was also able to sell the same customer additional items that he wanted but which it heretofore couldn't supply.

4. *A rumored plant closing.* Rumors that one of the paper mills was going to be sold had had a depressing effect on morale. When they surfaced at the conference, everything came to a halt. The silence demanded affirmation or denial. In a hurriedly called recess, Alex worked out with me exactly what it was he would have to demonstrate to relieve the concerns. The major points were:

- He would be completely honest and open regarding any possible sale of the mill.
- He would respect what had already been done in the way of cost reduction.
- Key economic and supply problems at the mill were out of control of the personnel involved.
- He would be open to suggestions for making the mill economically viable.
- If the mill were sold in the future, the employees would be treated not only fairly, but generously.
- Employees did not have to rely on rumors but would be kept informed on a regular basis.

These and other points were openly discussed. It was as though someone had said to the mill personnel for the first time, "Look, we are being honest with each other. Our problem is not going to be solved fighting each other, but rather by searching for a solution together. However, we must continue to respect that our responsibility to the stockholders is the overriding consideration." (When the mill was finally sold, Alex believed that every manager and employee felt she or he had been treated fairly and honestly.)

5. *Relations with New York.* If the LAR companies could gain the respect of headquarters, New York might be willing to inject much-

needed cash for modernization, and they might also begin treating LAR people with respect.

Because LAR's performance was so poor, New York had decided not to infuse any more capital until there was evidence of a turnaround. This, of course, simply created a "Catch-22" situation: without cash, there couldn't be a turnaround.

The LAR managers openly discussed the dilemma, and they developed a plan demonstrating that money was not recklessly requested. They would inform New York that the building of a warehouse would be delayed because they'd found adequate rental space.

A key part of the plan was for the mills and plants to make a long-promised $500,000 payment to Deltron, despite a crippling bank strike. In other years, such a strike would have been considered justification for default. This year, the company on an island with the strike worked out an arrangement with a sister company on another island without the strike to borrow money and send it on to the home office. Transfer of the funds would be made on the last working day of the month in which payment had been promised.

By repaying the note, they would demonstrate to New York that they weren't simply lazy leeches but took their responsibilities seriously. The LAR companies would also vigorously pursue a $40 million contract from a European prospect that sales had previously felt it had no opportunity to win.

At the end of the conference, Alex beamed and said, "I never could have imagined these guys working together like this. The feedback session and opportunity to develop a common plan gave them the inspiration and hope they needed to begin working together as a team. If we can make the plan happen, and I believe we will, I think New York will sing a very different tune about LAR."

I agreed, but I placed the credit back with Alex. After all, as the client, he would need the support and encouragement to apply the process to other challenges that would undoubtedly occur in the future. I then prepared to fly back to Boston with my team. This turned out to be the hardest part of the assignment. The day we left Caracas it was 85 degrees. And what was the forecast for Boston? The temperature would be 5 degrees below zero—with a wind chill to minus 25!

The Fruits of Our Labor

To make sure that the conference would *not* be a one-shot pop, we held a follow-up session to evaluate the results and reinforce the application of the methods. The happy ending was that just six months later, LAR was able to meet the profit plan. At the end of the year, return on investment had gone as high as 16 percent. The year-end dividend was equal to the initial capital investment in the entire area.

With all this good news, New York did indeed begin singing a new tune about its Latin American *associates*. Receipt of the $500,000 payment truly shocked Deltron's president of international operations who at first thought it was a joke. But no one talked about jokes when LAR reported that it had brought the major oil companies to their knees; it had negotiated a deal for fuel oil that was better than any deal ever cut by Deltron for *North America*! New York even asked if it could send a team down to learn how LAR had accomplished this feat.

But clinching the $40 million contract was what truly changed Deltron's opinion of its Latin American region. It gave LAR more autonomy and even agreed to accept 8 reports per quarter—2 more than LAR managers demonstrated they felt necessary, but a vast improvement over the 42 that had been required previously.

The effect of its various successes was like a shot of adrenalin for LAR; one achievement begat another. Objectives that had formerly been seen as impossible suddenly became attainable. For example, LAR had previously regarded bidding on linerboard requirements of a large shipping company as a waste of time; everyone assumed that competition had the account locked up. Now, using Steps 7 through 10 in particular, it prepared an aggressive proposal, and the sales team took it out and returned with a lucrative $90 million contract.

With its increased revenues, LAR was able to purchase a new shipping system that enabled the mills and plants to reduce material inventory from a 10 months' supply to 2. Indirect overhead dropped to levels below that of five years ago, even though volume had almost doubled. Finally, measures were taken to eliminate bad debt and steer clear of questionable accounts.

Why did this turnaround succeed? In Alex Clark's words, "by developing a common language and common vision of the critical success factors, we were able to get the LAR managers to focus on and think through goals, objectives, and problems at hand, rather than focusing on each other and their animosity toward New York. In the process, we developed trust and managing tools that allowed decisions to be made at the lowest possible level."

Case Notes

1. As this case demonstrates, people involved in an organizational conflict often can't "see the forest for the trees." That's because they

tend to look at a situation from the standpoint of how it affects *them* personally rather than from the logic of a larger "system." It became apparent that in this case the centralized structure was the culprit. Both Alex and I were aware of this fact, although as Alex spent more time getting immersed in the company, he would soon become an insider and lose a bit of perspective himself. Because of this increasing lack of proper perspective, it's imperative that whoever is trying to resolve the conflict do everything possible to maintain objectivity. Reconstructing the crime (Steps 1–4) helps you to zero in on the significant data, incorporating typically both the micro and the macro considerations.

2. It's easy to forget that there are two (or more) sides to every conflict. In this case, the people in the LAR simply focused on their overbearing New York parent. The people in New York likewise simply focused on their wayward and deficient "children." Had the LAR people stopped to think that New York had good reason for pushing centralization—it worked in North America and other parts of the world—they might have approached the problem differently. Rather than seeing themselves as oppressed, they might have seen their task as one of finding better ways to *educate* headquarters about why the LAR was different from other situations. Similarly, with so many successful plants in different parts of the world, New York might have looked for causes other than "laziness" or "stupidity" to explain the poorly performing LAR plants and mills.

As a conflict resolver, it's very important to "pull back the curtains" and reveal the big picture for everyone. Only when people understand each other's frame of reference and values (Step 5) can logjams be broken and effective solutions found.

3. People in conflict generally fall into one of two categories. Either they assume that the situation is hopeless and that the best they can do is live with a (sometimes) unlivable situation, or they want immediate gratification and they're ready to fight for it tooth and nail. In this case, the LAR people were frustrated and, until the retreat, accepted the status quo and stopped being innovative in their problem solving. The New York people with the power, on the other hand, were readying themselves for immediate relief by jettisoning the LAR plants and mills. As in this situation, the catalyst-mediator should determine whether a double-win approach (Step 6) is desirable. If so, he or she should immediately move with the protagonists into Step 7, which entails developing a list of APA criteria as a set of specifications to be met by solutions to the problems.

4. In an organizational conflict, the catalyst-mediator is responsible for opening multichannel communication. In addition to making sure that the

parties involved understand each other, the catalyst-mediator must ensure that the messages are being received; people have to really *hear* what is being discussed. A helpful technique, which we used in the LAR work conference, is to sometimes ask people to repeat in their own words what they think people have just said. (*Note*: This technique has to be done carefully so as not to insult the participants' intelligence. Phrase the request as "testing whether the communication was received as intended.")

5. One of the most challenging tasks facing the catalyst-mediator is dealing with a situation in which there is a great economic or educational disparity among the parties. In such instances, the catalyst-mediator needs to make sure that the party with the higher economic or educational status does not convey, verbally or nonverbally, any disdain for the other party. The people in the LAR clearly felt treated like second-class citizens, and the executives in New York took no pains to make them feel otherwise. Had our feedback session involved New York and LAR people, I would have held a special session with the New York staff to make them aware of how destructive their attitudes and communication style had been and could be.

A key point that people forget is that *how* they communicate is just as important as *what* they communicate. New York's style communicated a simple message to LAR managers: you're lazy and stupid, and you don't care. And as we saw in the actual situation, nothing could be farther from the truth. The LAR people had a wealth of experience and ideas that could benefit the company. And they did care. Their status in the community as better-paid workers and the fact that the community depended on the success of the plant or mill made "caring" a high priority.

6. If you apply the 10-step method, you can sort out even the most convoluted and complex situation. Here, we had a three-ring circus involving MBAs, people with no more than a high school education, operational problems, a mix of languages, and so on. Yet the method enabled us to sort out the main issues and develop double-win solutions. Actually the solutions were triple-win ones—New York, LAR, and each of the individual island and other communities all emerged as victors!

Postscript

I'm sure there are still some "island fever" jokes cracked now and then in New York, but they are probably more in reference to how the Deltron executives feel when visiting the plants during the dead of winter than about the performance of LAR employees.

8

Warring Fiefs: Managing Interdepartmental Conflicts

Case Study

ExecuTrak File 1143:
"As the Milk Sours"

At one time, Eastwood Dairy Company was a happy "family." Headquartered in Atlanta, and with farms throughout the midwest, the company enjoyed a steady rise in profits since the mid-fifties. It was becoming clear, however, that national and multinational companies were taking over the industry from local and family-run firms. Advances in technology and regulatory changes in the trucking industry permitted national companies to become key players in many markets.

After purchasing two smaller firms, which enabled Eastwood to extend its line into cheeses, frozen yogurt, and various gourmet fares, the company was acquired by food-produce giant A. B. Franklin, Inc. Franklin forced the resignation of Eastwood's CEO and founder; while searching for a new CEO, the acquiring company sought a new vice president of sales, John Benton. Benton agreed to the job, with the priority task of moving the sales force within the following 6 to 12 months to Sacramento, Franklin's national headquarters.

By the time that the new CEO, David Burke, joined the group, the sales representatives, who were southerners with no connection to California and couldn't see any benefit to the move, were threatening to resign en masse rather than move. Among many reasons for their intransigence were the facts that, if anything, "being at the seat of the bureaucracy will drain us"; "a number of major accounts are east of the Mississippi"; and "the three-hour time difference to California will hurt our responsiveness to customers and brokers."

Eastwood's top management would later regret caving in to the sales group, because it simply made the salespeople feel invincible. The sales force, which many others in the rest of the company had always considered prima donnas, was led by Walter Krueger, a dynamic "supersalesperson" who didn't let anyone push him around. Not only did Krueger's people flout a new centralized system that Burke installed shortly after joining Eastwood, but they constantly demanded that Eastwood's production operation continue to dance to their tune and juggle priorities to meet (unrealistically) promised ship dates.

They also sent customer service up the wall by offering special deals to certain major accounts, or to new accounts to win business from competitors, without getting approval from headquarters. Sometimes they didn't even notify anyone of the changes, making accurate billing difficult and customers and brokers upset. And they rebuked the new marketing VP's attempts to turn Eastwood from a sales-driven to a marketing-driven company.

On the one hand, over the years, the sales division had a spectacular track record, one that would make any competitor green with envy. But the mutually destructive warfare between sales and the other functions and departments was demoralizing the company. It had already led to several resignations of key corporate and plant people who simply couldn't stand the hostile atmosphere. How could Eastwood's new CEO, David Burke, keep its cream-of-the-crop salespeople without spoiling the rest of the company?

Overview of Interdepartmental Conflicts

The sixth class of conflict, interdepartmental, is probably the most common of all conflict types. It involves strife between divisions or functions that should be working together rather than fighting each other for resources, turf, autonomy, compensation, prestige, power, recognition, and so on. Interdepartmental battles are common in virtually every organization. Take, for example, the friction that frequently occurs between the marketing and sales arms of a company. At one large meat-processing producer, we heard the following complaint from the sales force: "They [marketing] design programs at the national level as opposed to designing them at the regional level. This approach hinders us. You often can't translate programs from one region to the next."

Another conflict that often takes place occurs on the production side of a company. Sales and even marketing often want product faster than manufacturing can deliver it, while manufacturing feels that the sales department makes impossible promises just to get the business and pump up commissions.

Other typical conflicts include customer service versus sales and accounting, merchandising versus store operations, research versus engineering, production and sales versus inventory control (logistics), hospital administrators versus medical departments, and institute researchers versus finance and administration.

We witnessed a striking example at a hosiery manufacturer. There, sales clung to the philosophy of relationship selling: if you develop a close relationship with a buyer, he'll take more product and give it more prominent display than he gives to other products. Marketing felt the company should forget about the buyer and create *consumer* demand instead: the buyer will have to buy it, or consumers will go to another store.

So there was a real "push–pull" conflict here. Marketing was not daunted by demands and wishes from sales, and it proceeded to develop various merchandising programs to accomplish its goals. Unfortunately, the sales reps simply refused to get behind the products in question. They felt they knew the market better than marketing. Neither side was willing to listen to the other. The company, of course, was the big loser.

Through our interviews and feedback sessions, we were able to get to the root causes of the polarized positions (Steps 1–4) and make people aware of the self-inflicted wounds everyone was causing. By the time we had gotten involved, so much damage had been done that all we could do for the marketing director was to interview him after his resignation. Fortunately for the client, our feedback and work conferences helped develop a common vision among the warring departments and players, and a sense of how best to focus the sales force on a "consumer pull" rather than a "company push" strategy.

While sales and marketing are often not on the same wavelength, and sometimes at each other's throats, finance often finds itself at the hub of a fray as the "bean counters" who are viewed as only thinking in terms of "pinching pennies." We saw a particularly interesting example of an interdepartmental conflict involving the finance division of an industrial-equipment manufacturer. (Actually, the situation involved yet another underlying problem type, management process.)

In this case, we were hired to help a new CEO, Bill Retke, settle into his job. In reviewing the situation, it was clear that the new chief was particularly impressed with the company's CFO, Brian Dodge. But when we conducted interviews to obtain general feedback from middle and top managers (always essential for shrinking a new CEO's learning curve), we were surprised to learn about a great deal of hostility toward finance in general and Dodge in particular. We heard comments such as, "This is like working in a police state." and, "We feel that we can't do our jobs. The 'Dodge boys' are involved in making decisions that are none of their business. They're compromising our ability to develop and market products. They're hurting our ability to compete."

Retke confronted Dodge, who vehemently denied that his department was obstructing any other department. I suggested that we interview some of Dodge's own people. Dodge became furious and refused. "Arnold's feedback stuff is just a bunch of @#$%!!" Retke persisted, demanding that finance go through the interviewing and feedback process. As I suspected, Dodge's people felt tremendous pressure from him to act like watchdogs—actually, more like attack dogs guarding the corporate coffers.

When I first met with Dodge, providing him with our findings, he responded with even more anger, demanding to know who in his department was spreading such "libelous ideas." I suggested that "perception is the reality with which you must deal," and that "where there's so much smoke, there's got to be a fire." Dodge refused to accept the validity of what we'd been told by so many of his own finance group. Yet I believe that he secretly recognized the reality of the situation. He chose to resign rather than try to change his attitude and management style. Interestingly, when a new CFO, hired from the outside, took his job, his own "due diligence" validated what we had already reported. We helped him change the climate and a number of inimical policies and procedures in the department, and we helped his finance managers, eager to make amends with others in the company, to strengthen their working relationships with the other departments. Within a month of the common-vision conference, new procedures were in place, and finance quickly came to be regarded as a partner, not a "wicked stepmother."

Nonprofit organizations are particularly prone to interdepartmental conflicts because people are less often rewarded (if at all) with recognition and prestige. As a result, turf battles are likely to spring up. Nowhere is this more evident then in health-care and research organizations. Physicians and scientists often feel that their hands are tied by administrative and financial rules and red tape. Many often believe that since they're involved in the lofty intellectual pursuits or noble purposes that serve humankind, they should not be constrained by irritating directives and procedures from administrators who have no technical knowledge and who don't appreciate patient care.

Consider the case of Mentor Hospital, which experienced a near-fatal interdepartmental conflict. Physicians and administrative staff clashed on a daily basis. At the mundane level, the heads of surgery and neurology, for example, complained about the bureaucratic procedures that robbed them of important patient time, about purchasing's running late and holding up desperately needed supplies and equipment. The physicians also complained that they didn't have a sufficient role in decisions affecting their departments. At the macro level, another controversy involved the mission and direction of the hospital; physicians and administrators argued about whether the hospital's focus should be on teaching or on patient care.

The fiercest battles, however, concerned whether or not physicians practicing in the hospital should own their laboratories or, in the case of radiologists, their own diagnostic imaging centers. One administrative study showed that prior to a radiologist's purchasing his own imaging center, about four patients per day were referred to an outside CAT Scan center. With the opening of the radiologist's center, the number jumped to 15! Administrative staff accused the radiologist of funding his new center with marginally necessary scans. The medical staff responded with outrage at the accusations.

Fortunately, we were called in before the best talent from the medical or administrative sides left for more peaceful pastures. We started off interviewing heads of medical departments and key administrators as well as the board of directors of the hospital. A joint-feedback session allowed everyone to see the "whole elephant." They agreed on a mission for the hospital as well as a joint-decision-making process that would allow all factions to resolve the "crunch" and shared accountability issues in a mutually satisfactory way. Things aren't perfect at Mentor, but physicians and administrators alike have commented that the sparks are no longer flying. The main emphasis is back where it should be—on making sick patients well again.

Finally, interdepartmental conflicts often give way to an interesting subspecies, *intra*departmental conflicts. In these cases, factions develop within specific departments and divisions, each vying for resources, credit, and so on. When this happens, the players fail to realize that the department suffers as a whole because it can't play an effective role in the company. Everyone loses.

At one manufacturer that retained us, teamwork within the engineering division had vanished, which led to invalid schedules and late deliveries. A counterculture developed, in which an informal engineering information system evolved. If you weren't part of the "in" group, you simply didn't get access to information necessary to develop the product. For this and other reasons, time to market for new products was a significant weakness. Engineering designs typically came late, so the pressure was on manufacturing to make up the lost time. Consequently, many problems arose and some customer shipments were up to two years late!

Talk about sibling against sibling! (We did help them arrive at a common vision that eventually broke down the we-they barriers and put the company on a healthy track again.)

Effects of Interdepartmental Conflicts

This type of conflict can take place at a high or line level. Division managers, directors, and vice presidents may fight for who has final say over a particular procedure (which can easily transform into or be derived from a responsibility/authority/accountability conflict; see Chapter 5). They may also fight over resources if it appears that top management is showing a bias toward or against a particular department. The conflict may also be felt at the grass-roots level, when managers and workers feel that their counterparts "down the hall" or over the partitions are getting more resources, credit for joint projects, higher compensation, and so on.

While interdepartmental conflicts are often started over small issues, they can be terribly destructive. As people begin to view their fellow departments, functions, and employees as the competition, the company is less able to focus on the real competitors. The conflict may go as far as unintentional acts of sabotage (sales refusing to show a particular product line, engineering taking additional time to make a necessary change or failing to notify manufacturing of it, etc.). Ultimately, the organization will operate as a collection of independent "rogue elephant" departments.

Guidelines for Resolving Interdepartmental Conflicts

1. With interdepartmental conflicts, people tend to forget who the enemy really is. They see the competition as the people down the hall or across the site rather than across town under a different company's roof.

When this happens, the company as a whole will suffer. So it's critical for the conflict resolver to focus on helping the warring factions to achieve a common vision. Unfortunately, accomplishing this is often difficult because layers of divisive fingerpointing and acrimony obscure the facts. Also complicating matters are the facts that everybody has been labeled as "good" or "bad" and the real roots of the problem have long been buried. Therefore, pay special attention to reconstructing the "crime" (Steps 1–4). And when you're doing so, make sure that people have the opportunity to "vent." While the real culprit may be a reward system that encourages individual over team actions and departmental over companywide actions, or a management style that rewards people for deflecting problems to others, people need to express their emotions before they'll believe that the cause of the strife is *not* their colleagues (read "adversaries") in another department.

2. Interdepartmental conflicts are similar to operational conflicts in that people feel that the cause of their particular problem is outside their department. But from an emotional standpoint, this type of conflict is very different. With an operational conflict, people feel that they're fighting a "system" that doesn't understand their needs or that makes their work hard (or impossible) to do. With an interdepartmental conflict, people ascribe motive or intent, usually to another department or function whom they perceive to be actively plotting against them. Again, the solution is to agree on a common vision so one department can work beyond the perceived competition with another.

Let's say that sales and manufacturing are at odds. The sales force complains that manufacturing is sabotaging their efforts to clinch deals and offer speedy service. "They can't produce the right product of the right quality in the right amount at the right time," is a common lament. The manufacturing wing, on the other hand, might complain that "salespeople give away the store. They'll tell any customer anything she wants simply to get a commission, whether it means changing the specifications without checking with us to see if it's feasible, committing to an unrealistic schedule, or whatever."

In fact, the conflict resolver must get everyone to agree to a triple-win solution (Step 6) spread among the two departments and the customers. The goal changes from "How can I get those fools down the hall to see the light?" to "How can we satisfy the most customers given our current resources and operations, and what can we do to strengthen our operations in the future to become even more capable of meeting customers' needs?"

3. People involved in interdepartmental conflicts tend to jealously guard turf. The catalyst-mediator, or whoever is committed to resolving the conflict, must realize that people are holding onto some-

thing that they feel they've fought hard to get—which represents power and authority. By getting them to "play ball" with other people, functions, and departments, you're in effect asking them to risk surrendering that power and authority. Since human beings don't readily do this, you have to make sure that they feel that by making a deal they'll get something better than if they didn't. In other words, they must perceive some value, some "win" for themselves (Steps 5 and 6), or they'll quit, "lean back on the oars," or resort to "sabotage" of some sort. So it's critical to make sure that people aren't just accepting the situation but are perceiving that they'll "win." You cannot afford to assume this for them (that is, that they indeed will automatically feel this way).

4. When you deal with a company with geographically remote operations, you're bound to experience a variety of interdepartmental strife when there are "fuzzy," conflicting objectives or overlapping objectives. In such cases, you'll likely find a responsibility/authority/accountability problem underlying the interdepartmental conflict. Again here, reconstruct the "crime" (Steps 1–4) and flesh out the achieves, preserves, and avoids (Step 7) that are especially critical to the resolution effort.

5. In some cases of major warfare, smaller departments—for example, customer service, production control, or logistics—get caught in between the crossfire and become "civilian casualties." What is the best solution to this dilemma? Get information from each of them (Steps 1–4). Then get them together and share all the information with them at once so they realize that each has seen only "part of the elephant" and now they can see the whole "beast."

Interdepartmental conflicts are, in a sense, like autoimmune diseases in which the body turns its defense mechanisms against itself: normal functions weaken, and the body may fail, or even die. Similarly, a company with an interdepartmental conflict fights itself, and its ability to compete declines. If the company becomes too weak to compete, it too may die. Fortunately, you can resolve interdepartmental conflicts before they become fatal by applying the 10-step Arnold Conflict Resolution Process within the context of the above guidelines. Let's see how we did that at Eastwood Dairy Group and prevented a "disease" that might have proved fatal.

Yogurt on the Walls

As described above, Eastwood Dairy was having its difficulties. Not only were competitors encroaching on its turf, but the market was changing. To stay competitive, Eastwood would have to develop new product lines such as frozen yogurt (projected to be the "hot" dessert item of the 1990s). With the internal strife, it would be difficult to maintain current accounts let alone branch into new areas.

To add fuel to the fire, many Eastwood veterans were deeply upset about the firing of Eastwood's founder, Charles Kent, after the acquisition by A. B. Franklin. Kent was an "old-school" type who had been wise enough to buy two small yogurt firms, but he didn't have the vision Franklin believed was necessary for the company to remain competitive, let alone grow. And there was no clear successor in-house.

The executive search firm that had served A. B. Franklin determined that of four candidates, David Burke would be the best person for the job. Their decision was based on his reputation for rationalizing operations, achieving high productivity, and easily grasping marketing.

Still, three months after Franklin hired David Burke as CEO of Eastwood, Eleanor Lane, a forward-looking member of Franklin's board of directors, suggested that Burke contact me regarding all the changes he was making. Certain members of the board were concerned that possibly Burke was overwhelming the operations with so much major change. For reasons discussed above, competitors were making significant inroads with some of Eastwood's key supermarkets and chains, sales were down, and profits had begun to sag. These facts were not enough to trigger alarm bells, but they were enough to warrant concern at Franklin and among the board. Several years earlier, Eleanor had observed me working with another of Franklin's acquisitions, which suffered from major external and management process conflicts. That company is today one of the star performers in the Franklin "family."

Burke took Lane's suggestion, and he invited me to meet with him. After I described what my firm does, he said, "Well, Arnold, I've already brought on board a strategic consultant, a manufacturing consultant, a sales consultant, and an MIS consultant installing a new computer. You'd be the *fifth*. Why should I hire you, too?"

I laughed and said, "Well you do certainly have a lot of consultants. But each one has a specialty—and no one is providing you with a satellite's eye view of the company and the people in it: what they're thinking and feeling, especially given all the massive changes you've been making. What you really need to do is to get them to pull together under the mantle of a common vision. And I'm not talking about shallow, 'rah-rah team building.' I'm talking about you creating an organization in which people feel a deep sense of commitment and excitement to a plan they can make happen!"

Burke liked what I had to say and agreed to hire my firm to interview key managers, vendors, supermarkets, and chains; provide him with a private feedback session followed by one for his management group;

then lead an intensive work session in which the key players would develop a shared vision for the company and agree on what needed to be done to solve the key issues. Whether or not there would be further "sounding board" work and conferences would depend on the outcome of the shared-vision session.

I thanked Burke for the opportunity to work with him. Then I flew back to Boston and spent time with my staff designing a business value survey and interview process. I also advised Burke how to position the project with his people and outsiders so it would not seem like "overkill." ("Good grief, not *another* damn consultant!!") Then, following Burke's project announcements (sent by telephone, voice mail, fax, and courier), ExecuTrak people departed for various parts of the country to interview the key internal and external players in what would turn out to be an exciting corporate drama.

Shades of the Wild West: Sacramento

Several of us headed for Franklin's (and now Eastwood's) Sacramento headquarters to interview a number of key executives. My first stop was Burke's office, where I had arranged to spend a good two hours discussing his views of Eastwood's problems.

An energetic man in his late forties, Burke came to Eastwood with considerable experience in consumer products and solid credentials from Stanford Business School. Within weeks of taking the position, Burke realized that the company needed "overhauling" in a number of areas, such as pricing. He then instituted a number of sweeping changes to "put things aright," such as "bracket pricing" that standardized Eastwood's pricing for all customers throughout the country. He also instituted radical cost-cutting measures and major changes in logistics, and he decided to close two production plants (to name just a few of his major actions). But the various measures didn't seem to be working as fast as he hoped, and in some cases, they weren't working at all.

Burke was also astonished at the resistance he was getting from Krueger and the sales force. A descendant of a well-to-do and patrician San Francisco family, Burke simply couldn't fathom the Southern mentality, nor was he that comfortable relating to people who didn't share advanced academic training. Most of the sales force had, at the most, undergraduate degrees.

Now, I always listen carefully, probe for my understanding, and take copious notes during interviews; in some cases I provide instant feedback. And in this situation, for Burke's sake, I couldn't wait until the private feedback session a good month or more down the road to share some of my thoughts with him. (As a conflict resolver, you too will have to decide on a case-by-case basis whether to offer immediate recommendations or wait for the formal feedback session. If the protagonist could immediately benefit from your advice, or if he or she could avoid making the situation worse, then by all means offer your thoughts on the spot.)

I did offer some thoughts: "You know, David, you're shaking up the lives of everybody in your whole organization. You're like a Greek god who's hurling thunderbolt after thunderbolt at the mortals below. And you're doing it with full confidence that you're doing the right things. You don't have as much experience in this industry as some of the veterans. You're relying on a group of outside consultants to tell you what to do. No wonder things aren't coming together as fast as you hoped! And no wonder you're at odds with people who have helped the company to grow during the past three decades."

I also commented to Burke that he had really spent too much time holed up in his office with consultants and not enough time in the field: "You're spending too much time talking about Eastwood's deficient infrastructure and lack of centralization, of 'benchmarking' and 'continuous quality improvement.' In fact, you've got a lot of core issues that have to be resolved. The best 'infrastructure' and 'centralized plan' doesn't mean a damn if you don't have people committed to making the company grow and prosper. You're not betting your grade in a B-school case exercise. You're betting the future of the company and your career. You can't win unless you pull everyone together."

Burke was surprised at my candor and then admitted, "Yeah, I guess I am throwing out a lot of change. But I just assumed that since I didn't hear any complaints, people were swallowing it. I'm a firm believer in the 'silence is approval' philosophy. I'll be curious to see just what your interviewing turns up!"

I shook his hand as I left and thought to myself, "Of all the 'parachuted-in' CEOs I've ever worked with, this guy is the most business-school-minded and consultant-addicted I've ever met. He hasn't gotten nearly enough out into the plants and field to discover what's happening in 'the real world.' At the advice of consultants, he has initiated one major change after another, and then he sat back waiting for information on what was happening to be filtered (by subordinates) back to him. In essence, he's playing a theoretical chess game while the real pieces are getting up and walking off the board." I then made my way across the headquarters complex to talk with the vice president of sales, Richard Benton.

Like Burke, Benton had an impressive pedigree. He also seemed incapable of understanding people who didn't have his educational background or credentials—people like most of his sales force back in Atlanta. Benton had been the sales manager for another food-processing company, but I began to suspect that the closest he'd ever been to a cow was the milk in his morning coffee.

Benton was clearly disturbed that he hadn't been able to establish a "close rapport" with Walter Krueger, and he knew that getting a nod of approval from Krueger was essential to gaining respect from the rest of the sales force. If anything, my interview revealed that he was intimidated by Krueger—and with good reasons. Krueger had nearly 25 years of experience in the industry, and he was treated as a living legend by the rest of the sales force.

"Yeah, Walter can talk a cat off a meatwagon," Benton admitted. "But the S.O.B. just won't play ball. He won't come here for meetings, and his reports are always late. He's just not a team player."

I read between the lines that Benton's plan was to wait until he gained the confidence of CEO Burke before doing anything about Krueger; clearly, making any kind of move to oust Krueger now would be a losing proposition. Once Benton made it clear to Burke, who would eventually "understand" the new "Eastwood ballgame," Benton would make his move against Krueger on the grounds of insubordination. He would try to paint Krueger as a loose cannon who would ultimately harm the company because he wouldn't play by the new rules.

I left Benton's office feeling sorry for him. I thought, "This guy will be shoveling cow manure long before Krueger even gets a slap on the wrist. It's a good thing we're here to resolve this conflict before the straw flies!" (*Note*: I have stressed throughout this book the importance of remaining objective, of not letting your own emotions cloud your work. Still, even conflict resolvers are human, and we will have definite opinions and reactions to people and situations. The key is to develop a level of self-awareness that enables you to know when you're injecting your own emotional response into the situation.)

After interviewing Benton, I took a lunch break, then headed across the courtyard to visit Larry Trent, vice president of marketing, to see what he had to say about Eastwood's problems.

Not surprisingly, Trent was out of the same mold as Burke and Benton. He had a lot of experience in the food industry and quite a bit in the dairy sector. While this gave him some credentials with the sales force, his slightly academic and standoffish manner put him at odds with Krueger and his "good ol' boys."

Trent's first mistake was to actively campaign for a more "marketing-driven company." (I groaned at this buzzword from the 1980s. Trent's ideas made textbook sense: do lots of market research and find out what, for example, customers really wanted in a yogurt or new kind of cheese. Let the customers pull the company rather than pushing products down the customers' throats and seeing if they like them.)

Not surprisingly, the sales force strongly protested Trent's attempts to make the company more marketing-driven. Trent characterized them as "unsophisticated hillbillies" who thought they knew what the customers wanted just because they were there. "They want all the resources to wine and dine the buyers, provide special incentives, and produce more point-of-purchase displays," Trent complained. "They joke about focus groups, and they constantly complain that the company is wasting time and money on market research studies. They just don't understand that there are professional ways of managing a company. If Eastwood is going to grow, we need a sales force that thinks beyond their immediate accounts and keeps their eyes on a *national* focus."

I noted Trent's comments, but didn't offer much in the way of confirmation or rebuttal. While I respected his opinion, I also thought he was "throwing out the baby with the bathwater." Eastwood's sales force might not be the most sophisticated group of reps in the world, but they undoubtedly had a wealth of experience, knowledge, and wisdom that was probably a lot more solid than a philosophical game plan. It was now clear that an important goal of the work conference would be to get the opposing factions to recognize each other's merits and end up marching to the beat of the same drummer.

Late that afternoon, I flew to Atlanta to meet with the infamous Walter Krueger. Although I was only meeting with Krueger, while members of my staff were interviewing his sales force, I knew that he represented the hearts and minds of 80 salespeople who worshipped the ground he walked on.

On to Peach Blossom Country: Atlanta

Usually our interviews last one-and-a-half to two hours, once in a while going to two-and-a-half hours. I expected my session with Krueger to last a bit longer but not a total of *four-and-a-quarter* hours. A dynamic and handsome man in his early fifties, Krueger certainly looked the part of a "can-do" salesperson who could "sell the Brooklyn Bridge" or, as Trent put it, "talk a cat off a meatwagon."

I spent the early part of the interview asking him about his experience in the industry. It soon became clear that he had milk in his veins. He'd started in the business in his early twenties, and he simply loved making dairy deals. Eventually we got back to Eastwood, and I paid special attention to his body language as he described the changes in Eastwood as it grew, particularly when we were discussing Franklin's takeover. His anger, though under control in his dialogue, was evident in the way he clenched his fists and stiffened his neck, particularly as he described how Charles Kent, the founder of Eastwood and still a golf partner, had been forced to resign after the company was acquired by Franklin. "They told Charlie he'd continue to have a major operational role," said Krueger. "Then they just made it impossible for him to stay. Charlie built this business from a small company to one of the larger dairy products companies in the region. He was the best."

Our discussion then turned to the current problems under Franklin. Krueger complained about all the red tape under Burke, Benton, and Trent. He particularly disliked Benton and also felt that Burke was out of touch with the rest of the company: "Both talk about a lot of 'highfalutin' theories that have nothing to do with running a dairy products company."

Krueger explained that the attempt to move the sales force to Sacramento was Benton's major mistake. "That was just crazy!" he snorted. "Seventy percent of our business is east of the Mississippi. What good is it going to do us being on the West Coast when the action is right here? Besides, Sacramento is so damn out of the way. With just one flight a day, it's a full day's travel just to get in and out of there. [I hadn't arrived in Atlanta until after midnight, so I knew what he was talking about.] And instead of getting some 'customer benefits' from corporate meetings, I hear of changes they expect me to sell to the sales force that *take away* customer benefits to improve our bottom line. They cost us volume—that's what!"

Krueger said he refused to go to Sacramento because it required a great deal of effort, and he was sick and tired of wasting his time in nondecisive meetings. "He [Benton] wants me to come all the way to Sacramento when I have a full schedule with supermarkets and food brokers. I don't want to think of how many orders we'd lose while I was transferring flights. Why can't they just come here if they think it's so important to meet face to face? Let them kill a day while I'm out getting orders."

Krueger also expressed anger that neither Burke, Benton, nor even Trent really understood Eastwood's segments of the dairy marketplace. It was annoying having to spend so much time educating them. "What value do they bring to the party? All they can do is think up ways to waste our time with meetings, reports, and other things that chew up time when we could be making sales calls. Besides, the three-hour time difference is awful. We need information at eight-thirty in the morning, not noon when they get in. By that time our accounts have gone out to lunch and have bought from our competitors."

A lot of what Krueger had to say made sense, and I suggested at the end of the interview that people in Sacramento probably didn't realize how much he cared about the company. His seeming "insubordination" was really just his way of making sure that he got his job done. Krueger just smiled wryly when I suggested this, indicating that the work conference was going to be one interesting affair.

And Elsewhere in the Midwest

While several of my staff and I were interviewing Eastwood's top managers, others had been wending their way across the country interviewing the sales force, plant managers and their quality-assurance managers, food brokers, and supermarket chains. They presented an interesting picture that to some degree vindicated Burke. While everyone commended Eastwood's sales force as being hardworking, many brokers complained that they were too aggressive and sneaky, sometimes going behind their backs and selling directly to supermarkets, cutting them out of the picture. Then there was the unevenness of the pricing. In some cases, several stores of a chain would get a lower price than the remaining stores, depending on how toughly the buyers negotiated. Burke had attempted to correct this by instituting bracket pricing based on the volume of business done with a customer. But there were all kinds of things wrong with this new system and the way it was implemented. The following are just some examples:

- "There has been great confusion over the bracket pricing. Would you believe that exceptions have been made about 90 percent of the time? So we're right back in the same boat as before, only now customers are confused and our morale is terrible. Our top 200 customers today are just where they were before the bracket-pricing structure."

- "We had flexible pricing. Now the pricing spread between brackets is too great. Even big customers haven't space to store what they must order to get better prices."

- "We used to sell service, now we are trying to dictate both prices and programs to our customers."

- "We dramatically changed our pricing, and we tightened terms and conditions, which are now apparently inflexible."

- "The contract with the broker stated that he would receive 2 *cents* per pound on cheese and 5 percent on all other items. However, when the pricing contract came out from Sacramento, it specified 2 *percent* on cheese and 5 percent on all other items! This was a costly mistake. We lost $300,000, and it caused great confusion."

Some of the complaints were directed at the company itself. Quality was a major issue, depending on which plant produced the goods. Short shipments were also the norm. Eastwood apparently thought it was better to make just a partial shipment if the company couldn't fill a whole order, which was often the case. Buyers, unfortunately, weren't warned of the situation. Customer service was a problem too: calls were going unreturned, billings were done incorrectly, and so on. Finally, many customers with accounts complained of slow payments. If a supermarket ran a promotion, it might have to wait 120 days before it saw a co-op advertising check from Eastwood.

All of this pointed to a company that was ripe for being picked off by competitors who realized the importance of product quality and customer service. And Burke was right in trying to address these issues before many more accounts became too fed up and actively sought better service elsewhere. But how could I bring him down from the clouds and at the same time expand Walter Krueger's rather parochial view and narrow vision? That was the challenge of the upcoming feedback and work sessions.

Showdown in Denver

Once ExecuTrak completed the interviewing, we spent a good three weeks analyzing the data and assembling our report. This process was not extremely complex (as in the case of the Bergstrasse file; see Chapter 6), but there was a great deal of data to compare, given the number of brokers, supermarkets, chains, and people (managers, sales and customer-service reps, etc.) we had interviewed. My game plan was to hold a private session with Burke, then lead a work session on neutral turf. Denver seemed attractive to both the corporate and salespeople as a place to meet for the conference. After all, the travel to Sacramento was so provoking to Krueger and his people that holding the conference at headquarters would immediately start things off on the wrong foot. A neutral meeting place, somewhere in between, would be a gesture from Burke and his staff that they were willing to meet Krueger and his regional managers halfway, at least. (Given the location of corporate and plant managers, Denver was also a more cost-effective site to hold the conference than Atlanta.)

When our report was complete, two of us held a private session with Burke. In a way, there was not a lot new. I had already told him that I thought he and much of what he had initiated was the problem; the report strongly validated my assessments. I really think that he was hoping that the data would prove me wrong and would vindicate his approach. Now he was dismayed and for a few moments speechless. Finally, he spoke.

"Wow. I didn't realize that I was really the cause of so much trauma here, John. I really believed that I was doing things that would prevent a major collapse at Eastwood. Strategically, I think many of the changes made sense. The major problem was the number—and their execution. I thought the organization could assimilate this much change. I guess I was just naive. What should I do now?"

"I'm sure you did mean well, David," I said soothingly, "but it's all history. All that counts is what happens from this moment on [a key concept that keeps people from stewing in the present]. The most important thing we have to do is prepare for tomorrow's feedback session with your key people; then we should decide on the mission, objectives, and agenda of the work conference."

I stressed the fact that he had to "come clean" at the beginning of the session by admitting that his approach and ideas had obviously put the organization all at once under too much strain. He had to admit that he'd been too focused on cost reduction, productivity, and uniform policies and pricing for customers at the expense of not demonstrating any tangible benefits to customers and leaving them with the feeling (supported by comments to brokers and customers by the sales force) that "Eastwood no longer cares; it's forgotten that you're the ones who provide the paychecks!" He also should state that, if need be, he'd rectify certain policies and programs once it was verified that they were doing more harm than good. Equally important, he had to acknowledge that the sales force was an invaluable repository of experience and wisdom that could benefit the company. If he could harness that knowledge and energy to a larger strategic plan, the company could regain whatever ground it had lost and once again become the industry powerhouse.

At first, I think Burke was unnerved by the idea of baring his soul; it just wasn't his style to "defer" to his employees that way. But he became excited as I described the opportunity for energizing the whole organization and moving forward, for showing his people that he was ready to take "real-time" action—not unilaterally or on the basis of advice from high-priced consultants, but on the basis of input from the people who knew the brokers and customers. Soon he talked about his chance to use the work conference as a medium for analyzing problems, as an integrative mechanism, and as a way to empower his people to take actions that would benefit the company as a whole.

There was one issue that he still felt uneasy about—Walter Krueger. "John, this guy holds a tremendous amount of sway over the sales force and others in the company. And he is damn good; we can't afford to lose him. But he's our national sales manager, not the vice president of sales, let alone the president and CEO. If he can't be a team player, we can't have him on the team. And he's so awfully difficult to deal with."

"Well, David," I responded, "I've spent some time with him. I honestly believe that I'd act somewhat the same way he has if I felt 'yanked around' by a group of people who don't know the industry as well as he does and who he believes don't add value to customer satisfaction. No wonder he's adopted a win-lose attitude. Yet Walt really cares about his company; he thinks he's protecting it as well as the future of his salespeople—whom he also cares a great deal about. He's a practical businessman and wants to make sure that you draw on his knowledge and experience rather than acting solely on the advice either of consultants who've never seen the inside of a buyer's office or, frankly, of your vice president of sales. Krueger feels—and, as you've seen by the feedback, others feel—that Benton doesn't add value and seems to be a roadblock to progress. They also perceive that he filters important information, preventing whatever he fears won't make him look good from reaching you.

"Most important," I continued, "is that beneath the hostilities, you really have the basis for a double-win situation [Step 5]. You and Krueger both want the same thing: a better, more prosperous Eastwood. All you need to do is find a modus operandi that works for everybody. And I really think you'll find Krueger to be a decent person if you lay your cards on the table as we've discussed."

By the end of my feedback session, David was exuberant at the potential opportunity he had before him. He commented that the "fog" had lifted: "John, since I've been here I've felt like there's been a thick haze between me and the rest of the company. I guess that's part of why I felt the need to stay close to my office with outside people. But I see now that the real fog was a little cloud around my own head. Tomorrow, let's clear the skies for everyone."

We continued our discussion on the plane flight to Denver, and afterward we enjoyed a casual dinner together free from any talk of business. (The nonbusiness talks are always important for developing rapport and further building trust with the main protagonists.) The next morning, we entered the work conference refreshed and ready for a profitable session.

People chitchatted in the hotel conference room until Walt Krueger and his salespeople sauntered in 10 minutes late; at this point the silence became palpable. Krueger himself sat with his arms crossed and a slight smile on his face, staring straight at Benton, which is an extremely effective technique for disarming an opponent. Having found Krueger to be a highly competitive yet decent human being, I assumed that he was acting on "autopilot" rather than out of malice. In any case, Benton started looking up, down, sideways, and everywhere but in Krueger's direction. "Gotcha! Take that!" I imagined Krueger's mind thinking at a very subconscious level. (The more conflict resolutions you conduct, the more you'll become aware of such "psychodramas." Such an awareness can help you steer your feedback sessions and work conferences from pitfalls and traps onto a productive course.)

When the last of the 26 managers had arrived and settled in, Burke made a number of opening, tone-setting remarks: "We have a lot of issues to review here, and since a lot of them stem from my office, I'll go first." Burke candidly talked about his approach to running the business—and how some of it had been ill-timed. He openly admitted that he'd spent too much time listening to consultants and not enough time in the field listening to managers, vendors, and especially brokers and customers."

He mentioned one example: "Sixty days ago I introduced a bracket-pricing policy. It's clearly not working. The concept, I believe, is sound. It's execution is faulty. Let's get some more facts and figures. If we have to, we'll modify it. We'll even rescind it, if that's what's best for our customers and this company. If we wind up with some egg on our faces, I'm big enough to admit a mistake."

When he finished, I explained the process all of us would go through to capitalize on the feedback and explained that to open everyone's "opportunity lens" and thaw out feelings, we would run through a business simulation. (See Chapter 5 for an example.) We then passed out the feedback reports for everyone to study section by section. After they read the cover letter the managers were asked to identify what they saw as crucial issues or opportunities in our summary and then in each part.

But before opening the feedback reports, Krueger asked to speak. Everyone had anticipated that he had come to Denver looking for a gunfight. He was clearly unprepared for this peaceful turn of events. He cleared his throat and expressed surprise.

"David, I really didn't think I'd ever hear corporate talk about its mistakes. Yeah, we've been tough to deal with, maybe even obstructionists at times, but if you can start with that level of honesty, so can we. I really respect you for it."

With the tone set and with the "purging" underway, we were able to move on to identifying the key issues without expressing hostilities or pointing fingers. For example, the Atlanta sales force expressed some of the following concerns cited in the report:

- "Marketing designs programs at the corporate level as opposed to designing them at the regional level, which hinders our ability to take advantage of opportunities we know about. And there is a corporate company attitude rather then a regional one. You can't have one corporate program that translates to different regions in our particular market niches."

- "Marketing's programs are not exciting. We need more things to increase same store sales, such as demos and incentive trips. We need more innovation."

- "With all the Sacramento controls, we're losing more and more opportunities. Structural price lists and the like are killing our ability to move entrepreneurially and responsively. We're far less flexible. We're becoming 'bureaucratized.'"

- "Promotions work better when they can be altered slightly to reflect needs of different accounts."

- "Sacramento doesn't listen to us. Our customers feel they are getting less for more money. We in the field are not selling as much as we are administering the changes in product pricing, minimum orders, and so on. And, we know from experience that once we lose a customer, it takes two to three years to get that person back. With increasing competition today, we'll be lucky ever to get that customer back."

- "Sacramento should focus on better merchandising support for the trade. More interesting sales promotions are needed. We must decrease to three weeks maximum the turnaround time on promotional payments to our customers. We need to decrease to 48 hours turnaround time between the field and Sacramento on program promotions."

- "I sense a fear of too much 'marketing' coming down the road. Will we be inundated with tie-ins with other food programs and companies? We've built our business on good products and prices. But what are these tie-ins trying to be? Unless marketing knows what the competitive advantage is, then what's the point of this 'marketing'—that is, 'do this, do that'—promotions? Customers know what they want, and they don't want to screw around with some merchandising gimmick that's not directly relevant to their needs."

- "Customers want deals cut in their office. 'Relationship selling' is what counts, especially now that we're being undercut by 'Johnny-Come-Latelies.' But with bracket pricing and the like, our authority has been stripped from us. We lose face with our customers. They're not waiting days, or even weeks, for approval from Sacramento to a request. They're going to competitors."

Twenty-five of the 32 insiders not from sales described the sales force's negative attitudes, including such comments as:

- "Our sales force doesn't accept many of our changes. They aren't running with the ball."

- "The sales force doesn't have much enthusiasm. Frankly, some of those guys may have been in the business 20 years, but it seems like it's the same year 20 times over."

- "The salespeople are committed to doing business the old way, tailoring things to customers' needs regardless of whether those things are feasible or will even make a profit. Salespeople just won't let go of their historical ways of doing business. There is a strong feeling that you can't nationalize the business. And a pervasive attitude of 'why change?' persists even when sales are falling off."

- "The sales force seems to make up its mind that a promotion is not good enough, and then they don't promote it to the customers. In fact, I get feedback that they're undercutting some of these changes and promotions."

- "We have a problem with sales management: Benton's philosophy is not consistent with it, and it even runs counter to that of his subordinates. This, in part, explains why we've had such difficulty implementing some of the major changes. The sales force doesn't respect his [Benton's] leadership. I don't think he'll make it."

- "The low morale of the sales force impacts our performance. If the sales force is only 60 percent behind our 'ideas,' the customers won't be behind the promotions either. This reflects a weakness in our sales organization and its leadership, both here and in Atlanta."

Another area that came up in the feedback report concerned lines of authority. Fifteen insiders (including several from Sacramento) claimed that at least some degree of decision-making authority needed to be put back into the field. Three of the comments from these people included:

- "Before, salespeople ran their territory as if it were their own little business, and the salespeople keep hoping they'll be able to do this again. It's an entrepreneurial focus."

- "We need to give people back authority to deal with customers from their particular area on an *individual* basis. Flexibility is needed for each region. Our customers demand a choice, and if we can't give it to them, they'll go to our competitors who will."

- "I'm afraid the consultants have done a grave disservice to Burke and our company by introducing so many changes that adversely affect customers. It's changed our sales force and brokers from 'yes' people to 'no' people who have been stripped of authority. And it's charged them with bringing bad news to Sacramento, or serving it upstairs, which no one likes to do."

Only four insiders claimed that there was too much authority delegated to the field. This attitude was typified by this statement: "Even though we said we had to get rid of small customers who couldn't carry their rightful load [i.e., pricing brackets], our sales group couldn't execute our strategy. They just don't understand the underlying economics—or they don't want to. They 'roll over and play dead' with the customer to retain his or her business. Too much authority has been delegated to field sales!"

Finally, a number of issues about plant rationalization were raised by 14 of the 50 insider respondents. Said one manager, "We never asked, 'Where is our capacity? Who are our customers, and how will we serve them?' Plant-closing decisions were based on money. We must become more sophisticated, and base those decisions on marketing and customer-service strategy, not on sales."

Another asked, "How are we going to meet the commitments of our sales force? We have to be able to deliver, or our customers will not trust or believe us. If you are up-front with your customer, you can achieve a win-win even if you can't meet your commitments." And yet another comment was made that "we haven't made good business decisions. Closing certain plants was a bad decision. It's now getting too expensive, for instance, to service the Northwest from Kansas City. We had a good plant and good people there. Why did we shut it down? Four of the people who got canned are now each in business for themselves or competitors, which takes business away from us!"

Yet another commented, "We built our reputation on a regional basis. Now we've rationalized the plants, taking customer service away from them. Their link with the customers is gone, except for sales, which constantly harangues them regarding orders. So now the plants enjoy making life miserable for Sacramento, because they are sick and tired of sales bludgeoning them."

Finally, consider a typical lament from sales: "Why haven't production problems been resolved—after all the money and 'experts' thrown at them?"

We listed comments such as these on wall charts throughout the afternoon, and by 4 p.m., they were covered with key issues in 11 different categories. We helped the 26 managers boil them down to six key issues that would be discussed at the first work conference a week hence by the top 14 managers. These included:

- Achieve greater trust, teamwork, and commitment to decisions and plans taken at the conference.

- Resolve (i.e., achieve agreement on) both Eastwood Dairy's and its key functions' missions.

- Resolve Eastwood's key performance areas and "deliverables" in several of the key performance areas.

- Resolve what will be basic strategies for achieving the objectives.

- Resolve *how* best to "drive Eastwood into the black."

- Agree on the communication and action plan to install the process and output of the conference and feedback session lower in the organization to ensure mutual understanding, trust, and commitment to the effective execution of any decisions that will be made.

The feedback session had started at 7 a.m., and by the end of the day (6 p.m.), everyone felt exhausted but optimistic. Sure, there was still some cynicism, but the major barriers had been broken down, and at least Krueger and his "people" could shake hands with the Sacramento staff. This was a good omen for the upcoming work conference. Here are some parting comments of the group:

- "For the first time we have identified the magnitude of the real problems, rather than superficial symptoms, in virtually all facets of the business from an internal and external perspective. These have provided a framework for delving into the root causes of the problem."

- "We defined the depth of our problems with some real emotional significance, and we illuminated the need to quickly change the perceptions both within and outside the company. We also developed what I think is a realistic action plan to resolve these problems and causes."

- "We really have a much better understanding of how our customers have suffered at our expense."

- "We've placed the major issues on the table for everybody to see and have gotten behind the facades. At the same time, I'm proud of how every person handled some very sensitive issues."

■ "We're all a bit humbled...."

Peace in Denver

The top 14 people attended the first intensive four-and-a-half-day work conference (again in Denver; the neutral turf seemed to please everyone), and got right to work. I was pleased that there was no bickering and fingerpointing, and the focus remained on the issues—as it should have. The group first agreed on a common mission: to ensure customer satisfaction and long-term profitability through superior products and innovative services delivered by the industry's most responsive and knowledgeable people. While this sounds like "motherhood, God, and apple pie," they defined what the terms meant and agreed to focus on three major areas:

■ *Customer satisfaction*   (on-time, complete delivery; quality that meets the product and customer-service specifications, and good relationships)

■ *Profitability*   (good return on sales and ROI, overhead restructuring, etc.)

■ *Management process*   (strengthening top management, role clarification, heightened sense of urgency, detailed action plans, and employee buy-in)

By applying Steps 6 through 10, they were able to make key decisions in a number of areas. For example, to improve customer satisfaction, the conference established a logistics management team that would be dedicated to improving on-time delivery and filling of orders. Changes in suppliers and in formulations were to take care of some key quality problems. Profitability would be addressed by special sales and broker incentives, a further reduction in administrative and sales headcount, and the closing of one, rather than two, plants. Finally, management processes would be addressed through three work conferences in which appropriate functional and cross-functional teams would analyze and resolve other major issues. They would also negotiate their respective missions, key performance areas, deliverables, strategies, and action steps for each major function in order to support the corporate goals.

The group was also able to resolve some of the major issues between the sales force and headquarters. First, everyone agreed that leaving the sales force in Atlanta made the most sense. But a great deal more coordination would have to take place. In addition, marketing people would go out on sales calls and learn from the reps, then jointly discuss plans for promotions. In other words, sales versus marketing would become sales *and* marketing. Responsibility, authority, and accountability (RAA) lines were clearly drawn, especially concerning pricing. Eastwood did maintain bracket pricing, but they completely revamped the structure and let the sales force *buy in.*

Finally, there was agreement about regularly scheduled meetings. Krueger would fly to Sacramento once a month to meet with the vice presidents of sales and marketing and participate in certain executive staff meetings. In the event that he had crucial business with customers, he could send a delegate.

Eastwood held a second work conference two weeks later, and a third conference with forty managers a month later. Shortly after the end of the third conference, senior management rolled out a complete "Mission Momentum" communication and implementation program that involved extending the work-conference approach throughout the entire organization, nationwide. As part of this program, five managers learned and eventually were licensed as ExecuTrak Systems® client consultant–trainers to execute the Arnold Conflict Resolution Process. Eastwood would then have an in-house team capable of heading off conflicts whenever possible, and they could swiftly deal with issues before they became crises. (*Note*: Chapter 10 presents part of an in-house slide presentation that the licensed Eastwood managers completed as part of their training.)

When we officially closed the file back in Boston, we celebrated in the most appropriate way—with champagne and frozen yogurts!

Case Notes

1. As the Eastwood situation demonstrates, whenever a top official throws massive changes at an organization, interdepartmental conflict is likely to occur. That's because not all departments will see the changes as being in their best interests. So they tend to build walls around themselves and fight to protect what is "rightfully" theirs. In the process of doing so, they may well see their fellow departments as potential enemies in an "every-division-for-itself" war. Moreover, when change has an adverse effect on people's personal lives, they tend to look for scapegoats, and the people "over the wall" are likely targets.

2. The Eastwood situation also underscores the damage that fuzzy RAA lines can wreak on an organization. In the case of Eastwood, marketing and sales felt they had claim to the same authority with regard to

certain kinds of decisions, and each wanted it removed from the other's "jurisdiction." This created a tug of war. In addition, the plants felt that customer service should be their responsibility. (At one time customer-service operations were located in the various production centers. After the acquisition, Franklin consolidated customer service in one operation at headquarters.) This resulted in yet another RAA war, with sales jumping into the fray. The reps felt that moving customer service out of the plants would simply lengthen the whole process of filling orders. And what is the moral of this story? Always look carefully at RAA lines as a probable cause when trying to sort out interdepartmental clashes.

3. An interdepartmental conflict has two levels of reality. The first is the actual situation in which you can readily determine who did what, and what needs to be changed. The other is what I call the "mythic level." Departments in conflict create "mythic" villains and heroes, acts of treachery and acts of heroism (in which the ends justify the means). The job of the catalyst-mediator is to shatter the mythic reality and bring people back to earth so they can deal with real issues, causes, and resolutions. "Dream-world" resolutions don't work in the workaday world of business.

4. As in Eastwood's case, interdepartmental conflicts often involve class boundaries. From the 1960s to the late 1980s, it was felt that the grass-roots managers couldn't hold a candle to professionally trained MBAs. Then in the late 1980s, we began to see a backlash against both MBAs and investment banker–types running companies. In part, this backlash reflected the wider reaction against "yuppies" and a new national revulsion for the "Age of Greed." Today, the lines between elite professional managers and grass-roots managers are drawn more tightly then ever, so it's critical to be sensitive to the value differences that underlie so many interdepartmental conflicts. Often the conflict has more to do with people's stereotypical ideas than with the situation itself. The catalyst-mediator must be careful to help the protagonists sort out those ideas from the issues at hand.

Postscript

As I expected, John Benton's career would go sour when the many negative perceptions about his lack of leadership were accessed through the feedback report. Although the "quotable quotes" from the interviews were carefully edited to give Benton as much benefit of the doubt as possible, and although all inflammatory statements about him (and others!) were exercised, Benton tendered his resignation two days after the feedback session. This "cleared the air" considerably and reduced CEO Burke's fury when he realized how much Benton had shielded him from the serious problems with the sales force and customers.

Following Krueger's enthusiastic and significant contributions to the first two work conferences, and because of his tireless commitment to overcoming customer and broker disgust with Eastwood, Burke appointed him vice president of sales. Krueger accepted the appointment, with the provision that he could spend at least 70 percent of his time in the field. Burke eagerly agreed once he and Krueger agreed on Krueger's management "deliverables."

Trent stayed on as the marketing manager and actually became quite knowledgeable about yogurt, cheeses, and the field. As for Eastwood, it took six months of hard work to undo the damage done to customer and broker goodwill by the lack of support of the sales force and some of the changes initially instituted by Burke. But at the end of the seventh month, Eastwood had regained its volume and, for the first time in over a year, it showed a profit.

The company now appears to be on a winning streak, with both "hardpack" and "soft-serve" yogurts (a new product for them), soft-flavored dessert cheeses, and low-fat natural cheeses coming on strong.

9

A Question of Values: Resolving Value-System Conflicts

Case Study

ExecuTrak File 321: "Doing Well by Doing Right"

Just after World War II, the United Fellowship Society, based in Philadelphia and affiliated with the Belmont Hospital Center, was created to provide health care to people in need, particularly the elderly. Affiliated with a major religious organization, the Society grew steadily and without event until the late 1980s, when it found itself in a major conflict over its mission and direction. While there had always been some dissent among board members as to where the Society should be allocating its energies and resources, the board members had never clashed openly about the issue.

But with the retirement of several board members and the addition of several young "hotshots" to voting positions, the landscape began to change. One new member, Bill Casperi, a lawyer by trade, was particularly interested in "revitalizing" the organization and making it more profitable. His enthusiasm, in turn, stimulated

Martin Douglas, Belmont's president, to take a more aggressive role in suggesting various expansion strategies.

The talk of "profits" and "expansion" sent shivers up the spines of some of the more conservative members of the board, particularly Orlan Carver. He believed that profits, mergers, and talk of expansion had nothing to do with the charitable spirit of the Society. And another board member, Sarah Hauster, felt that, if anything, the board should be focusing on housing for the elderly, not on "business talk."

With Casperi pressing hard for reform, and Carver digging in his heels, the chairman of the Society's board, Paul Kryzminski, faced the difficult task of finding a peaceful resolution and getting on with the Society's business.

Overview of Value-System Conflicts

This category of conflict has to do with disagreements over philosophical issues relating to a company's value system. These conflicts have traditionally involved such issues as speed versus quality; responsibility to stockholders versus responsibility to employees; profits versus protection of the environment; research and publishing versus teaching; breakthrough products versus integrity of research; and customer education versus proselytizing.

Years ago, I was involved with a major computer company struggling with one of the most common types of value-system conflict, output versus quality. Actually, no one wanted to intentionally create shoddy products; management's edict was "meet the delivery date without fail come hell or high water, even if you have to build quality into the product in the field."

The decision to ship a product that engineers knew might well need immediate fixing right after it was unpacked caused great internal strife. It resulted in at least one key manager being fired and several resignations that hurt the company and caused morale problems.

This "get it out the door on time" approach was a built-in corporate value system. The company had a large customer engineering group whose role was to fix problems in the field. For example, they often fixed computers that failed to function the way they were supposed to from the moment they reached the customers.

Why did customers put up with this kind of nonsense? They did so because this company was the premier supplier in its market segment. If you wanted to do business with it, you accepted this mentality. To be fair to the company and its superior cadre of customer engineers, they satisfied customers as quickly as possible after shipping the machines. The fact that the customer engineers traveled constantly, which caused stress because they were away from home and families so often, was sometimes painfully discussed in the conferences. But *their* value system placed this type of work ahead of the impact on their family life.

Today, total-quality management (TQM), a philosophy widely adopted in most U.S. industry, is reducing, to varying degrees, the problems caused by value clashes in the field and on the factory floor. Interestingly, however, when values get completely wrapped around achieving the highest state of quality at the expense of other business considerations, the results can be disastrous. Consider the case of Wallace Company, an oil-pipe company that won the 1990 Baldrige Award; afterward it found itself teetering on the brink of bankruptcy. How did this happen? When quality became the sole value, management forgot to pay attention to the basics of running the business and found itself experiencing financial difficulties. The situation with Wallace is worth remembering, because it illustrates how bottom-line thinking can clash with top-line values.

Sometimes value-system conflicts involve a tremendous amount of ego. Consider the case of a film manufacturer whose new sales manager actually insisted that his representatives *physically* resemble him. (This was a tall, hefty order, given the fact that this person was 6 feet 6 inches tall and weighed nearly 260 pounds. Talk about values!) The company's human resources director and others charged with screening candidates dutifully complied. Only "hulks" with a similarly intimidating and bullying presence were recruited. While sales from the photographic shop rose for several years, they suddenly took a nosedive when the uniqueness of a product represented by a sales force of Goliaths wore off. The reps might have been able to bench-press 400 pounds, but they simply did not know how to maintain accounts of resentful customers once a key competitor developed a similar product.

Value-system conflicts can be particularly gut-wrenching because people involved in them often feel trapped. We once worked with a leader in the chemical industry that was putting together a new agricultural-chemicals group. The company had just introduced a new pesticide that some staff scientists felt posed an unacceptable degree of human risk. While the substance itself had met the criteria of the forerunner of the Environmental Protection Agency, the scientists feared that if the directions for its use were not followed to the letter, the application of the pesticide could lead to terrible consequences. As one chemist told us, "I hate myself. This stuff should never see the light of day. I'm fearful that it's very possibly a killer. We need a longer research period to really determine its long-range human impact. But I'm stuck.

I'm in my late fifties and have two kids in college. I have medical bills for my wife. I just can't afford to get another job. Besides, what company is going to hire me if I bail out of here because I disagree with the corporation's decision? The product will probably make a lot of money— and perhaps kill a lot of people before its degenerative effects are discovered years later."

While this scientist stayed on, at least for the duration of our project, you can be sure that the company never got 100 percent from him. Others in the organization were terribly conflicted by the continual warfare: speaking out against what they believed was a potential evil to the human race versus doing what the company wanted and continuing to earn a good paycheck. In time, that product did prove to be far too dangerous for general use, and it was banned from the U.S. market. So what did the manufacturer do? Like too many other American, Japanese, German, and other companies, they sold it to Third World countries with little or no environmental regulations.

Increasingly, companies will celebrate corporate decisions to phase out environmentally hazardous operations. For example, Northern Telecom, with 60,000 employees, became the world's first large electronics corporation to meet a public commitment to eliminating dangerous chemicals—ozone-depleting ones in this case—from its manufacturing operations.

A more recent example can be seen in the controversy over the Dow Corning silicone breast implants. One of the developers, Thomas D. Talcott, believed early on that the devices weren't safe, and he resigned as a protest. His values had locked horns with Dow Corning's to the point where he felt that he had no choice but to leave. Talcott lost a job, and Dow Corning lost a 24-year veteran employee. (Dow Corning also created a formidable enemy; Thomas became a nationally known whistleblower whose efforts helped put a temporary restriction on the sale of implants.)

Finally, for an extreme example of how top-management goals and lower-management concerns can throw a company into turmoil, just think back to the *Challenger* disaster. We all know the events leading to the tragic launch and subsequent death of six astronauts. The incident and subsequent hearings also created shock waves throughout Thiokol, the company that made the infamous, defective O-rings which caused the explosion. The furor led to resignations, firings, and a permanent black eye that will dog the company for a long time to come.

Another type of value-system conflict concerns the way that a company treats its employees and suppliers. Even today, in many manufacturing companies, people on the line are considered to be warm bodies who check their brains at the door when they punch in each morning. While some employees may do just that to get the product out the door, others are growing increasingly discontent. Just read the stories of employees who complain of being treated like robots who perform the same repetitive tasks every day.

Suppliers, too, want to be treated differently than they have been in the past. This fact is often difficult for executives to accept if they've been steeped in the old school of playing one supplier against another and then squeezing until they've wrung out the most concessions, lowest prices, best turnaround, and so on. In an increasing number of companies today, however, there is a recognition that the treatment of suppliers as partners results in better double-win performance.

Effects of Value-System Conflicts

Value-system conflicts tend to be the most gut-wrenching of all conflicts, because they're so personal and because they challenge people's belief systems. Also, people tend to approach philosophical, ethical, or other "soft" business issues with a strong bias regarding right and wrong. This makes them less flexible and more likely to think only in terms of win-lose rather than double-win relationships: "The only solution is for you to change and adopt my way of looking at the world."

Some situations are undoubtedly right or wrong—for example, a company knowingly withholding important product-safety information or cheating the government is wrong. But other situations can't so easily be judged; conflict resolution in such cases can lead to a double-win outcome. Consider the case of a department store chain that retained ExecuTrak to get at the cause of sagging sales. We quickly found that the sagging sales were the result of dispirited store managers and employees who, in the words of several store managers we interviewed, said they felt like just a pair of hands: "The district manager walks into my store and says 'grab your pad and take notes.' He marches me along like a dog on a leash continually pointing out what he thinks is wrong with cleanliness, displays, presentation of merchandise, and so on. The fact that our sales are up over this time last year, and against tough competition, doesn't even get mentioned. I can't wait till the bastard leaves my store; he humiliates us." Other managers and store employees said that headquarters treated them like "mindless robots."

Our feedback report convinced management that they had to change their basic attitudes about their people. If they wanted enthusiastic managers and store employees who truly wanted to create pleasurable shopping environments and who would go all out to provide top-notch customer service, they would have to develop a double-win attitude and working relationship among the regional, district, and store managers, as well as between the home office and the field. Training in several key facets of store operations and management skills would also be required. The compensation and reward system would also have to be changed. For their part, store managers would have to inculcate into their employees that *"customers* are the ones who pay your biweekly paychecks"—the employer merely "writes and distributes them—and customers need to be treated like guests, not like nuisances."

Guidelines for Resolving Value-System Conflicts

Value-system conflicts are easy to spot, but they can be very difficult to resolve because people have so much of themselves invested in them. After all, when people truly care about their company or organization and the work they do, you're going to have a difficult time asking them to reconsider and do something contrary to their fundamental beliefs. Therefore, bear the following guidelines in mind when you set out to handle a value-system conflict.

1. Values are deeply ingrained in people, and they're not likely to change without a major shock to the system. Or, to use contemporary management terminology, resolving value conflicts involves making a "paradigm" shift, a paradigm being a collection of ideas and assumptions about the world at large. Historically, paradigm shifts have not gone down easily; in fact, the first response to "anomalous data" is to violently reject it. Just look at how great scientific geniuses have often been ridiculed because they challenged the current paradigm; only later, often posthumously, did their theories became the core of a new paradigm.

In business and in life, the same thing occurs. When a faction feels that its core assumptions are being challenged, they have a knee-jerk reaction. Unfortunately, in business we don't have time to wait for history to sort itself out, and people must be shown why their world view must be modified. That's where the formal conflict resolution process comes in. First reconstruct the "crime" (Steps 1–4); then check values (Step 5), probe the degree of interest in a double-win solution (Step 6), and get participants to identify what they are trying to achieve, preserve, or avoid (Step 7). Finally, get participants to agree on priorities (Step 8). If you follow these steps, in virtually all situations people are more likely to accept a change in their belief structure and concur on a resolution.

2. In a value-conflict situation, pay particular attention to your "crime" reconstruction (Steps 1–4). Often the values that people espouse do not relate directly to the "crime." Many people frequently do not focus on the precise identity, location, or time (or magnitude of each) of the actual situation or on the true conditions and facts; rather, they abstract and see, hear, and report what they *expect* or fear. True dimensions of the issues and the real causes must then be specified and teased out before progress can be made.

3. Be prepared to let people "vent," since value-system conflicts often spark knee-jerk reactions. In the case that follows, the very mention of the word *abortion*, which tangentially entered the conversation at one point when discussing the option of potentially acquiring a clinic, triggered a violent reaction from otherwise peaceful people. Similarly, the words *merger* and *downsizing* can throw people in the business world into a tailspin, even if they haven't considered the real issues and advantages.

4. Remember that you're dealing with what people believe is "right." (In the computer industry, you'll hear people talk about "goodness," which means "key value.") People approach value-system conflicts with a religious conviction (which in fact is what happened in the case that follows). The corollary is that everyone outside a faction's or a person's frame of reference may be considered a threat, even as "evil," and the more persuasively the "opponent" argues, the more evil he or she is perceived to be. Therefore, be very careful about the language with which you frame questions so as not to trigger a reflex and concomitant violent response.

5. While it is important for the catalyst-mediator to know his or her values when trying to resolve any type of conflict (Step 5), it is absolutely critical when he or she is dealing with value-system conflicts. That's because it's so easy to take sides when you're dealing with "goodness" and other issues of great personal meaning. If you cannot sort out your own personal values, you can't possibly do an unbiased and fair job of resolving the conflict. Mediator—know thyself!

6. Resolutions to value-system conflicts often involve double, triple, or even quintuple wins. These types of wins are very challenging to structure—you must juggle many groups of conflicting APAs (achieves, preserves, avoids). So pay particular attention to Step 7 and make sure you know what everyone believes is at stake. Remember, in a value-system conflict, people at first have an inclination not to budge, for fear that giving an inch is simply the first step toward complete surrender of a deeply held belief—and capitulation.

Consider the above guidelines as you read through the details of the United Fellowship Society (UFS) conflict. You'll see how deeply a value-system conflict can divide an organization, and how the catalyst-mediator must very gently coax everyone into a position in which he or she can begin to appreciate alternative views. As is so typical in value-system conflicts, in the UFS case everyone had the same end point in mind, from a "macro" perspective; they just had very different means of getting there.

Board Games

When Belmont Hospital's CFO, Frank Kloss, made his annual presentation to the Society's board regarding funding for the hospital, he could see that there was no small degree of controversy and argumentation. He also could tell that Paul Kryzminski, chairman of the UFS's board, was having difficulty with his fellow members. After the meeting, Kryzminski confided in Kloss that meetings were interminable, tempers got frayed, and decisions were never reached. Kloss, who had recently read one of my books, suggested to Kryzminski that he consider having me help him develop a decision-making process. We could work through some of the board's problems to arrive at a common mission.

A week later, Kryzminski told Kloss to interview me by phone. If he liked what he heard, he could have me fly up to meet him. Kloss did just that, and two weeks later I flew to Philadelphia to meet with Kryzminski and Kloss in person.

The three of us met in Kryzminski's office for nearly two hours, talking primarily about Belmont and the issues it was facing. When Kloss left, Kryzminski confided in me that the real potential client was the Society, the parent of the hospital.

"UFS drastically needs a decision-making process," he said. "John, have you ever worked with a religious organization, and particularly the board of directors of one?"

"Well, I have in fact worked with several church groups," I replied. "I've also worked with many civic and governmental organizations and various 'crisis intervention' groups. All these are similar, except that the people in religious organizations really have deep-seated beliefs—which can often make things even more sensitive—but the task is not necessarily more difficult." Then, placing the ball back in his court (which is a good way to get a consulting project moving), I asked, "Now, as for UFS, can you tell me more about the situation?"

He thought for a moment, then said, "We're grappling with many issues, but several stand out in my mind. First, the role of UFS is greater than just overseeing the [various medical] entities. We need to lock into the Society's needs and filter them down through the entities by looking at programs that can broaden the Hospital's services, increase income, and help out people. Also, we should be in a position to take action on any of the entities, to ensure compatibility. Too often, one entity has little, if any, concern with a sister organization. Another issue concerns the structure of the Society. If UFS were a corporation, then doctors could share in the profits of Belmont hospital.

"Then there's the whole issue of planning," he continued. "We need to get into opportunistic areas to protect investments and plan for expansion. We have to start thinking of the goal of the Society as planning for the overall system.

"And, of course," he finished, "we must never forget the theme that we are a charitable organization and everything we do must be in the spiritual tradition of the church."

We chatted about other issues, such as profitability versus the outreach activity (particularly elderly housing), after which I asked him to describe the people on the Society's board. Kryzminski laughed and shook his head, then reeled off what could have been the description of the cast of a soap opera. Among the 11 members, he described the following 7 as the most influential:

Rosalyn Bargett, extremely community-oriented. She runs a subsidiary foundation and generally sides with Hauster.

William Biddle, also extremely conservative, very religious, and antichange. While much less vocal than Carver, he follows Carver's lead and always votes lock-step with him.

Orlan Carver, extremely conservative, very religious, and antichange. He is very outspoken, and known to clash with Casperi and Vogel. He's also the oldest board member, at 76 years of age.

Bill Casperi, the Society's very sharp, outspoken, articulate attorney "who's decided he'll help the group 'stay on track.'" He is the youngest board member, at 38 years of age.

Harold Glarskov, often quiet, with no leadership qualities, but he tends to cast the tie-breaking vote.

Sara Hauster, very involved as a community activist. She is the most politically active of the group.

Jack Vogel, energetic, with strong leadership abilities. He contributes a great deal to meetings.

When he finished his list, Kryzminski said, "In general, Casperi and Vogel clash with Carver and Biddle, with Hauster and Bargett running a sideshow with their own community agenda. Glarskov can take sides with any of the three groups, sometimes unpredictably. The other four will generally not make waves, and they'll often sit in silence. You never can tell what they're thinking or how they'll vote. Now, John, you can appreciate the situation. How can you ever get your hands around all this?"

"Actually, Paul," I said with a smile, "it's not that difficult at all. I have a process that works in all kinds of situations." I then explained how we design a survey, interview key inside and outside people, hold a private feedback session with the employer (Kryzminski) and then with the board, and then move into a work conference and consulting mode. Kryzminski was intrigued and thought it just might work. But I'd have to pitch the program to the board first. He felt that even though the board was leery of consultants, the members were frustrated enough that they just might give it a try.

After dining with Kryzminski, I returned to Boston. One week later I flew back to Philadelphia to present my process to the board. One condition I made was that community leaders and other competing hospital presidents be interviewed as well as UFS and Belmont Hospital senior officers and medical department heads. The Society's board would need data from these sources to properly determine its mission, direction, objectives, and appropriate strategies. Sometimes, the protagonists in a conflict are reluctant to hear the comments of people who seem removed from the organization; however, as in this case, those comments can be crucial to painting a complete and accurate picture of the situation. If you feel that outside feedback is essential, be insistent, as I was in this case, that it be obtained.

As Kryzminski had warned me, Carver and Biddle were the naysayers. Carver, the more vocal of the "dynamic duo," said, "I've used consultants in my company, and all they do is ask for your watch and then tell you the time." Biddle nodded: then he scowled at me. I smiled back. (Years of experience have taught me: never respond to general attacks by protagonists. That will compromise your position of neutrality. If a protagonist raises a specific issue such as, "Isn't this just team building?" answer with a definitive, factual response. Otherwise, just grin and bear it.)

But Casperi and Vogel were very excited at the prospect of "breathing some life and direction into this board," and asked encouraging questions. Hauster and Bargett also seemed enthusiastic, and even silent Glarskov showed signs of life as I spoke.

When the last questions had been asked, Kryzminski said that the board would take up the issue after I left, and he escorted me to the elevator. On the way, he said that Carver was really the only person against my program, that in the end he thought he, Kryzminski, could get enough votes to make it happen. He thanked me for the presentation, and he said he would call the next morning before breakfast.

I flew on to Chicago to work with another client. The next morning at 6 a.m., as arranged, Kryzminski called me to say, "You're on!" I thanked him for the opportunity for me to serve the Society, and I laid out my plans for the project.

The Philadelphia Shuffle

In Boston my staff and I developed an appropriate values survey to administer to the Society board and to senior hospital administrative and medical heads. Then I headed southward with two staff members to begin interviewing members of the hospital and of the Society's board. Outsiders such as other hospital presidents from the area, the mayor, the local congressional representative, and the managing editor of the leading newspaper were interviewed as well. All of these people had valuable perceptions of the hospital in its environment (although they might not have been knowledgeable about its parent, the Society).

There was a total of seven days of interviewing, and the process was generally pleasant and straightforward. There were a number of concerns but no vitriolic reactions. (This situation was in stark contrast to some of the other situations mentioned in previous chapters, such as at Bergstrasse; see Chapter 6. There, I was nearly drawn and quartered during the interviews and especially during the feedback process.)

Back in Boston, we developed two feedback reports—one for the Society's board, which included our feedback on the hospital, and one just for the administrative and medical heads, which didn't include many references to the Society, since UFS was the parent. In three weeks our report was ready, and we prepared to present the findings, initially to Kryzminski.

One-on-One with the Chairman of the Board of the Society

After completing our review of the report, Kryzminski looked up and said, "There really aren't that many surprises, John." This was one of the few times that I believe there were no truly significant surprises for the CEO. (Again, contrast this situation with earlier ones, in which CEOs such as Tomlinson and Hemmerl were shocked to hear about the breadth and depth of the issues at their companies.)

The Society's chairman then went on: "I'm really pleased at much of the findings. You've captured what I have felt but haven't been able to put my arms around, and you've stated the emotional issues in a very task-focused way that shouldn't trigger a lot of sensitivities. If you're as good as this report suggests you are, you're going to be able to help the Society members and senior staff and medical department heads of the hospital deal with the appropriate issues successfully. So this is really quite promising, John."

I thanked Kryzminski for his endorsement, and reminded him that access to the organization (as would be the case in any organizational conflict) made the report possible. He then went on to say, "But is this report ever loaded with conflicting issues and sharp contradictions! It's clear that we desperately need a decision process if we're going to make any progress."

Kryzminski also admitted to being "alarmed that outsiders' perceptions of our medical staff are so poor. Unquestionably, the Society's board must be deeply involved in change, in terms of both the Society and the hospital."

I agreed with Kryzminski's observations and conclusions. Then I helped him troubleshoot what could go wrong with the feedback session with the Society's board. We speculated that one pitfall was that factions might read the report and try to interpret it in support of their own pet issues, or "hobbyhorses," so it would be important to impose strict ground rules.

One of the ground rules would be that we would not accept silence as approval; if someone sat without talking for more than an hour, it was incumbent on anyone in the group to ask, "Where are you? What's going on in your head? This is your opportunity to put your cards on the table rather than 'try to reshuffle the deck' when you leave."

Facing Reality: The Feedback Session

Normally we start feedback sessions in the morning and work for a solid day, unless it's a very large report or unless the group has more than 16 people. I had advised Kryzminski that we should kick off the group's feedback session the same evening as his feedback session— tonight—and hold it outside the city. So, at 3:30 p.m., we left for a conference center in Princeton, New Jersey; the get-together started at 5:30 p.m. with [nonalcoholic] cocktails followed by dinner. I thought it would be best for everyone to ease into the feedback and open up their "opportunity lenses."

After dinner, and Kryzminski's tone-setting remarks, I reviewed what we discussed we were going to be doing the next day. I then involved the board members in a simulation. (See Chapters 6 to 8 for descriptions of how simulations work.) After the exercise, I asked the members to look at how they performed in the simulation and to try to determine how their actions were relevant to the feedback.

Several of the board members raised their hands. Said Casperi: "Well, my team was too focused on its own agenda and basic beliefs. We didn't trust those folks on the other team." Other people made similar remarks.

I then said, "From an attitudinal and listening viewpoint, what do you *have* to do differently to capitalize on the feedback you'll get tomorrow?"

"We have to listen to one another better, and allow only one speaker at a time," said Hauster. "We also ought to cut off the windbags" (shedding a glance at Carver).

"And we have to stop 'hobbyhorsing' around," broke in Jack Vogel.

"Oh, am I glad you said that!" I exclaimed with glee as I reached under the table and pulled out a long pole with a toy horse head at one end. "This is a key mediating tool. Any time anyone in this room thinks someone is riding his or her pet steed, regardless of whatever else is going on in the room, challenge that individual by saying, 'I think you're on one of your pet subjects; you're off track.' Or, 'We already put that issue to bed.' Or, 'You've already talked for three minutes about the same issue!' If more than 50 percent of the group agrees with a challenging statement, the person challenged must take the hobbyhorse and hold onto it until someone else starts 'riding' his or her 'hobbyhorse.' If the group agrees, the toy should then be passed on to that individual."

Everyone laughed at this very concrete prop—one of many you can introduce to drive home a point. We covered a few more ground rules, then passed out the reports and asked everyone to sign for them. Then the group was asked to read the cover letter, which shows the purpose and format of the project and report and demonstrates how to read the latter. Next, we had everyone read the table of contents, and then pass back the reports to us. (The idea was to whet their appetites for tomorrow.) Needless to say, the men and women handed them back to us reluctantly. We had built an air of expectation!

The next morning, we began bright and early with the board members. We discussed first the executive summary and then the feedback report, section by section. Here are some of the key feedback issues concerning the board:

- "I see the Society as really being the ones who should have the 20-year vision. This plan should encompass more than just the hospital; it should involve all of the entities as well. Each of the organizations working below the Society would then be able to make their plans accordingly, and the Society would be assured that it is congruent with our charter. This would be a new role for this organization."

- "The hospital is highly successful without the board. The board seems to have lost track of where the hospital is going, although it expresses no dissatisfaction with hospital management. In fact, after raising questions about management requests, the board always approves what the hospital requests."

- "Some board members say that hospital management is 'lucky' because everything is going so well."

- "To me the board appears to lack a valuable role. It is a very socially and culturally oriented group of men and women who, for the most part, are middle-aged, with the oldest member being 76 years old. At its present level of functioning, it doesn't serve a valuable purpose—but it could, and it needs to."

- "The board treats hospital management as administrators, not as managers."

- "A board meeting must go to 10 p.m., or board members consider it not to be a good one! There's plenty of talk, no action."

- "The Society is at a level that looks down upon the goals and objectives of all who report to it. They are a centralizing function and must coordinate the subsidiaries to ensure that their mission is fulfilled. The Society has a role of periodically assessing where their subsidiaries are going. Is everyone moving in the same direction? Are they still on track? Do the various entities need to refocus?"

- "While the board doesn't challenge or confront management, members do seem to have a lot of pent-up frustration."

- "The Society was made to be a 'paper-shell' organization."

- "It's my impression that the Society is no longer as dominant a force as they once were. Everyone still respects them, but they're kind of out of the picture."

After openly identifying these and many other issues, the board members agreed on the priority ones. Then they "moved" to approve my proposed evening and two-day "Common Vision/Issue Resolution/Modus Operandi" work conference two weekends hence (they had already penciled this event in their calendars). They also ratified the issues that would be discussed at the work conference. I then introduced my decision-making system at this time, to demonstrate how they could use it to solve the major problems faced by the Society.

The following key issues were identified as topics for the work conference:

- *A new mission and roles.*   The society should be able to update its own mission and roles and provide the complete framework for Belmont to perform as an entity. Once agreed on its own mission and roles, UFS should provide the "reason for being" of the hospital and its mission within this context. It must also be responsible for the results.

- *A review of the centralization.*   The Society should take a look into the future for its entire holdings, including the hospital. Included as subissues would be whether tactical maneuvers and execution of day-to-day control should be done at the operating level of the organization.

- *Long-range planning.*   Just how should UFS be an integral part of the long-range planning of all its subsidiary corporations? Certainly it must focus in on the goals, objectives, and services it wants to provide; then it should determine which of these should be implemented by which of the subsidiary corporations.

- *Board membership.*   The role of the Society is either to appoint or to ratify the appointment of directors of the subsidiaries and to see that the subsidiaries are marching to the beat of the same drum. But it is not the responsibility of the parent to make decisions for the children (i.e., subsidiaries). Do we still feel this way? If so, how do we influence the subsidiaries to move in the right direction? If not, then what do we do?

- *Communication.*   UFS should be responsible for communicating with the board and various religious committees about what is going on in the different UFS organizations. What mechanism should be used to accomplish this objective?

In addition to these issues, the group identified a number of opportunities for enhancing the scope and effectiveness of the Society. These would be explored at the conference. Included were:

- Improvements in ambulatory-care services so the hospital services could compete more effectively with services offered elsewhere.

- Joint ventures with physicians and with other hospitals and universities that would give the Society access to new technologies and research.

- HMOs. Perhaps the Society should consider becoming a health maintenance organization (HMO) or joining forces with an existing one. As one person put it, "The hospital of tomorrow will have salaried physicians. Right now, we have no control of the medical physicians. As an employee, an HMO would serve the board better."

A list of key issues the board felt were facing the hospital was also ratified. These were to be communicated to the senior administrative and medical heads when they met in several days for a feedback session to review their hospital report. At that time they could compare their version of the priority issues facing the hospital with that of the board's. They could then determine how best to plan accordingly.

Surprisingly, Casperi, Vogel, Carver, and Biddle quarreled very little during the issue-identification phase. Perhaps the simulation of the previous night, combined with the optimism that the conflict resolution process just might lead to a double-win solution, kept their emotions in check. I knew that with this mindset, which is essential for truly productive sessions, we'd begin the first work conference with a real chance of developing effective solutions to the Society's problems.

Double Win: Work Conference I

Since the first work conference, tentatively scheduled for only an intensive two-and-a-half days, was designed to tackle all of the issues identified above, the board had approved my initial recommendation of extending it to a third full day. First, we focused on defining the mission of the Society (really Step 5 as well as Step 7 of the Arnold Conflict Resolution Process, since it was so value-laden). The board then ratified a new mission for the Society:

> In the tradition of our religious organization, the mission of the United Fellowship Society, a charitable corporation, shall be to encourage and support:
>
> 1. the activities of the Society and its member corporations;
> 2. the health-care and social needs of the elderly;

3. the health-care needs of all people in the immediate community;
4. the community-service needs of the surrounding areas.

Before the above statement was translated into measurable objectives, I introduced my decision-making process. (Fortunately, the group had read my book during the interim since the feedback session.) They used the process (Step 7) to set strategic objectives, and then they began to tackle the major strategic issues. The key issue, of course, was to determine the best ways for the Society to fulfill its mission and strategic objectives. While a complete analysis of the alternative strategies is beyond the scope of this book, let's briefly consider how the group evaluated the eight strategies they developed (Step 9 of the decision-making process). Here are five of the the eight options they evaluated:

1. Merge part or all of Belmont Hospital with another similar system.
2. Invest or participate in high-tech health-care ventures.
3. Increase investment in housing for the elderly.
4. Contribute more to revitalization of the surrounding community.
5. Employ physicians in group practices.

The board evaluated all eight strategies against seven key criteria upon which they had already agreed, which resulted from their discussion of what they wanted to achieve, preserve, and avoid (or APA; Step 7):

1. Preserve the spiritual tradition of the Society.
2. Avoid susceptibility to involuntary loss of tax-exempt status.
3. Avoid draining or straining our scarce organizational resources.
4. Over the next three to five years, *optimize* earnings and asset growth (minimize risk).
5. Over the next three to five years, *optimize* growth in potential services offered by our organization for meeting unfulfilled community needs while preserving the dignity and quality of life.
6. Enhance our reputation for quality.
7. Avoid loss of control to outsiders.

Each of these seven criteria had been prioritized (Step 8) and were used to evaluate each of the alternatives. What was the winner? By a margin of 15 percent, it was the third option: housing for the elderly. Secondary emphasis would be placed on the runner-up, the second option: invest or participate in high-tech health-care ventures.

By reviewing the decision matrix shown in Figure 9-1, which captures the logic behind the evaluation, you can understand the board's rationale for their decisions. Criteria (C) through (G) have been assigned "values" of desirability—the most desirable being 10 on a scale of 1 to 10. The criterion's value appears in brackets before the statement. The alternatives for these criteria are assigned ratings (the figures in parens) on a scale of 1 to 10—the best receiving a 10 and the other alternatives rated relative to the best one. The points allotted to each alternative are determined by multiplying the value by the rating. The alternative with the most total points is tentatively considered the best subject to a risk analysis. (You'll find a more detailed explanation of the evaluation process in my book *The Complete Problem Solver*.)

At the end of the conference, board members felt that they had a mission and direction and some basic strategies that would best meet their objectives and serve the community at large. They also felt that the Board had adopted a strong leadership position, and it now enabled the Society and related medical entities to change with the times without compromising their beloved core values.

I was particularly pleased when Orlan Carver came up to me, held up his wrist, then pointed to his watch and said with a grin, "Hey, young fella! Got the time?"

Case Notes

1. The Society's situation was particularly interesting from several respects. Even though there was a chairman, this was more of a collegial and democratic group than you'd normally find in a business setting. While the working atmosphere is generally pleasant in such situations with volunteers, in some ways it is not at all. At least in a situation with a hub-and-spoke autocratic leader, you know where the problems are—and what decisions will be made. And in a situation in which people are at each other's throats, at least you know where the flashpoints are. Here, we had some antagonisms, but the nature of both the organization and the democratic process—especially in the absence of an explicit decision process—fostered an atmosphere of constant argumentation about "pros and cons." No decisions were made, and much frustration was generated.

2. A corollary to the preceding point is that the board members here were all volunteers. In value-conflict situations in which people's careers are on the line, there is an added incentive to "play ball." In this case, the board members assumed some degree of freedom from formal rules. While no one would actually verbalize it, I believe there was a cer-

Criteria	Alternative 1 Merge part or all with another similar system.	Alternative 2 Invest or participate in high-tech health-care ventures.	Alternative 3 Increase investment in housing for the elderly.	Alternative 4 Revitalize surrounding community.	Alternative 5 Employ physicians in group practices.
Absolute requirements:					
A) Preserve the spiritual tradition of the Society.	Yes, if we demand it be structured that way	Yes	Especially, yes	Yes	Yes
B) Avoid susceptibility to involuntary loss of tax-exempt status	Yes, if we structure it properly	Need more data	Yes, if plan is structured properly	Highly likely	Highly likely
Also should:					
C) [10] Avoid draining/straining our scarce organizational resources (achieve effective organization).	*Positive:* If we were prepared, it could help us become a major player and give us an umbrella under which to put other subsidiaries. *Negative:* It would strain our resources, adding more layers of inefficiencies. *Overall:* Negative (3) 30 points	*N/A:* We could hire an outside expert. *Negative:* We lack resources to know what to invest in. *Overall:* Negative, but less negative than alternative 1 (10) 100 points	*Positive:* Management requires relatively few people; not much strain on staff. *Negative:* We lack the organization. We can hire necessary expertise. It would take up some volunteers' time. It would take financial budget time and administration. (5) 50 points	*Negative:* Long range: Big strain Short range: Not as much strain (2) 20 points	*Negative:* Another organization that needs to be managed for the short and long term (4) 40 points

D) [8] Over the next 3 to 5 years, *optimize* earnings and asset growth (minimize risk).	*Positive:* Main premise is to develop assets and earnings. Very few/select partners are available, but potential is there, especially given current trend. *Negative:* Risk if partner is not right one. (5) 40 points	*Positive:* If it were the right investment, risk can be positive over the long term. *Negative:* High risk (venture capital included) (6) 48 points	*Positive:* Does increase assets. *Negative:* Will this increase earnings and rate of return? (10) 80 points	*Negative:* 3 to 5 years is not doable as profit base (4) 32 points	*Positive:* Opportunity to enhance out- and in-patient services. Investment in people (5) 40 points
E) [7] Over the next 3 to 5 years, *optimize* growth in (potential) services offered by our organization to meet unfulfilled community needs, while preserving the dignity and quality of life.	*Positive:* Would result in increase of services. Ability to deliver strong services to another hospital and vice versa. *Negative:* Long process (6) 42 points	*Positive:* This meets unfulfilled needs. Better short-term feasibility than alternative 1 (5) 35 points	*Positive:* Does a good job of meeting dignity and quality of life. There are unmet needs. We're already doing a good job. (10) 70 points	*Positive:* Concentration in the community. There is a need, as there are lots of gaps in what's being provided today. If we don't do it, our community will continue to deteriorate. *Negative:* No growth, only protection of assets. If we do nothing, that's a negative. (4) 28 points	*Positive:* Meets unfulfilled needs and will help to build. (7) 49 points

Figure 9-1. The decision matrix. *(Copyright 1986 by John D. Arnold, John Arnold ExecuTrak Systems, Inc., Waltham, MA. All rights reserved.)*

Criteria	Alternative 1 Merge part or all with another similar system.	Alternative 2 Invest or participate in high-tech health-care ventures.	Alternative 3 Increase investment in housing for the elderly.	Alternative 4 Revitalize surrounding community.	Alternative 5 Employ physicians in group practices.
F) [6]Enhance our reputation for quality.	*Positive:* If we had control, we wouldn't lose as much business (8) 48 points	*Positive:* In-house equipment will allow better-quality care. Technology sells our reputation. *Negative:* This is not hands-on. It's more passive. (4) 24 points	*Positive:* Hands-on, direct relationship with people, and visibility is good. (6) 36 points	*Positive:* Visible and seen in the community. (3) 18 points	*Positive:* If we have control, we can influence the type of doctors we get. (10) 60 points
G) [4]Avoid loss of control to outsiders	*Negative:* Worst overall (1) 4 points	*Positive:* 60% as good as alternative 4 (6) 24 points	*Positive:* Good control (8) 32 points	*Positive:* Most control (10) 40 points	*Negative:* High risk (3) 12 points
TOTAL POINTS	164	231	268	138	201

Figure 9-1. (*Continued*) The decision matrix. (*Copyright 1986 by John D. Arnold. John Arnold ExecuTrak Systems, Inc., Waltham, MA. All rights reserved.*)

tain sense of "I'm doing this out of the goodness of my heart and my convictions to the Society, so don't push too hard or I'll lend my services elsewhere."

3. This example of the Arnold Conflict Resolution Process, like the others in the five preceding chapters dealing with various types of conflict, demonstrates that "smoking out the issues" is the most effective way to start off a meaningful conflict resolution process (Steps 1–4). Unless people can see and agree on the same "beast," they most likely will not reach agreement on effective strategies for getting the organization beyond its current problems.

4. As a catalyst-mediator, you must get everybody to recognize their "spheres of ignorance"—that is, what they *don't* know. With value-system conflicts, accomplishing this task can be especially difficult, because people's beliefs are strongly grounded in a set of assumptions that they hold dear and true. Here, we had some people who felt that the only way to truly fulfill their religious convictions was not to worry about being profitable; others saw profitability as the only way to reach the greatest number of people and assure the survival, let alone growth, of the holding company (the Society) and its subsidiaries. In fact, there was a path that enabled the Society to both be profitable and focus on a mainly charitable issue (housing). In the for-profit world, value conflicts will often be resolved with multiple-part solutions, too, so that everyone's concerns are addressed.

5. The catalyst-mediator or conflict resolver must keep in mind the "Holy Trinity" (quite an appropriate term to use with the preceding situation!): *"why* before *what* before *how."* If you find that people are arguing about the "how," ask, "Why do you even consider these actions? What is it you're really trying to accomplish?" And if there's argumentation about the "what," again ask, "Why bother? What's the raison d'etre, the 'why?'—the purpose for doing anything, for doing what you are trying to do?"

Once the group has agreement on the "why," it can better address "what" needs to be accomplished in order to fulfill the purpose, the mission. Only then can it begin to determine "how" to accomplish these things.

Postscript

The Society conducted a major capital campaign that resulted in their obtaining enough money to both increase investment in elderly housing and fund a new wing for Belmont Hospital, complete with the latest in certain high-tech diagnostic and therapeutic equipment.

We also conducted a separate project with the constituencies of the hospital. New programs evolved that enabled the Society to expand its outreach, supported by wise investment decisions.

Over time, Belmont's image improved significantly, primarily because of the increasing quality of its medical staff and service, and because of greatly improved hospital administration and medical staff cooperation and effectiveness.

Orlan Carver retired, and William Biddle, now free to think for himself, became a "radical thinker." The "hotshot" Casperi settled down and realized that he could effect change without a heavy foot on the throttle. And Paul Kryzminski enjoyed working with a board that could make decisions—in less than an hour!

PART 3

The In-House Conflict Resolver's Guide

Up to this point, you've been reading about conflict situations involving organizations that may be very different from your own. You've probably been wondering how my method can be applied directly to your situation. This section of the book provides an in-depth discussion of what you can do as an in-house conflict resolver. I suggest that you start off with small conflicts, rather than a "you-bet-your-company-and-career" gambit.

Becoming a proficient conflict resolver takes time and experience. But as you conduct your own in-house interviews, feedback, work conferences, and consulting, you'll become an expert in your own company. You'll learn how to better serve its needs and help it move beyond the kind of squabbling that can erode performance and degrade the quality of life.

If you get stumped, reread the examples in previous chapters that refer to the type of problem you are solving. If you start by asking the right questions to define the situation and reconstruct the "crime," the likelihood is higher that you can proceed through the method to arrive at effective solutions.

Finally, take to heart the principles described in Chapter 11. While organizational conflict is, invariably, inevitable, you can take steps right now to minimize its frequency and impact. I call these steps "organizational preventive maintenance (OPM)." With your skills as a conflict resolver and a commitment to OPM, you'll help your company chart a smooth course toward higher productivity, customer satisfaction, and profitability.

10

How to Conduct Organizational Conflict Resolution in Your Company

The Unabashed Conflict Resolver

One of the great joys of conducting a successful conflict resolution is leaving people with the skills to work out their own problems. In a way, it's a variation of the old saw about giving a starving person a fishing pole rather than a meal—as a catalyst-mediator, you give both a meal *and* a fishing pole. Your job is first to solve an immediate crisis, big or small, then to put in place the mechanisms for the organization to work out future conflicts. In this chapter, we'll examine the mechanics of the techniques I've applied in earlier chapters.

1. Selecting a Conflict Resolver

Based on our 24 years of organizational conflict resolution work, we have found that the following characteristics are very important for playing the role of catalyst-mediator:

- High standards of integrity, both ethical and intellectual
- High conceptual skills
- High analytic skills
- High energy level with good traction
- Practical orientation
- Being perceptive
- Superior listening ability
- Excellent interpersonal skills
- Ability to put situations in perspective
- Ability to handle conflict and not "personalize" it
- Good sense of humor
- Sensitivity to the feelings of others
- Trustworthy

The last point is especially important; whoever is selected to be the in-house conflict resolver must win the trust of everyone involved in the situation. As you've read in previous examples, I am often treated with suspicion because my staff and I typically enter a conflict situation under the wing of the CEO or another top executive. Many people initially fear that we will report both their names and their comments to the boss and give our opinion as well—neither of which we *ever* do. Perhaps they've suffered such an experience at the hands of another consultant, so they're distrustful of us. However, once I've helped the clients develop and announce a few ground rules (such as strict confidentiality will be maintained; a feedback session, typically for the whole senior management group and often for a wider population, will be held; and my role will be as a facilitator who helps the group reach their own choices), they tend to feel more at ease and optimistic.

This brings up a related point: whoever serves as the conflict resolver must be prepared to be a "punching bag." (Refer to Chapters 5 and 6 for good examples of how three company presidents used me as an outlet for their frustrations and anxieties.) In other words, you can't take things personally, and you have to be able to suppress any reflex reactions.

Finally, the conflict resolver must also do some deep soul searching and ensure that he or she has no axes to grind. Ask, "What's in this for me?" If you do find a hidden agenda, deal with it, or find someone else to do the job. Any biases you introduce will derail the whole process, and any attempt to manipulate a situation will probably be transparent.

As it is, protagonists may suspect you of having your own hidden agenda and be looking for overt signs of your manipulation.

2. Anticipating Pitfalls

Based on the previous six chapters, you can see that, right at the beginning, the conflict resolver faces two potential objections from the people involved in the situation. The first is that you are going to reveal deep, dark secrets that will either stunt their careers or get them fired outright. The second is cynicism: "Here we go again. Not more superficial team building crap. We've tried that before, and we're worse off than ever!"

To overcome these barriers, you must market your program. In other words, even though you're an "inside" person, you still must sell yourself as a "competent catalyst" to the organization. This entails deciding what role you feel is required and you want to fulfill. Imagine that the possibilities are rungs on a ladder, the bottom one, "informing (top) management of the problem," being the least influential. The next rung is "provide detailed information of some type." Then you come to "counseling," followed by "facilitating," "guiding," "achieving," and "ensuring" (ensuring being the top and most influential rung). With each rung, you'll need more credibility. (After all, it doesn't require a whole lot simply "to inform.")

If you feel that your role is to guide, you'll really have to prove your credibility. Facilitating is less influential and therefore may require less credibility. (The worst that can happen is people will say, "He [or she] can't hurt anything, and we can always ignore him [her]."If your goal is to achieve, you're making a commitment, and your career may be on the line. You may feel that you achieved the task, but if you fail to achieve resolution in the eyes of the key players or your own boss, you'll be in big trouble and may well make the situation worse. And if you're going to ensure, that means you have to make a *guarantee*; you must have the credentials to prove not only that you're capable of delivering, but that you actually *can* deliver. Assess the risks carefully!

The key, then, is to tailor your internal "marketing" to the type of service you wish to provide the organization. You must also tailor your ability to prove that you have the credentials to make the project happen.

3. Designing an In-House Interview

The first step in designing an in-house interview is to decide the mission and objectives of the project. These will determine what kinds of questions need to be addressed. You'll also want to look for two kinds of information on the interview: content and process. Content concerns the issues involved with reconstructing the "crime," the strengths and weaknesses of the organization, and so on. Process involves questions about how the organizational structure may be blocking effective functioning, what needs strengthening about the decision process and communications, and so on.

Let's say that you are attempting to resolve an interdepartmental conflict as we did at Eastwood Dairy (see Chapter 8). Your mission will be to unify the warring factions and get them focused on the job that needs to be done mutually. Typical interview questions might include:

- What do you view as the critical problems, issues, and/or opportunities facing your company in the next 6 to 12 months? In the longer term?

- When, how, and by whom was the issue first recognized? Can you tell me anything more specifically about the issue? Was [X] part of the issue or concern, or not? Has this been an issue all the time since then, or have there been periods when it wasn't? Has it occurred anywhere else?

- What do you view as the organization's principal strengths, distinctive resources, and capabilities with regard to these issues?

- What do you view as its principal weaknesses, vulnerabilities, and constraints with regard to these issues?

- Is there anything else that you believe *should* happen that isn't happening for your company to achieve its mission, goals, and objectives?

- What are the most promising business/productivity/profitability opportunities available to your company in the next 6 to 12 months which, to your knowledge, are *not* being addressed as you believe they should be?

- What, if any, values, prejudices, sacred cows, wishful thinking, and so on, do you believe are interfering with the effectiveness, profitability, and growth of your company and the professional satisfaction of its members?

- In your opinion, what responsibility, authority, and accountability issues, if any, are blocking more effective functioning?

- ETCETERA!

A typical conflict resolution interview of an hour-and-a-half to two hours will, in our experience, consist of 12 to 16 such questions. Some may also have subissues, as you've seen in the first questions above.

As a general rule, never ask directed, leading questions, such as, "What do you think of the new vice president?" or "What's wrong with the manufacturing process?" The interviewees will feel forced to come up with an answer, even if they don't have an opinion. Also avoid questions that force a yes or no response. Asking them implies that there is either a *right* answer or, more ominously, an answer that the boss wants. This politicizes and therefore invalidates both the process and the project.

A better format is to ask open-ended questions in which you don't insinuate or lead the interviewee to believe that there is an approved answer. For instance, the following question would allow the interviewee to talk about *anything*: "What do you see as the most crucial issues facing the organization in the next 12 months?" Or this question would allow the interviewee the option of reporting a number of different things: "In what way, *if any*, does the organizational structure impede progress?" The responder might determine that the structure is alright as is, but other things are problematic.

Finally, if you have too few questions, then you probably don't know exactly what you're trying to achieve. On the other hand, if you have too many questions, you might have built-in redundancies or you might not have focused carefully enough on the project objectives. Remember that every question adds additional time to the interview, to the data analysis, and to the feedback reporting.

4. Designing a Survey

There are three basic types of self-administered surveys we have developed over the years and applied to many conflict situations with clients: (1) a business values survey; (2) a functional interaction survey; and (3) a total-quality management/continuous-process improvement/change managing survey. Here's a description of each:

1. *The business value survey.* This type of survey measures what people perceive the values of the organization to be vis à vis the other organization(s) that are key protagonists in the conflict, and vis à vis what values they feel *should* drive the organization in the future. Examples of typical business values that are ranked by each individual include: meeting of shipment schedules; high-quality products and services; fair dealings with customers, suppliers, and employees; high integrity; and

teamwork. Depending on the project's mission and objectives and on whether or not you developed this list of values with the client, you will generally present 10 to 12 items for self-administration. If you can determine the values, you'll understand the perceptions of how each organization functions at the senior management level. By the perceptions of the respondents you can then compare what really drives different functions and departments.

In a conflict situation, if two or more units are at war, ask them to rate the values for each unit; then ask them to rate values for their own unit. The comparison may well reveal the distinctive nature of the underlying conflict. Sooner or later, you may have to deal with these basic beliefs and values, so why not save time, energy, frustration, and cost by "smoking them out" at the beginning of the process?

2. *The total-quality management/continuous-process improvement/change managing survey.* This type of survey measures to what degree the organization is focused on customer satisfaction and problem prevention versus to what degree it is focused on reactions to problems. The survey asks respondents to rate on a scale certain items as to how well they describe the current climate and how important it is to correct the situation. Comments to be rated could include, "We're too busy firefighting to take time to anticipate and prevent new fires from breaking out," or "Our plans are always consistent with our goals," or "People are not held accountable for the things that have gone wrong in their area of responsibility." Together with the business values survey, this type of survey is very useful in changing both the culture and climate of the organization and in repositioning people's attitudes toward a problem prevention mode.

3. *Functional interaction surveys.* This type of survey pairs comparisons of how well each pair of departments and functions now mesh with how well they need to mesh. The result is a matrix that shows people exactly how well or how poorly functions are working together. This survey also helps in determining the best ways to resolve the conflict and strengthen interaction.

5. Selecting Interviewees

Clearly, you can't interview everyone in the organization and everyone outside with a stake in it. So you have to make sure you have a representative sample of both groups. Again, the project mission and objectives should direct you in determining who should be interviewed both within and outside the organization.

Inside the organization, look at all the people involved as well as at two to three levels of subordinates, peers, and superiors. How far down in the organization you go is determined by such factors as the type of data you need to collect, the time available, and the costs involved. If sister divisions are involved, they, along with the people at the corporate level who may interact with one or more protagonists, should also be interviewed.

Outsiders include customers and vendors, as well as, when appropriate, government officials, investment analysts, industry and trade associations—any constituencies that may have a stake in the organization or any knowledge of it. (For example, in the case of the United Fellowship Society, discussed in Chapter 9, the mayor was important, since the Society provided extensive health-care benefits to the immediate community. The editor of the leading newspaper was also relevant because the Society wanted to demonstrate its perspicacity and receive favorable press for any decisions that came from the projects.)

In general, there are three criteria in selecting interviewees:

1. Whom should you tap into for relevant data?

2. From a "goodwill" and public relations standpoint, which influential figures do you want to satisfy by asking them to participate and "buy into" the project?

3. Who, of importance, would truly be "bent out of shape" if they weren't interviewed?

Finally, make sure that people understand why they were or were not included on the interview list or else people who aren't on the list may assume that they're about to get their walking papers or that they're second-class citizens.

I'll never forget one situation in which an executive (let's call him Jorge) in a former project called me and announced he had recently been made president of a new group. That group was about to make an acquisition. Would I help do some conflict prevention work that would smooth the transition? I agreed, but I was dismayed when I met him and he said, "I know most of the key guys in the company I'm going to buy. I want you to interview this guy but not his boss, these three peers, but not the fourth...." "Whoa!" I said, "You'll be sending all kinds of signals here."

Jorge responded by saying, "Who cares? I know pretty much from industry and trade association meetings who I'll keep and who I'll let go. The 'good guys' will be assimilated into my group."

I asked, "Why bother to go through this charade if you've got your mind pretty well made up?"

"Because," he responded, "you can get information that I can't—and I can learn what the issues are faster and more objectively through you than by any other means."

"Jorge, you'll stir up a hornets' nest if you do it this way. It's wrong."

Jorge got angry. This was *not* what he wanted to hear! "If you're unwilling to do the job, Arnold—which ought to be worth lots of money to you—there are plenty of consultants who will!"

The result was that I gave up a lucrative consulting opportunity because I wouldn't have my integrity violated, and he wouldn't budge.

My former client did indeed hire a consultant from right here in Boston (!) to carry out his orders. During the interviewing process so much distrust was created that several key people quit. Within four months, Jorge became a former employee of his own company!

6. Troubleshooting Problems Before You Begin Interviewing

If you troubleshoot what can go wrong before you start, you'll maximize your chances for a smooth conflict resolution process. Look at the mission and objectives again, and ask, "What could interfere with achieving these?" You should come up with a fairly lengthy list! Being forewarned is being forearmed.

First, consider yourself as a conflict resolver:

- You might be perceived as an inappropriate person for this role.
- The role itself may not be clarified or legitimized, or people may have differing and conflicting opinions of what your role really is and isn't.

Next, consider the internal client:

1. Will your project really get the high priority it deserves? If not, you can do the best job in the world, but you will be doomed to failure.
2. The internal client may already know the solution he wants, and he may just manipulate you to be the "bad" person to help him accomplish something he can't bring himself to do. Or, he may suddenly find during the project that he doesn't like the way it's going and wants to scuttle it, while you feel things are on track. (The constituencies you're helping might be coming up with answers that they and you feel are right, but your client may not want to hear them!)

3. Your client may see this as a one-shot inoculation rather than as a continuing process. And even if the client initially buys into the plan, he or she may feel it's going too slowly, it's taking too much time, he or she can't afford to have so many people involved, and so on.

4. Logistics—"brushfires" and travel schedules—may prevent your internal client or other key players from being there at crucial times, so you'll have to lay down milestones and get commitments to the schedule. If not, people might say, "Hey, this really isn't that important to the boss. I won't put myself on the line if the boss can't even show up!"

Finally, consider the follow-through. Let's say that the project is successful. What will happen? If there's no follow-through, people will look back and get angry that they bared their souls and put their cards on the table, walked out of the room feeling great, only to find that—nothing has changed! When that happens, there's no hope that you'll ever get them back to the table again, and it's doubtful you'll be invited back.

7. Announcing the Project

It's critical that your "internal client" announce the project in the proper way, through face-to-face meetings, phone calls, and electronic mail (E-mail). If your "client" does use phone calls and E-mail, be sure he or she backs them up with written memos. A good announcement will contain the following elements:

- An introduction describing the challenges facing the organization
- A disciplined approach to resolving problems and for enhancing the organization's capabilities
- A statement of purpose for the project—that it is designed to help everyone arrive at a set of shared objectives and an action program to resolve issues identified
- The mechanics of the process (how long it will take, what kinds of questions will be asked, etc.)
- Assurance of *total* anonymity
- Heartfelt thanks for the group's participation

8. Conducting an Orientation Session

Once your project has been announced through proper channels, you should schedule an orientation session in which you explain the "whys," "whats," and "hows" of the project. Make sure you cover the following points:

- The mission, the objectives, and the expected results of the project
- The mechanics of the process (what, how, why, who, when, where, etc.)
- The ground rules
- The benefits for the participants and what they can realistically expect from the process
- The time frame
- A distribution and explanation of the surveys and a discussion of how they are to be self-administered
- Some examples of the interview questions (which are *not* to be handed out but read aloud to give everyone a "feel" for them)

9. Administering the Interview

Plan to spend one-and-a-half to two hours per interview for insiders, and an hour to an hour-and-a-quarter for outsiders. (You don't want to impose on the latter for much more time than that. However, if you've properly positioned the project and explained the reason for your requesting their participation in it, they may well be motivated to invest more time and attention to the interview.)

Here are some basic interviewing tips:

1. If you think people are a bit nervous, ask them about their understanding of the project and how they feel about it. Certainly, clarify any misunderstandings and reinforce the ground rules (nonattribution, etc.). Also, ask permission to take notes, stressing that no one else will see them. *By no means tape record!!!! There is no better way to get people to clam up!*

2. Start off with one or two general questions before diving into the issues, strengths, weaknesses, and so on. There is a pitfall to this: If you ask people about their positions, and if they wax on, you often cannot gracefully ask them to stop and move on, which may put you under a severe time crunch. Therefore, avoid asking these types of questions unless you have a definite purpose in mind.

3. If you don't understand something, or if someone stops short of a

complete answer, ask, "Can you give me an example of what you're talking about?" Or, "Let me tell you what I think you've said, and correct me if I'm mistaken."

4. Feel free to ask, "Can you say a little more about what you've just described?"

At the end of the interview, ask people any other questions, concerns, suggestions, criticisms, and so on, that they haven't discussed that should be mentioned at this time.

The more you interview, the more proficient you'll get, and the better will be your sense of when someone is holding back or has additional things to say.

10. Analyzing the Data and Compiling a Feedback Report

From the surveys and interviews you will have both qualitative and quantitative data. You will need to tabulate the data by categorizing the information; then you will need to take a statistical reading to find out what each constituency sees as the key issues. In effect, you'll be able to hold up mirrors to see how a particular group sees itself, how it is perceived by others, and how it perceives the other protagonists involved in the conflict.

Once you complete your statistical analysis, you can then flesh out the issues with representative samples from the interviews. Only include those quotes that illuminate the issues. You may need to do some editing to protect the identity of people speaking, and, as appropriate, to tone down statements that may be so inflammatory that they will take the focus off the issue and make the feedback session too emotionally charged. In short, use your good judgment and common sense to determine what will lead to productive discussions and what will simply spark a firefight.

11. Conducting a Private Feedback Session

As you've seen from the previous chapters, the private feedback session with whoever sponsored or sanctioned the project is critical. There may be portions of the report that will be upsetting; therefore, be prepared to be sensitive to the feelings and values of the recipient.

Early in my career, I used to be surprised and disappointed that so many CEOs would say, "You organized this report well: it reinforces what I thought was wrong, but there's no real surprises." In fact, I knew there were many surprises. To prevent this type of defensive reaction from occurring in CEOs, I now administer a brief 10- to 15-question "litmus" test before every private feedback session. The questions basically ask the client to answer a series of multiple-choice questions about what he or she thinks people reported in terms of the areas of concern. Then, I present the actual answers. This makes it impossible for the sponsor to say there were no real surprises! In fact, most executives answer relatively few questions correctly, even though the questions relate to some of the biggest issues facing the organization! (I've had many instances in my 20-plus years of employing this technique in which CEOs only answered one or two of our questions correctly!) This fact demonstrates how often senior executives do not receive vital information because it is filtered out before it reaches them.

Therefore, consider devising your own kind of litmus test so that your in-house client will understand the extent to which his or her perceptions of the issues are accurate. It will also protect you, too, from receiving an emotional letdown.

Finally, once you've gone over each page of the feedback report with your in-house client, and once you've helped him or her finalize the process, you should together troubleshoot the project in terms of what can go wrong and how you and he or she can prevent problems from happening. You should also go over a plan with your in-house client for presenting the data to the management group.

12. Conducting a Management Feedback Session

Once everyone is assembled, the in-house client should offer some tone-setting remarks that put people at ease. You should then review the "roadmap" for the day—where you are going together and how you will get there safely. Depending on the dynamics of the situation, you might want to either use a simulation to make people feel at ease, as described in earlier chapters, or, if the group is at ease already, you might want to delve directly into the feedback report.

Even in the latter case, you probably want to present an executive summary, perhaps with slides or transparencies, that gives everyone a sense of what's to come during the session. Then you should work through the report section by section, asking people to respond and identify what *they* believe to be the real issues. As they speak, make sure that you capture the responses on chart paper or an electronic copyboard, categorizing the answers. Also make sure that administrative people are available to transcribe or enter on a word processor what has been said. During breaks, the session participants should receive a printed copy of the responses to edit and to ensure that these accurately reflect what they believe and will commit to.

To prevent tempers and emotions from running high, or to keep people from using the session as a gladiator contest or an opportunity to grandstand, develop and implement with the group ground rules such as:

- Only one person should speak at a time.
- There will be a penalty for derogatory comments.
- No "hobbyhorsing" is allowed (see Chapter 9).
- No sidebar conversations are to take place.
- Stay on track.

By the end of the session, you should have helped the group boil down perhaps as many as 100 or 150 issues to a vital few. Everyone should then be able to agree on the process and the plan for addressing these issues.

This process may sound democratic, but, in fact, it may not be if a key executive feels that his or her decision should be the final and accountable one. Rather, think of the process as a highly *collaborative* one. Very often, in the final analysis, one person will make a decision about which plan will be used for tackling the issues. However you arrive at the decisions, the key issues will serve as the basis for subsequent work conferences.

13. Holding Work Conferences

Prior to starting an actual work conference, you should decide who should attend and what information they should bring. There should also be agreement on the format of the information people are to bring with them or send out beforehand (e.g., slides, overhead transparencies, or handouts). A work conference should deal sequentially with each issue identified in the feedback session [generally from mission/direc-

SUMMARY

THE PAST

EASTWOOD HAS BEEN HEMORRHAGING SINCE THE HALCYON DAYS OF THE MID-EIGHTIES, DUE LARGELY TO SELF-INFLICTED WOUNDS

- In '89 through '91

  - Management processes deteriorated and information systems were inadequate (and in the case of sales data, systems were decommissioned)

  - Costs (operations, sales and administrative) increased significantly

  - Product quality deteriorated and manufacturing facilities became uncompetitive

  - Customer service declined and relationships were not maintained

  - Labor costs put pressure on our core component program

  - Competition increased as competitive manufacturers became more aggressive and our primary program matured

  - Company employees became disaffected and apathetic

  - Customers were alienated and sought alternative suppliers as sales fell nearly 15%

Figure 10-1.

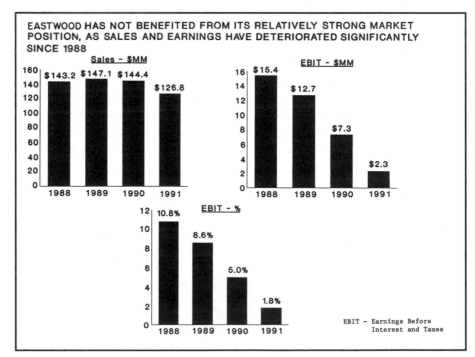

EASTWOOD HAS NOT BENEFITED FROM ITS RELATIVELY STRONG MARKET POSITION, AS SALES AND EARNINGS HAVE DETERIORATED SIGNIFICANTLY SINCE 1988

Sales - $MM: 1988 $143.2, 1989 $147.1, 1990 $144.4, 1991 $126.8

EBIT - $MM: 1988 $15.4, 1989 $12.7, 1990 $7.3, 1991 $2.3

EBIT - %: 1988 10.8%, 1989 8.6%, 1990 5.0%, 1991 1.8%

EBIT - Earnings Before Interest and Taxes

Figure 10-2.

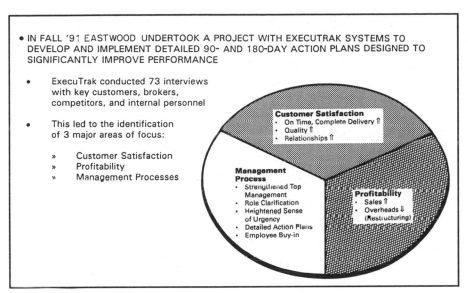

- IN FALL '91 EASTWOOD UNDERTOOK A PROJECT WITH EXECUTRAK SYSTEMS TO DEVELOP AND IMPLEMENT DETAILED 90- AND 180-DAY ACTION PLANS DESIGNED TO SIGNIFICANTLY IMPROVE PERFORMANCE

  - ExecuTrak conducted 73 interviews with key customers, brokers, competitors, and internal personnel

  - This led to the identification of 3 major areas of focus:

    » Customer Satisfaction
    » Profitability
    » Management Processes

Customer Satisfaction
- On Time, Complete Delivery ⇑
- Quality ⇑
- Relationships ⇑

Management Process
- Strengthened Top Management
- Role Clarification
- Heightened Sense of Urgency
- Detailed Action Plans
- Employee Buy-in

Profitability
- Sales ⇑
- Overheads ⇓ (Restructuring)

Figure 10-3.

- MAJOR ACTIONS INCLUDED:
  Customer Satisfaction
  - Improved customer service
    – Establish logistics management team to improve on–time delivery and order fill. Both are now in 98.5–99% range

  - Improved product quality:
    – Changed four key suppliers
    – Modified two ingredient formulas
    – Implemented raw materials inspection program
    – Modified shipping containers and palletization to reduce damage
    – Improved appearance of six key products by process and Q.C. changes

  - Improved customer relationships
    – Top–to–top customer meetings

  Profitability
  - Special sales and broker incentives fielded
  - Took salaried head count down 25% vs last year (despite the addition of new functions)
  - Plant shutdown in conjunction with another plant's reconfiguration

  Management Processes

  - Strengthened top management through addition of six new key managers

  - Installed ExecuTrak action planning and monitoring system throughout the company

  - Built essential, accurate and timely business information systems

- RESULTS FOR JANUARY AND FEBRUARY: EBIT ahead of Plan.

Figure 10-4.

tion/objectives, through market and product strategies to organizational structure, RAA (responsibility, authority, and accountability), etc.]. *Do not move on until each issue has been resolved or until an action plan to resolve it has been agreed upon.*

A realistic action plan with milestones and accountability should result from the discussion. If you conclude with a set of vague intentions, no real change will come about. Therefore, the onus is on you, the conflict resolver or catalyst, to ensure that the work conference results in a solid work plan with measurable, "doable" objectives and steps that can be acted upon.

14. Showing Results

Once people have accomplished the tasks shown in the plan, it's important for you to demonstrate the organization's achievements to your in-house client (not to validate yourself, but to prove that the organization can indeed work as a team and achieve results). The slides shown in Figures 10-1 through 10-4 were prepared by an in-house conflict resolver licensed through ExecuTrak Systems. They exemplify the kind of concise reporting that top executives seek. At a glance, you can see exactly what issues the organization faced, what it wanted to achieve, and how well it did so. And the implicit message in the slides is that the in-house conflict resolver did an excellent job as a catalyst!

Now that you have a sense of how to prepare a strategy and process for resolving organizational conflict, and now that you know *how* to serve as an integrative mechanism to accelerate conflict resolution, you're ready to think about a complementary action: conflict prevention. As you'll learn in the next and final chapter, the ultimate goal of conflict resolvers is to reduce the likelihood and impact of organizational conflicts. As the old saw goes, an ounce of prevention is worth a pound of cure.

11
Conducting Organizational Preventive Maintenance

Where There's Smoke...There Need *Not* Be Fire

Throughout this book, I've stressed that organizational conflict is inevitable. You simply cannot expect a group of human beings within an organization to work together harmoniously day after day and year after year, especially since they often have conflicting objectives and pressures. The wonderful diversity that makes people unique also guarantees that they will, at some point, clash over values, expectations, likes and dislikes, misconceptions, and misperceptions.

The good news, though, is that through anticipatory thinking and organizational preventive maintenance (OPM), you can lessen the severity and frequency of organizational conflicts. In addition, you can learn to spot organizational conflicts when they're still in the early, "smoke" stage, rather than waiting until they become full-fledged conflagrations.

In this chapter, you'll learn how to conduct OPM, through which your company can detect emerging problems and resolve them before they become serious. Doing this does not require you to develop a crystal ball or psychic powers; rather, it involves drawing on your basic knowledge of people in general, your company's own people in particular, and the means of resolving conflicts with a disciplined, problem-prevention planning process. Why not refer to the 10-step Arnold Conflict Resolution Process *before* trouble begins?

Organizational Preventive Maintenance (OPM): The Basic Concepts

The concept behind OPM is simple. Just as preventive medicine makes our bodies less susceptible to disease (but not infallible), OPM can enable us to analyze what makes an organization healthy, then avoid those things that tend to make it "sick." The analogy with medicine is apt, I believe, because corporations have their own ecology, much like a living creature.

If we can anticipate and analyze the forces or events likely to occur that could cause an "autoimmune" response in an organization, in which it tugs and pulls and fights itself from within, then we can also take corrective action, and apply the right remedy, or "medicine." (I sometimes think of conflict resolution as a healing process in which the "patient" is more than the sum of the parts. The job of the catalyst-mediator is to mend the entire fabric of the organization by harmonizing all of its internal constituents. In other words, he or she acts like a holistic doctor.)

The key to OPM is "anticipatory thinking"—being on the lookout for emerging or potential changes in the company that will likely affect its people. As an in-house conflict resolver, you should be looking for what I call "flashpoints," or "hotspots," that could lead to either immediate or "delayed-action" conflicts. In general, these flashpoints fall into two categories: external and internal.

External and Internal Flashpoints

To keep abreast of external flashpoints, you need to have a keen sense of national and international events and how they affect your company and plans for mergers, acquisitions, strategic alliances, and other deals. You also need to be in touch with the competitive arena and any plans to restructure the organization, executive turnover, and so on.

To identify the internal flashpoints, it's critical for you to "take the pulse" of your entire organization. You have to know the players, the personalities, the key pressures and fears, the desires, and the objectives. In other words, you must be a "connoisseur" of your own company. Here are some common external and internal flashpoints:

External Massive Changes

1. *Acquisitions.* Any time one company is acquired by another, the opportunities for major conflicts are ripe. As you've read in the preceding chapters, cultural clashes can lead to *any* of the six conflict types, not just external. The two opposing cultures may have very different values, leadership and management styles, strategies, and operations. No wonder studies show that 7 out of 10 acquisitions fail to meet the acquirers' objectives and that more than 1 of 3 are outright failures; also, within two years of the deal, 90 percent of CEOs and 52 percent of the executives in the acquired firms leave their companies. To describe this sad state of affairs, I've long used the "DATE" acronym: Date to Mate to Delegate to Alienate to Abdicate.

There's a lot of truth in another acronym I coined in our work in more than 100 merger and acquisition projects: MAD (Mergers and Acquisitions are like marrying a blind Date!).

As conflicts resulting from organizational clashes escalate, trust and confidence wane, robbing the acquired company—and sometimes the parent—of its ability to compete effectively. Therefore, if an acquisition is contemplated, the in-house conflict resolver of the acquiring company should be looking at how the cultures will interact and how people will respond to the "marriage." Think the unthinkable, and imagine the worst-case scenario; you can never do enough organizational preventive maintenance when an acquisition is involved.

2. *Competitive assaults.* Any competitor can potentially throw your company into a state of conflict. For example, a competitor may offer a breakthrough technology that renders yours second-rate or even obsolete. Sales and marketing may panic and put extreme pressure on engineering or R&D to develop a similar or competitive product. R&D and engineering might in turn put extreme pressure on manufacturing to quickly retool, possibly for products that cannot even be produced!

Another situation likely to cause conflict is a competitor who initiates a price war. While major companies routinely engage in price skirmishes, upstart competitors often cause more problems because they are often willing to take a bigger gamble. When a company is faced with a potential price war, sales and marketing are often eager to jump into the fray; after all, they have to retain the accounts. But top management may feel that meeting competitors on price either will erode margins too much or simply might not be fitting for the product. (For example, when a Japanese or American car dealer pits a midpriced car against a Mercedes-Benz in terms of performance, the venerable German company is not about to respond with a drop in sticker price!) The result can be a strategic direction conflict in which the people who sell the product feel that they are being robbed of the very tools they need to be competitive—in effect, having the rug pulled out from underneath them.

Examples of the above are legion. The in-house conflict resolver thus needs to consider the impact of changes in the competitive arena; by interviewing those people immediately impacted by a new technology or price war, he or she can often head off internal strife that can be more destructive than the actual competition with rival organizations.

3. *Government intervention and regulations.*   Every company is subject to some type of federal, state, and local regulations. At times, new laws have a major impact that can cause tremendous internal trauma. Your product may suddenly find itself banned because of previously unforeseen dangers. Entire product lines may be dropped, jeopardizing people's careers and dashing their hopes for the future. People in product development may feel that those people in the company who deal with regulatory issues didn't keep their eyes on the ball; people who sell the product may feel that they've lost a key component of their sales arsenal; people in R&D may become pariahs for developing an "evil or dangerous product."

Another type of government intervention concerns deregulation. In some industries, deregulation has brought sweeping changes that not only have altered the competitive landscape but have radically transformed the way that people do their jobs. Just look at the massive changes in the banking, airline, food, telecommunications, pharmaceuticals, insurance, electronics, and other industries.

Yet another type of government intervention is bans on the export of technology. With former enemies of the government collapsing left and right, and former friends becoming current enemies, people in the business of high technology can find themselves being pulled in many different directions. Never knowing when the direction will change can cause unrest and anxieties that translate into organizational conflict.

In short, business and government have traditionally been in adversarial roles in terms of regulation. When actions are taken in response to government policy that change the way people do their jobs or affect the company's ability to make a profit, anger and ensuing organizational strife is likely.

4. *Changes in the economy.*   Every company, whether it is product-,

service-, or information-based, is subject to changes in the economy. At one extreme, we see massive layoffs, such as those announced by so many companies in 1991 and 1992. The in-house conflict resolver needs to constantly take the pulse of the economy and be aware of how it will affect the people in her or his company. For example, suppose that leading economic indicators are pointing toward a recession. People might start "hunkering down" and looking for ways to protect their own position; of course, the opposite actually needs to happen—they need to find ways to make the company more cost-effective so that it can survive the rough times ahead.

The international economy must also be monitored so that internal strife in reaction to it can be avoided. For example, if your company sells heavily in foreign markets, then fluctuations in the exchange rates can have a significant impact on your products and services. All of a sudden, the Europeans may not be able to afford your products and your company may lose potential market share. Sales and marketing may then respond with a desire to drop prices or lower production costs; others in the company may take a "hold the fort" approach, leading to an interdepartmental or strategic direction conflict.

In any event, it's critical to take the pulse of the economy and project how it may affect your company's people in terms of their personal well-being and their positions among the various departments.

5. *Political changes.* Changes in the political arena can have a definite impact on companies, especially those that do business overseas. While domestic changes in the political climate tend to have a gradual effect, through legislation, major changes in the international arena, such as coups and skirmishes, can instantly turn once-lucrative ventures into ones generating only red ink and lost opportunities. (In the case of Kuwait, profits literally went up in smoke!)

Whoever is responsible for conflict prevention should therefore take into account how world and political events can affect the morale and psyche of people both at home and in the host countries. Look for changes that can cause significant shifts in the way a company does business.

Internal Changes

1. *New technologies.* The introduction of new technologies into the workplace can have dramatic effects on everyone in the company. We all know the impact of new management information systems (MIS) that don't work "out of the box." People complain that they can't get the information they need, and they point the finger at MIS people for

"screwing up." Or they simply register disgust at the company's leadership for putting them through such hardships.

When new technologies and systems are installed and they haven't yet been debugged or people haven't adapted to them, departments blame each other. Sales, order-entry, and customer service may be at one another's throats, for example, each claiming that the other is at fault for the lack of information or for information that was not entered properly. Or purchasing may find itself in a clash with manufacturing or finance. The list goes on and on.

When your company is contemplating a new technology, be assured that it *will* cause conflict. By troubleshooting the "hotspots," you can reduce the conflict to a minimum.

2. *New management systems.*   A related issue to the previous point concerns the adoption of companywide systems, such as just-in-time (JIT), cross-functional management (CFM), total-quality management (TQM), flexible manufacturing, concurrent engineering, and others. If any of these systems are implemented without employees being adequately educated or motivated to use them, people may have very strong negative reactions. Too often, companies attempt to do a "cold turkey" implementation in which they decide to implement the system on Friday at 5 p.m. and then surprise everyone Monday morning. When this happens, people feel as if they've just experienced a massive earthquake. All of a sudden, familiar ground has shifted or vanished; their routines may be in shambles; and the very nature of their jobs and working relationships may have changed.

3. *Changes in leadership.*   Inevitably, leadership within an organization changes. A CEO or chairman may die or retire unexpectedly. The board or a new parent may without warning replace a president or CEO. Regardless of the cause, a change in leadership is extremely stressful. (Just look at how the firing of a president led to an uproar in the company cited in Chapter 4!)

Changes at the top cause a ripple effect, like a rock being thrown into a pond, chain reactions occurring down through some or all of the organization. In the same way, promotions at the vice presidential or middle-management level can cause internal strife in their respective spheres because of resentment and/or jealousy on the part of people passed over. Factions often develop in support of one candidate or another, which can lead to serious intradepartmental conflict.

Any time a change of leadership is expected or has been announced, the in-house conflict leader should be prepared to head off a possible negative reaction.

4. *Geographical expansion or retraction.*   Any time a company expands

or retracts its operation, there will be some type of conflict. In the case of an expansion, some groups of people will have added responsibilities. Communications will become more critical and perhaps more difficult. Life may suddenly become more complex, and the opportunity for interdepartmental strife escalates. The new plant "across the country" may become an enemy of the "original" people; the new sales territory may become the company's "wicked stepchild," or the new distribution system on the opposite coast could become an "energy sink" and the perceived cause of everyone's problems.

Retracting business also can cause tremendous conflict, as people fear for the immediate and long-term prospects for success. In some cases, people are likely to see themselves pitted against management in a vicious strategic direction or values conflict. Criticism might be intense: "How could they put all those people out of work?" "How could they have pulled the floorboards out from under that whole community?" or, "Those fools! If they would just wait until the economy turns, there would be no need to pull out of Dallas!"

When any change in business scope is contemplated, you can be sure that some faction will find itself at odds with the corporate vision. As the in-house conflict resolver, you need to stay one step ahead and learn how people will deal with proposed changes—*before* they happen.

5. *Restructuring and reorganizations.* Next to picking up and moving a facility, nothing can generate internal chaos and conflict so much as a reorganization or restructuring. The very nature of such actions demands that some people will feel pleased with the changes and many others may well feel "screwed" or threatened. Fortunately, you can help minimize the impact of pending corporate restructurings and reorganizations by getting people to discuss how the changes will affect their lives, their jobs, and their performance. Prepare them for adopting a double-win mindset.

The OPM Process

Once you've identified the potential flashpoints in changing situations, the next step is to develop an interview for the people who are most likely to be in conflict because of them. Then administer the interview just as if you were seeking information during an actual conflict. Of course, you'll have to change your phraseology to a hypothetical, "what-if" mode:

- What would happen if we were to develop a joint venture or strategic alliance with ABC Corporation? How do you think our cultures would mesh? What would be the trouble spots? Would we have management process or strategic direction conflicts? Why? Would the strife arise in manufacturing? Or would it arise in sales and marketing? Why? Would it be short- or long-lived? Why? Or, what would happen if *we* acquired XYZ Corporation—what would be the chances of crushing this entrepreneurially minded partner with our formal systems, causing an external conflict? Why would or wouldn't this happen?

- What would happen if our major competitor came out with a microprocessor-controlled version? What would that do to our current marketing program and our grip on the market? What would engineering and manufacturing have to do to keep up and exceed our competitor's development? Would the two likely engage in interdepartmental conflict? Why or why not? If so, what would be the likely distinctions of the conflict, and how would we smoke out the issues and devise effective resolutions?

- What would happen if the Food and Drug Administration forced the proposed changes in labeling? Who would have primary responsibility for ensuring that we complied with the law? Would it be the legal department, in which case marketing would be concerned about scaring off potential customers? Or would it be marketing, in which case the legal department might be concerned about meeting legal requirements? Would this cause an operational conflict because of blurred RAA lines? How would we envision the unique dimensions of the conflict?

- What would happen if the government passed the proposed air-quality legislation? How could we remain competitive with Third World nations with less strict (or nonexistent) environmental standards? Would certain contingents lobby to move our manufacturing operations to those countries, or would we subcontract to those countries? Would this lead to a value-system conflict? an operational conflict? a management process and style conflict? If so, how widespread would it be? How intense might it get? How deep in the organization would it penetrate? And how long would it continue? Why?

- What would happen if the new MIS system were installed? What kind of disruptions would it be likely to cause? Why? Who would be affected, and what would be the effects on customer service? Would we be likely to find ourselves faced with an operational conflict, an interdepartmental feud that degrades our performance, or both? Why? If so, how could we smoke out the issues before implementing the system?

- What would happen if our CEO retired early because of health problems? How would either of his two likely successors be apt to change the current strategic direction? Why? Would we have a strategic direction conflict? And what would happen if the new leader, internally promoted or parachuted from the outside onto the top of the organization, were perceived to be autocratic or turned out to be a poor decision maker? Would we then be challenged with a management process conflict? an operational conflict? a "hybrid" conflict? To what degree (scope) might the conflict be in contrast to our current situation, and what would be the likely effects? Why?

- What would happen if we expanded to Seattle, as we've been discussing? How would that affect our sales and marketing and order-fulfillment divisions? Why? Would the initial kinks in the system generate an operational conflict or an interdepartmental one? Why? If so, what would the likely dimensions of the conflict be?

- What would happen if we restructured as proposed? Would the new decentralized organization cause people to break into warring fiefs, creating a massive interdepartmental conflict? Why or why not? Or, if we closed one of our plants in Michigan, would people be likely to feel that we've destroyed an entire community, leading to a value-system conflict? How long would the resentment continue? Would it be companywide or just at a sister plant? Would the resentment fade, or would it hang with us like a cloud? How much of the organization would get swept up in this? Why?

When you're done interviewing people and asking them questions such as the above which help to reconstruct the "crime" (Steps 1–4 of the Arnold Conflict Resolution Process), and when you're done probing their value systems and basic beliefs (Step 5) for their underlying premises, then prepare a feedback report based on the interviews, just as you would normally do in an actual conflict situation. Present the findings to the in-house client, then to the management group. Smoke out the issues, then boil them down to the most essential ones. Since you're not dealing with an actual conflict session, you might not need to sponsor a work conference to resolve the key issues; just making everyone aware of them may be sufficient.

If, however, there is a high probability that the "flashpoint" events will come to pass, it's probably best to structure and implement a work conference. One of the objectives of the conference is to do the skill building and team building that will be necessary to keep people together and ready to cope when the anticipated change happens.

The conference can also be used as a forum for thinking things through. By applying the 10-step process and beginning to put solutions in place, you can enable the group to deal with expected change when it first occurs without experiencing conflict and adverse impact.

Make sure that you have "intelligence agents" out there scanning for the first signs of the "flashpoints" coming a company's way. Probe the organization's inside people and get external resources who are in the best position to anticipate and detect the arrival of events; also interview the company's managers who are most likely to be affected.

Preventive Thinking in Action

We have conducted a number of OPM projects for a wide range of industries, government and public institutions, communities, and nonprofit organizations. These projects have helped the groups to get operationally ready for a major acquisition (both acquirer and acquired need to be prepared) or for other kinds of major changes (such as all the changes that are necessary to spur economic revitalization of a region).

The following situation from the ExecuTrak files demonstrates how OPM can head off a massive conflict. In this case, the Prime Minister of Canada suddenly decreed a 20 percent budget cut among all federal departments. The department ministers, in turn, handed down the edict to their agencies and directorates.

Our client in the pollution-control industry, the Inland Waters Directorate of the Canadian federal Department of Energy, Mines, and Resources, received new orders. It had to cut its budget by 20 percent and initiate a hiring freeze. The freeze was retroactive to a date preceding the hiring of many new staff by the directorate. It would severely affect the directorate since the group had been preparing to respond to pending legislation that would expand its mission and responsibilities for the public welfare. The directorate was given a mere week to show "just cause" if it wanted to retain anyone whose position was eliminated by the freeze.

Unlike most organizations that respond with great trauma to a 5 or 10 percent, let alone a 20 percent, budget cut by immediately focusing in on the "whos" (e.g., "Who shall we cut?"), the Inland Waters director decided to take preventive action. He tried to head off a potential firestorm by division chiefs whose areas of responsibility were likely to take a major hit.

Rather than telling each division chief that within 48 hours he or she would have to produce a list of line items and people to be lopped off the rolls, the Inland Waters director quickly searched for a creative approach that would result in a peaceful double-win outcome. He wanted a win for both the directorate and Canada.

Learning of my prior work with the Canadian Federal Food and Drug

Department and with the director of air quality, the director called me, and briefly explained the situation. I suggested that we convene a three-day meeting that would include all of the division chiefs. ExecuTrak would help him lead his management group through an analysis of the issues and keep everyone focused objectively on what needed to be done. First he was advised to prepare his division chiefs for two things: alerting people in their divisions to the meeting; and phoning them, as the analysis unfolded, with questions to be answered as soon as possible.

In his opening remarks, the director discussed the serious nature of the meeting. He explained that the goal was not simply to meet the Prime Minister's directives, but to "determine, in the following sequence, what mission, objectives, agency programs, activities, and staffing are absolutely necessary, in our collective best judgment, to discharge our mandate to the Canadian public."

There had been no time to do all the important interviewing of the six division chiefs, their subordinates, and other key constituencies that would enable us to reconstruct the "crime" (Steps 1–4 of the Arnold Conflict Resolution Process). We were certainly well aware that this was a highly emotional situation, fraught with considerable anxiety and frustration. And, even though Canadians, in my experience, tend to be somewhat more polite than citizens south of the border, there was still the potential for win-lose antagonism. If people thought they had to protect turf and preserve the jobs of personnel in their respective divisions, fights could erupt.

Add to this situation the sense of frustration and guilt many people felt for officers who, at that very moment, were in transit from many places to their new assignment in Ottawa. Some officers were moving from such far-away places as Vancouver, Prince Edward Island, and Nova Scotia. You can certainly understand the potential for several types of conflict!

For this reason, I had successfully urged the director to allow us to not jump right into the fray by first looking at their mission and objectives and then looking at agency programs—let alone where to make necessary cuts. Instead, we were to begin with two simulations that would open up people (as described in earlier chapters). The simulations would serve to reduce possible defensiveness, get everyone to agree on possible problems with work productivity and on ground rules, and really get them focused on "What's best for discharging the responsibility of this directorate for the welfare of the Canadian public?"

After simulations, the director discussed with his six division chiefs what he felt they should try to achieve, preserve, and avoid in this difficult and complex exercise (Step 7).

The first issue was to rethink their mandate in view of the austerity program. What did they believe *had* to be the mandate, the mission of the directorate, at least during the time of the austerity program, to fulfill the agency's reason for being? After applying the "Hierarchy of Influence" verbs of activity and results (i.e., "inform" through "ensure") described in Chapter 10, the officers then agreed on what they felt should be the mission of the directorate in view of the 20 percent budget reduction. This newly stated mission established the focus and parameters of the second issue: establishing what *absolutely* had to be achieved, preserved, and avoided as problems, in their collective judgment, in order to *minimally* fulfill this mandate (Step 8).

These agency objectives became the key criteria for the third issue: determining which *programs* (with what scope) absolutely had to be filled so that the objectives could be achieved (Steps 9 and 10). These programs then became the basis for determining which *positions* absolutely had to be filled so that the objectives could be achieved by sufficient staffing of these programs (Steps 7–10).

The last point is particularly interesting. Prior to our arrival, the group had already begun writing a series of job descriptions for some of the positions they hoped to salvage, setting forth the activities and responsibility of each one. We counseled that *what* people do, or would be doing, is a much weaker justification for keeping positions than *why* they would be doing it. We helped the officers shift from a focus on activities to results of these activities in each program. Using these results criteria, the officers could then determine which positions were necessary and should be "reprieved," and which should be curtailed (Steps 9–10). These proposals would demonstrate the group's responsiveness to the Prime Minister's call for severely reduced spending.

This penetrating "telescopic" process continued to evolve, with each major program's results in turn being translated into the key criteria in determining what professional staffing was *absolutely* necessary (Steps 8–10). Finally, this in turn suggested the key criteria for determining the most appropriate organizational realignment.

Unfortunately, too many executives and consultants, when faced with a reorganization problem, start by deciding how to reorganize. Instead, they should tackle this issue much later. Decisions about reorganization should flow from higher levels of decisions made during the continual application of Steps 7 to 10: the best mission, objectives, programs, major results, and staffing positions. The best new organizational structure will then evolve.

Throughout this series of five major decision analyses, with criteria basically preprogrammed by the prior decision (one of the many time-saving benefits of this conflict prevention process), various division chiefs at one time or another said, "I can see where this program (or these results, or, in one instance, not only my function but my entire organization!) is no longer significant for the immediate future of this agency. I'm sure I speak for my division in saying we'll be pleased to do whatever proves to be in the best interest of the public welfare."

ExecuTrak's face-to-face role in this extremely intensive three-and-a-half-day OPM conference ended early Wednesday evening. At this point, the group of highly dedicated and achievement-oriented Canadian government officials began preparing their agency presentation to the assistant deputy minister. They worked long into the night before they caught a few hours of sleep.

The director's presentation to the assistant deputy minister demonstrated his responsiveness to the austerity program. In it, he carefully explained the method he and his division chiefs had used to arrive at their recommendations. He talked his boss through the officers' analyses of the five issues, and he stressed why 66 specific professional positions had to be reprieved. These *absolutely* had to be filled if the agency was to meet the critical pollution-control problems facing the Canadian public.

As a result, this directorate was the only one that had its recommendations completely approved in the department of 20,000-plus employees.

When to Conduct OPM

When is the best time to give your organization a preventive "tune-up?" You should do it when things are going well! As the old saying goes: The best time to make a plan is *before* you need one. Likewise, the best time to resolve a conflict is *before* it happens.

Think ahead, think the unthinkable, and take action! Once you become proficient at this, you'll find that when you are in the midst of an actual conflict, it will be less severe and damaging than if it had just "dropped out of the sky" like a pestilence. Moreover, by making anticipatory thinking a standard operating practice, you'll reduce the frequency with which conflicts visit your organization. You'll spend more time doing things that make money, such as offering goods and services in the most competitive possible manner, delivered on time to the right specifications in the right quantity at the right location. In other words, you'll be "right the first time, on time, *every* time!"

Epilogue: Organizational Conflict— The Challenge of the 1990s

The 1990s have been—and promise to be—a decade of rapid change. Who could have imagined, for example, that we would see the collapse of the Soviet Union almost overnight, the unification of Germany, and the rise of a united Europe? Or who could have foreseen the near collapse of General Motors, a company that served for more than half a century as the symbol of American manufacturing might; or massive layoffs at giants like IBM, DEC, Hughes Aircraft, and so many other major American corporations? Or the demise of the American dream; or other "unthinkables"?

Change by itself, whether for the better or the worse, provides a culture in which conflict can thrive, much like an agar dish provides a medium that nourishes bacteria. Therefore, as we race toward the new millennium, it will be more critical than ever for business leaders to be sensitive to the conflicts that are likely developing within their organizations. Those who are blind to the strife will pay dearly in the future; those who recognize that organizational conflict is the major productivity issue of the decade and take appropriate real-time preventive action will gain a competitive advantage in the hearts and minds of their constituencies and in the global marketplace.

Perhaps the most daunting challenge facing U.S. companies in terms of organizational conflict involves inevitable linkages with other companies, both North American and international. The Age of

Consolidation has dawned, and linkages, whether through mergers and acquisitions, joint ventures, or strategic alliances, will become the norm. Few, if any, solo players will be able to compete with juggernaut companies emerging from Europe and the Pacific Rim. American companies must learn how to manage such relationships far better than they do currently. Studies indicate how poorly American companies bridge cross-corporate and cross-national cultural gaps, because they assume too often that "the American way is the right way to do things." Contrast that with the Japanese, who have a 60- to 70-year lead time of experience with *Keiretsu* (industrial groups), and with multilingual Europeans, who have also long engaged in corporate alliances and are often more skillful than Americans are. Corporate executives and government officials in the United States need more training and experience in cooperative competition and mutual-gains negotiation.

We'll also see more entrepreneurial partnerships during the remainder of the nineties. It is the rare large company, layered in bureaucracies, that can innovate fast enough to keep pace with world competitors. At the other end of the spectrum, small, breakthrough companies, though "fast on their feet," won't have the resources or access to the marketplace necessary to bring their concepts to fruition.

With each linkage, whether between giants or between "Davids and Goliaths," will come the inevitable massive external, strategic, value, management process/style, operational, and interdepartmental conflicts. As demonstrated in this book, conflict is just an artifact of the human condition; when people from different parts of the organization with very different values and philosophies are forced to work hand in hand, strife is a given.

In my 30 years of experience in business and industry, I can count on the fingers of one hand those companies that I think have done a good job of preserving their values *and* handling conflict well. For most of this period of time, Procter & Gamble and IBM have largely preserved their values, as has Digital Equipment Company; however, the latter two now find they have become too rigid and are trying to adapt so that they can perform better than they do now against fierce competitors. Hewlett-Packard, Matra in France, and a number of Japanese companies also manage organizational conflict well, but most other companies need to learn how to manage far better. Just look at how Jack Welch, CEO of General Electric, restructured his corporation. There was a tremendous amount of conflict and terrible layoffs. Now, the worst is over, GE hopes, and Mr. Welch has become "collegial" and "humanistic." The way layoffs are managed varies dramatically by country. Contrast the typical American way of massive layoffs in large industries, such as has occurred among automotive manufacturers, with the ways of the Dutch, the Germans, and many other countries with more humanistic laws. The major exception in the United States is small companies, which are usually more sensitive because they have to be.

Another source of organizational conflict is the rapid development of new manufacturing techniques and technologies. Twenty years ago, we began hearing about "panaceas" and "miracle concepts" from Japan, where they recognized the value of certain new concepts long before we did. There were quality circles, there were just-in-time techniques, there was statistical process control, and so on. And in the United States, a small percentage of companies began using manufacturing resource planning II (MRPII) and distribution resource planning (DRP).

Time has already begun to tell which are the best techniques and systems. Contrast the confrontation between IBM and Microsoft, at least at this point in time. Although Microsoft has aggravated suppliers, not to mention competitors, they have proven to be clever, canny negotiators; one part of the company does one thing while another does something entirely different. So far, they've been able to sustain conflict and absolutely have outmanaged IBM, who have been ponderous in confronting Microsoft.

One thing is certain right *now*—every new product development, materials engineering, manufacturing, distribution, and management approach has a change component that has the potential to engender internal conflict. Any time you introduce a radically new approach to any facet of an operation—from innovation and design through delivery and service to the end-user and customer—you run the risk that some constituencies will feel threatened as the ground shifts from underneath them. Unless companies deal with those insecurities and stresses, they may be faced with internal conflicts that diminish, and in some cases even negate, the benefits from the technologies. So I believe that in this era of cutting-edge technologies and techniques, some of which will determine winners and losers in the global marketplace, companies that aspire to world-class status will have to recognize the hidden dangers that attend any major change that causes people to do their jobs differently.

Yet another area sure to cause organizational conflict in the future is global networking. Advances in computer networks will enable people to work in new ways at their offices, at home, and in the field. People will have unparalleled opportunities to make their ideas known in electronic work groups and "virtual" conferences, to share ideas and insights with people down the hall or in remote locations around the planet. This opportunity not only opens exciting possibilities for drawing on "group brainpower," it also means that the shared beliefs and values, sentiments, desires, anxieties, and goals of entire constituencies will be heard by those whose ears are open. This information sharing will become essential as companies, out of necessity, make technological breakthroughs and create global work forces to increase their franchises around the world and exploit new opportunities.

At the senior level of American corporations, there will be a higher percentage of multinational managers who have proven their sensitivity to and skill in working with different national and corporate cultures. These people will be able to operate in the complex world of joint ventures and strategic alliances, both of which are so essential to the integration of product groups and geographically remote organizations for the achievement of global strategies.

Finally, think about the current trend toward "concurrent engineering" in organizations today. One of the most exciting developments is the breakdown of traditional boundaries. Rather than having information passed along in hierarchical fashion, through vertical chains of command, companies are finding that flatter management levels and lateral communication eliminates mistakes and boosts productivity. Techniques such as cross-functional management and fast cycle time are just two of the exciting manifestations of this trend. As companies begin to operate more cross-functionally and as their people are empowered to use their brains rather than just "checking them at the door," the corporation as we know it today will undergo a radical transformation.

Increasingly, as the world economy recovers in the 1990s, this positive transformation shift forward to management across the enterprise, as opposed to hierarchically down through the enterprise, will occur. When times are tough, organizations distort change programs to serve simple, "cut-the-fat" moves to restore short-term profit. Many of these distortions are dignified with buzzwords like re-engineering, slenderizing, workouts, and such, but the narrow focus shows through in implementation. True departures such as concurrent engineering force a market-driven reassessment of the firm across all functions and capabilities since the focus is on learning what customers, both external and internal to the organization, want and need. The impact is horizontal, not merely vertical, and highlights redundancies represented by the "silo" hierarchy of functions and departments. The future of the enterprise is helped, not hurt. And to the surprise of some traditional managers, short-term results occur as well since the marketplace and customers become the primary force for change. The test is not the buzzword introduced, but rather the results achieved. If parallel efforts across traditional hierarchical boundaries are encouraged immediately, chances are the results will be dramatic and lasting. However, if a small group of clever or hard-driving managers are perpetrating a new dogma on the firm, the results will be short lived. The former takes real leadership. The latter is often characterized by "theatership" rather than "leadership."

These management transformations will be necessary as the paradigms of business, government, and the military change. The U.S. Department of Defense, for example, must shift its paradigm from a waging war scenario to coping with weather, famine, and localized conflict management. As its mission and role change, so must its culture and business processes in order to implement multimission systems such as fighting a limited war while handling hurricane disaster relief. As industry, the military, and the U.S. government "rightsize," they will define different needs and values, reinforcing horizontal rather than stovepipe management to attain world-class performance. This horizontal paradigm, with the kinds of business processes exemplified by the 10-step conflict resolution process, will strengthen communication and cooperation across organizational and international boundaries.

So what will the organization of the future look like?

With fiercer competition from all quarters of the globe, customers' heightened quality requirements for products and services, and intensive time pressures, organizational structures will flatten and become more flexible and reconfigurable. The benefits of decentralized and autonomous business units will be "married" to the strengths of a centralized operation. Deregulation, middle-management downsizing, and globalization will increasingly require greater participation by and consensus of principals, employees, and other stakeholders in the many business processes and decisions that create successful endeavors. Group parallel-processing decision support systems, including electronic meeting systems and computer-supported cooperative work, will facilitate asynchronous meetings globally, increasing productivity electronically and expediting decisions that have the "buy-in" and commitment of all constituencies. Team structures—with an *explicit, collaborative* decision-making process and comprised of members with sharpened skills as prime integrators—will complement flexible, concurrent engineering processes and "agile" manufacturing systems with computer-integrated systems and reconfigurable factories to produce customized products in a vast array of choices.

I believe that the organization of the future will be one in which leaders meld their visions of the future with the basic needs, hopes, and aspirations of their various stakeholders. Their focus, too, will extend from traditional concerns with the bottom line to newly appreciated factors such as customers and their values to recently emerging issues such as management of the environment.

The new corporate vision will be one in which technologies and systems are assessed not just on the basis of whether they will get the job done profitably but also on the basis of the human conflict factor. To make this assessment, designers and engineers of the new technologies, systems, products, and services will have to work hand-in-hand with customers and others who must use their creations on a daily basis. When confronted with undeniable customer requirements, suppliers will have to focus on how best to meet them, or they will lose out to competition. Suppliers will then be forced to adopt a *learning* mode of operation rather than an NIH (not invented here), "we know best" engineering-, manufacturing-, and sales-driven approach to the marketplace.

This is the real benefit of JIT (just-in-time): It's not simply a way of reducing factory-floor inventory time nor a re-engineering approach but also a learning approach. When confronted with undeniable customer requirements, companies will learn how better to satisfy them. Those organizations that respond to the challenge with better management methods will increase revenue and profitability. For example, many Japanese bicycle manufacturers today are successful because they continue to make their product in high volume, yet a customer can get personally fitted for one; customers' desires are built into the way Japanese bicycles are designed and produced.

I also believe that "management" itself will be redefined to include the art and science of melding the disparate expectations of everyone within the business environment. For example, governmental trade policies now are no longer discussed just in terms of economics but are also discussed in the context of national character and cultural factors. Increasingly, such diverse forces as the customer value-satisfaction movement, the quality movement, and the ecology movement will converge to create such beneficial results as industrial ecosystems, recyclable "cradle-to-grave" products, and services that help humanity. Humanity and our planet are irrevocably one; organizations will recognize that narrow, short-term economic interests cannot predominate. There is no black hole where we can dispose of what we don't need.

Organizations that understand this vision have the best chance of becoming the "Future 500," the elite corps that can meet the challenges of the decade head on, creating radiant light, not sparks.

Index

About the Author

John D. Arnold is an internationally renowned expert in
organizational conflict resolution and prevention. During his
29-year career, Mr. Arnold has worked with 200 of the
Fortune 500 and for the past 24 years has been president of
the Boston-based John Arnold ExecuTrak Systems. He has
given numerous seminars, workshops, and speeches, and
has published articles and been quoted extensively in
Business Week, Fortune, The Wall Street Journal, and many
business magazines. Two of his books, *The Art of Decision
Making (Make Up Your Mind)* and *Shooting the Executive
Rapids*, have been selections of the Macmillan, McGraw-Hill,
and Fortune Book Clubs. He is also the author of *The
Complete Problem Solver: A Total System for Competitive
Decision Making*, a Newbridge Executive Book Club selection,
and *Trading Up: A Career Guide to Getting Ahead Without
Getting Out.*